SAINT PAUL AND CONTEMPORARY EUROPEAN PHILOSOPHY

Crosscurrents

Exploring the development of European thought through engagements with the arts, humanities, social sciences and sciences

Series Editor
Christopher Watkin, Monash University

Editorial Advisory Board
Andrew Benjamin
Martin Crowley
Simon Critchley
Frederiek Depoortere
Oliver Feltham
Patrick ffrench
Christopher Fynsk
Kevin Hart
Emma Wilson

Titles available in the series
Difficult Atheism: Post-Theological Thinking in Alain Badiou, Jean-Luc Nancy and Quentin Meillassoux
Christopher Watkin
Politics of the Gift: Exchanges in Poststructuralism
Gerald Moore
Unfinished Worlds: Hermeneutics, Aesthetics and Gadamer
Nicholas Davey
The Figure of This World: Agamben and the Question of Political Ontology
Mathew Abbott
The Becoming of the Body: Contemporary Women's Writing in French
Amaleena Damlé
Philosophy, Animality and the Life Sciences
Wahida Khandker
The Event Universe: The Revisionary Metaphysics of Alfred North Whitehead
Leemon B. McHenry
Sublime Art: Towards an Aesthetics of the Future
Stephen Zepke
Mallarmé and the Politics of Literature: Sartre, Kristeva, Badiou, Rancière
Robert Boncardo
Animal Writing: Storytelling, Selfhood and the Limits of Empathy
Danielle Sands
Music, Philosophy and Gender in Nancy, Lacoue-Labarthe, Badiou
Sarah Hickmott
The Desert in Modern Literature and Philosophy: Wasteland Aesthetics
Aidan Tynan
Visual Art and Self-Construction
Katrina Mitcheson
Proust Between Deleuze and Derrida: The Remains of Literature
James Dutton
Saint Paul and Contemporary European Philosophy: The Outcast and the Spirit
Gert-Jan van der Heiden

Visit the Crosscurrents website at www.edinburghuniversitypress.com/series-crosscurrents.html

SAINT PAUL AND CONTEMPORARY EUROPEAN PHILOSOPHY

The Outcast and the Spirit

Gert-Jan van der Heiden

EDINBURGH
University Press

Edinburgh University Press is one of the leading university presses in the UK. We publish academic books and journals in our selected subject areas across the humanities and social sciences, combining cutting-edge scholarship with high editorial and production values to produce academic works of lasting importance. For more information visit our website: edinburghuniversitypress.com

We are committed to making research available to a wide audience and are pleased to be publishing an Open Access ebook edition of this title.

© Gert-Jan van der Heiden, 2023 under a Creative Commons Attribution-NonCommercial licence

Edinburgh University Press Ltd
13 Infirmary Street, Edinburgh, EH1 1LT

Typeset in 10.5/13 Sabon by
Cheshire Typesetting Ltd, Cuddington, Cheshire

A CIP record for this book is available from the British Library

ISBN 978 1 3995 2172 7 (hardback)
ISBN 978 1 3995 2173 4 (paperback)
ISBN 978 1 3995 2174 1 (webready PDF)
ISBN 978 1 3995 2175 8 (epub)

The right of Gert-Jan van der Heiden to be identified as the author of this work has been asserted in accordance with the Copyright, Designs and Patents Act 1988, and the Copyright and Related Rights Regulations 2003 (SI No. 2498).

Contents

Series Editor's Preface	vi
Acknowledgements	viii
Introduction: Another Legacy of Paul?	1
1. The Dialectic Spirit of Paul	25
2. The Ghost of Nihilism	45
3. Meontology	68
4. Time, Event and Exception	96
5. Law, Promise and Grace	128
6. Community, Exception and Outcast	154
Epilogue: A Pauline Dialectic of Exception	179
Bibliography	202
Index	215

Series Editor's Preface

Two or more currents flowing into or through each other create a turbulent crosscurrent, more powerful than its contributory flows and irreducible to them. Time and again, modern European thought creates and exploits crosscurrents in thinking, remaking itself as it flows through, across and against discourses as diverse as mathematics and film, sociology and biology, theology, literature and politics. The work of Gilles Deleuze, Jacques Derrida, Slavoj Žižek, Alain Badiou, Bernard Stiegler and Jean-Luc Nancy, among others, participates in this fundamental remaking. In each case disciplines and discursive formations are engaged, not with the aim of performing a predetermined mode of analysis yielding a 'philosophy of x', but through encounters in which thought itself can be transformed. Furthermore, these fundamental transformations do not merely seek to account for singular events in different sites of discursive or artistic production but rather to engage human existence and society as such, and as a whole. The cross-disciplinarity of this thought is therefore neither a fashion nor a prosthesis; it is simply part of what 'thought' means in this tradition.

Crosscurrents begins from the twin convictions that this remaking is integral to the legacy and potency of European thought, and that the future of thought in this tradition must defend and develop this legacy in the teeth of an academy that separates and controls the currents that flow within and through it. With this in view, the series provides an exceptional site for bold, original and opinion-changing monographs that actively engage European thought in this fundamentally cross-disciplinary manner, riding existing crosscurrents and creating new ones. Each book in the series explores the different ways in which European thought develops through its engagement with disciplines across the arts, humanities, social sciences and sciences, recognising that the community of scholars working with this thought is itself spread across diverse faculties. The object of the series is therefore nothing less than to examine and carry forward the unique legacy of European thought as an inherently and irreducibly cross-disciplinary enterprise.

Christopher Watkin
Cambridge
February 2011

Acknowledgements

This study is a result of the interdisciplinary research project *Overcoming the Faith–Reason Opposition*, which ran from 2012 until 2017 and was made possible by a grant of the Dutch Research Council (NWO; Free Competition 360-25-120), for which I am very grateful. A special thanks goes out to the people who participated in this project: George van Kooten, Ben Vedder, Antonio Cimino, Ezra Delahaye and Suzan Sierksma-Agteres. I am especially thankful for our many enriching discussions, which significantly shaped and changed my understanding of the philosophical potential of the letters of Saint Paul, inspiring me to write this book. I would also like to thank the scholars who have contributed to this project with their thoughts on and contributions to our project's research questions and the philosophical turn to Saint Paul in general: Jussi Backman, Chantal Bax, Andrew Benjamin, Ward Blanton, Jeffrey Bloechl, Vincent Blok, Walter Brogan, Nikolaas Cassidy-Deketelaere, Simon Critchley, Marc De Kesel, Françoise Frazier, Tobias Keiling, Anders Klostergaard Petersen, Donald Loose, Erik Meganck, Teresa Morgan, Carl Raschke, Carlotta Santini, Joeri Schrijvers, Claudio Tarditi, Marin Terpstra, Morten Sørensen Thaning, Paul van Tongeren, Herman Westerink, Sanem Yazıcıoğlu, Holger Zaborowski and Peter Zeillinger.

NWO (Open Access Books 36.201.069) also provided the means for the open access publication of this monograph, for which I am very thankful. This book was first planned as a translation of the Dutch monograph *Het uitschot en de geest*. I would like to thank Joey Kok for her translation and publisher Marc Beerens for encouraging this project. Over time, however, the present book has become a rather substantial reworking of the original. Going back to the text a few years after having written it, I did not only feel the need to correct small mistakes, but also to significantly clarify several main arguments, to improve their presentation, and to add substantially new insights, including discussions with more recent publications on present-day philosophical encounters with Saint Paul. Moreover, I added a new, extensive epilogue describing the specific viewpoint this study offers to the debate on Saint Paul in contemporary European philosophy as well as to the question concerning the philosophical potential of these letters today.

I would like to thank the students participating in the research master course Philosophy of Religion in the Fall of 2021 for reading an earlier version of this study and for thinking along with this project, allowing me to make additional improvements. I'm thankful to the anonymous reviewers who helped me to further finetune this project. I'm very grateful to Carol Macdonald, head of editorial at Edinburgh University Press, and to Christopher Watkin, editor of the *Crosscurrents*-series, for thinking along with this book project, for carefully editing the manuscript, and for supporting its publication.

Introduction: Another Legacy of Paul?

> No, not that. You misunderstand. I'm not in a church because of God. One of the problems is that the words, the serious words, have been used up over the centuries by people like those rectors and vicars listed on the wall. The words don't seem to fit the thoughts nowadays. But I think there is something enviable about that otherwise unenviable world.
> Julian Barnes, *England, England*, 243

> The poetry of a poet or the treatise of a thinker stands within its own proper unique word. It compels us to perceive this word again and again as if we were hearing it for the first time. These firstfruits of the word transpose us in every case to a new shore.[1]
> Martin Heidegger, *Parmenides*, 18/12[2]

Since the 1990s, the letters of the apostle Paul have been high on the philosophical agenda, and since the turn of the century there has been an upsurge in publications on Saint Paul and contemporary European philosophy, continuing now for more than two decades. This development may be considered surprising for several reasons. The philosophers examining Paul's letters do not share his religious beliefs. Moreover, one might have expected – hoped or feared – that, after Nietzsche's devastating critique of the apostle, there would be no role left to play for Paul in philosophical thought, at least to the extent that it is not invested in specific religious or theological presuppositions. Yet, there it is.

The basic questions I would like to answer in this study is the following. Wherein lies the philosophical potential of the apostle's letters for thought today? And which philosophical legacy can be discovered in the apostle's letters for our current moment? This particular focus of this study's questions means that I am concerned with Paul among philosophers – not among dogmatists, New Testament scholars, religious scientists or historians of ancient culture. It may at times be difficult to maintain these distinctions. Yet, this focus implies that, even in instances where I do comment on or use other approaches to Paul's letters, the invariable aim is to clarify, defend, critically assess or question their philosophical impact.

Consequently, on one level, this study attempts to describe, clarify and criticise some of the most important present-day philosophical views on Paul and to bring these substantially different positions in discussion with one another. What is at stake, beyond the specific idiomatic or idiosyncratic appropriation of Paul's texts by individual philosophers, in this more general philosophical turn to Paul? On a second level, I aim to put forward my own understanding of the actual, present-day stakes of a philosophical turn to Paul.

Even though this study actively engages with the philosophical rediscovery of Paul's epistles in the 1990s and the early 2000s, it is important to note that the stakes of a turn to Paul have changed. The question of the end of history, which framed a significant part of the discussion twenty years ago, is not as relevant today as it was then. Nevertheless, our present-day socio-political situation is confronted with its own impending end of the world. Today, the groaning of the whole creation of which Paul speaks (Rom. 8:22) is more real and urgent than ever. Moreover, our present-day socio-political situation is marked by various outcasts, of which the ever-growing stream of displaced people offers a paradigmatic example.[3] The circumstances of the displaced have strongly deteriorated in the political climate of the last twenty years. Paul's self-identification with the outcast (Cor. 4:13) therefore gets a pressing, present-day sense. Against the background of these socio-political issues of today, a further and deepened analysis of Paul's letters may help us to think about a conception of the world, of being and of a mode of living in attunement with our present sense of an ending and attuned to those who have been cast out of the order of the world.

While my study does not offer concrete advice or analyses concerning these issues, I do aim to create concepts in my reading of Paul to help thinking about them. Or, rather, I aim to revivify the profound sense of some of the 'serious words' in his letters, to listen to them as the firstfruits they are. In this regard, my study offers its own turn to Paul. In it, I argue which Paul is, in my view, philosophically the most viable and productive one for present-day thought and the present moment, philosophically, culturally and politically. This introductory chapter is devoted to explaining some of the points of departure for my interpretations and assessments and some of the basic motifs of a proper philosophical reappreciation of Paul today. These also determine the systematic plan of this book that unfolds along the two axes that appear side by side in its subtitle and that I consider to be the two focal points of the modern philosophical legacy of Paul as well as the two serious words that need to be revivified today if we want to think our present situation: his identification with the outcast or the scum of the world and his appreciation of the principle of the spirit.[4] These two focal points, as I show in the course of this book, determine the elliptical orbit of a particular dialectic movement that can be discerned in the apostle's letters, namely a *dialectic of exception* that has a special philosophical fecundity for thought today.

RETRIEVING PAUL

Let us begin with a characterisation of the philosophical context of the interest in and debate on Paul arising in the 1990s. The discussion mainly includes philosophers belonging to post-Kantian European philosophy or continental philosophy. Given its historical moment, this characterisation immediately offers us a sense of its substance. In broad and somewhat vague terms, one might say that during this period the hegemony of a certain *postmodern* viewpoint is coming to an end.

This does not mean that authors who are often associated with postmodernism and its intrinsic relativism, such as Derrida or Deleuze, do not have any place in this discussion or that they do not have anything to say on Paul. In fact, important recent studies, such as Blanton's *A Materialism for the Masses* or Jennings's *Outlaw Justice*, show how Derrida remains a crucial partner in conversation; and Crockett's *Radical Political Thinking* contains an intriguing account of Deleuze as a reader of Paul.[5] Comparing these references, we see that Jennings offers a portrayal of Paul in which he, on several occasions, discerns an affinity with Derrida. Yet, I tend to side with Blanton and Crockett, who argue that both Derrida's and Deleuze's portrayal of Paul – each in its own way – remain too Nietzschean.[6] This means that they are not fully up to the task of a genuine reappraisal of Paul because, as Blanton eloquently notes, Nietzsche 'failed radically to transform – rather than simply to excoriate or lament – the ongoing cultural and political functions of the Pauline legacy'.[7] Guided by the two epigraphs of this chapter, one could rephrase this by saying that 'the serious words' of the Pauline legacy 'have been used up over the centuries', not only by 'rectors and vicars', but also by philosophers and their incapacity to read differently and 'to perceive', as suggested by the second epigraph, these words 'again and again as if we were hearing [them] for the first time'. In the turn to Paul, philosophy aims for a renewed engagement with this legacy in order to find another, present-day use for his 'serious words'.

This renewal is not only a matter of the apostle's letters and their interpretations, but also of contemporary European philosophy itself. For instance, it concerns the notions of relativism and particularism that are often associated with the all-too imprecise term 'postmodernism'. Relativism and particularism are among the motifs that return throughout this book, but for an initial orientation on their meaning, one could for instance think of versions we encounter in society today. Terms such as 'fake news' and 'alternative truths' are the pre-eminent contemporary socio-political expression of relativism – not only beauty but also truth is in the eye of the beholder. In addition, the universal battle fought around identity politics and the revival of national or group awareness in different forms eminently illustrate the societal and political impact of the emphasis on particularism. Some analyses hold that these phenomena are intellectually and culturally grounded in postmodernism. I tend to reject this rather bold claim because it seems to me the thought of authors such as Deleuze, Lyotard and Derrida, who are often seen as representatives of postmodern or relativist strands of thought, cannot be held responsible for this particular societal predominance of relativism and particularism. Nevertheless, I agree that it is important to consider more systematically whether alternative approaches are possible that overcome particularism and relativism in a more radical way than explored up until recently.

The degeneration of the postmodern project is one of the main reasons why, for instance, Badiou and Žižek began to consult Paul. In his letters, they discern a radical alternative.[8] For them, this degeneration is not an internal-philosophical or purely academic matter but takes place on the basis of cultural and societal developments. Badiou, for instance, views the neoliberal form of capitalism that rules our current economic and political world as the prime evil here:

> On the one hand, there is an extension of the automatisms of capital [... which] imposes the rule of an abstract homogenization. [...] On the other side, there is a process of fragmentation into closed identities, and the culturalist and relativist ideology that accompanies this fragmentation. [...]
> The two components [...] are in a relation of reciprocal maintenance and mirroring.[9]

In their readings of Paul, Badiou and Žižek engage with severe forms of relativism and particularism and venture to reintroduce their opposites: the absolute and the universal.[10] The literature on the turn to Paul demonstrates that precisely this development appeals to the (philosophical) imagination and inspires further reflection.

Yet, much more happened in the 1990s. Paul's appeal reaches much further than Badiou's and Žižek's commitments to the motifs of the absolute and the universal. Volumes with remarkably similar titles such as *Paul and the Philosophers*, *St. Paul among the Philosophers*, *Paul in the Grip of the Philosophers* and *Saint Paul and Philosophy* evidence a plurality of new perspectives on Paul, some embracing the alternative Badiou and Žižek introduce, others rejecting it or exploring other approaches.[11] All of the major continental thinkers interested in the importance of theology and Christianity for philosophy are in one way or another engaged in this discussion.

To get a sense of the diversity of commitments represented in the turn to Paul, let us consider the fundamental themes at the heart of what I consider to be the major texts published in the 1990s and which are much debated in the philosophical turn to Paul. Throughout the chapters that follow, a solid critical assessment of and dialogue with these texts allow me to position myself in the debate concerning the philosophical significance and potential of Paul's letters.

Heidegger's series of lectures on Paul's letters were presented in the winter semester of 1920–1, but were published only in 1995 as 'Introduction to the Phenomenology of Religion' in the volume *The Phenomenology of Religious Life*. For Heidegger, the basic issue is to contribute to a phenomenology of religion by analysing the early Christian experience of life and of temporality, especially based on Galatians and 1 and 2 Thessalonians. For him, the significance of this experience goes beyond the limits of early Christianity alone. That is to say, the experience of time as borne witness to by Paul can also be appropriated beyond the limited sphere of his cultural period. Crucial for Heidegger's reading is that Paul's letters offer an experience of time that can neither be found in the philosophical contemporaries of Paul nor in the founders of the history of metaphysics, Plato and Aristotle. The Pauline experience of time elucidates something that remains hidden in the philosophical account of time.

Much of the turn to Paul is concerned with socio-political issues, and one might want to reproach Heidegger for having neglected this dimension. Yet, unlike in the context of his personal life and parts of his thought, in the context of the turn to Paul this failure might be considered a benevolent one, since it shows most clearly that such a turn *also* concerns basic ontological questions regarding history and temporality. To borrow and extend Bloechl's remark, the ontology of Paul is important for present-day philosophy '*before and apart from any need to profile it in an explicitly political manner*'.[12] I aim to show that this ontology does have an impact for political philosophy. Yet, the ontological dimension comes first, and this seems to be forgotten in (the reception of) some of the other basic texts in the turn to Paul.

The second pivotal text also appeared posthumously, in 1993, under the title *The Political Theology of Paul*. In 1987, Taubes presents in a lecture series in Berlin nothing short of his spiritual testament. As Jerry Muller comments in his recent biography of Taubes: 'In 1947, the twenty-four-year-old Jacob Taubes revealed his aspiration to do for Paul what Heidegger had done for Kierkegaard, "to unchain this Christian content into something universal."'[13] Let me add to this comment that Heidegger has already done this for Paul as well and that, moreover, Taubes's interest in Paul also concerns a particular experience of time and urgency.[14] However, Taubes's emphasis is on Romans. His interest in the end of time is an interest in the apocalypse. This latter emphasis clearly determines his discussion with Schmitt. Whereas Schmitt fears the decline of political institutions and therefore invests in the Pauline political figure of the *katechon*, Taubes emphasises the Pauline theme of having no investment in this world and therefore salutes the end of time. Even though the end of time is the most pressing theme in Taubes's work, my reading will focus on another motif that tends to get obscured by the omnipresent emphasis on the theme of the end of history in the 1990s. Rather than Taubes's apocalyptic understanding of Pauline time, which I will criticise in the course of this study, I will emphasise and further his conception of *pneuma*, spirit, in Paul's letters and turn it into a linchpin of the apostle's dialectic of exception.

Although the historical context and the Talmudic method of Taubes's reading of Paul has only recently been comprehensively documented by Løland, the impact of Taubes on the debate on Paul is difficult to miss.[15] First, his engagements with the readings of Paul by Nietzsche, Freud, Benjamin and Schmitt have strongly influenced the way in which the discussion on Paul is staged. Blanton's aforementioned study shows how Nietzsche and Freud are (his) guides in the turn to Paul. Agamben uses Benjamin and Schmitt to structure his Paul. My study is no exception to this rule. Taubes's staging of Nietzsche and Schmitt offers an essential background for my own assessment of the ontological and political implications of Paul's letters. Second, Taubes's attention to the Gnostic temptation inherent in apostle's letters has already been widely acknowledged and developed. An important example in this respect is Critchley. He borrows Taubes's idea that Marcion's early, Gnostic interpretation of Paul strongly affects modern readings. He extends this claim to the readings of Badiou and Agamben, accusing them of crypto-Marcionism.¹⁶ As I aim to show in the course of this book, even though its motivation in Taubes seems to be mainly socio-political, the issue of Paul's Gnosticism concerns basic problems in ontology leading to the concept of the outcast. I will argue that Paul's solution to these problems is philosophically compelling and fruitful. Third, in line with my comment in the previous paragraph, I want to make the case that Taubes's true discovery is the Pauline principle of the spirit. Combined with the motif of the outcast, this principle inspires a specific Pauline dialectic unfolded in the course of this study.

Badiou's *Saint Paul: The Foundation of Universalism* from 1997 portrays Paul as a 'poet-thinker' of the revolution, of militant fidelity and of universalism.¹⁷ His attention to Paul's universalism is a brave attempt to listen to the words of this poet-thinker as if hearing them for the first time, although some readers might fear that in listening to these words, he mainly hears the echoes of his own *Being and Event*. Although Badiou is at the centre of attention in the renewed interest to Paul, the antidialectic commitment of his reading of Paul is highly problematic for several reasons, as I will argue. This has seriously damaging effects for the ontological, ethical and political reflections that follow from his version of Paul. This, however, does not mean that the important themes Badiou introduces are to be discarded. To save them, at least partially, I will engage with Badiou's work at some crucial moments alongside that of Žižek, who embraces Badiou's emphasis on universality and fidelity while placing them in a more dialectic frame. This does not mean that I will adopt Žižek's dialectic uncritically. Quite the contrary. However, his dialectic does help me to show how and to what extent some of Badiou's ideas on Paul can be integrated in a Pauline dialectic of exception. In fact, Žižek adds to Badiou's emphasis on universalism and fidelity another motif that conditions the possibility of fidelity, namely that of detachment or disengagement, that is, the ability to be freed from that which seems most important to us. This motif is so fundamental to him that he relates it to Paul's conception of God: '"God" is thus ultimately the name for the purely negative gesture [...] of giving up what matters most to us.'¹⁸ A form of negativity is indispensable in any proper dialectic.

Agamben's study *The Time That Remains: A Commentary on the Letter to the Romans* from 2000 collates the interpretations of Taubes, Heidegger and Badiou, sometimes critically, sometimes affirmatively. In this sense, his book offers an example of how a critical dialogue and discussion between these diverse positions can be initiated while developing a new perspective on Paul along the way. Moreover, his erudite reflections on important Pauline notions such as *katargēsis* and *chrēsis* are inspiring, and several of these reflections are taken up and developed into building blocks in my line of argumentation, leading up to a Pauline dialectic. I am less interested in his specific attention to the letters of Paul as a messianic text – for him, the letters are 'the fundamental Messianic text of the Western tradition'[19] – especially when it draws parts of his text into the context of Taubes's emphasis on the theme of the end of history.

PHILOSOPHICAL SELF-PORTRAITS AS PAUL

The reception of the turn to Paul and the accompanying discussion between philosophers, historians and scholars in religious studies has brought to light a specific methodological problem. In this section, I want to develop a particular stance towards this problem. In the discussions, it basically takes on the following form: do present-day philosophers, when reading Paul's letters, merely find themselves reflected in Paul's texts and thus impose their own thought on Paul, or do they find Paul's genuine, historical and theological points of view? Let me introduce this problem by referring back to how it has manifested itself so far, while keeping in mind that, *mutatis mutandis*, any philosopher's reading of Paul is confronted with a similar problem.

The more systematic works of the authors mentioned in the previous section are rather disparate, as can for instance be seen when comparing Heidegger's *Being and Time* with Badiou's *Being and Event*. Therefore, the assertion that each of these authors identifies structures and basic concepts of their own systematic thought in Paul's letters may easily arouse suspicion. Did they, perhaps, manipulate Paul to suit their own purposes and theories? Were they, perhaps, too selective in the passages they discuss and too violent in their interpretation? It is not surprising that this suspicion is expressed often and in different forms. Many times, this suspicion is instructive. At other times, however, it seems to lead to a rather massive criticism that casts doubt on the possibility of construing a meaningful present-day, philosophical Pauline legacy.

A succinct example of the latter can be found in one of the earliest books to stage a conversation between philosophy, theology and religious studies. In *St. Paul among the Philosophers*, which focuses primarily on the work of Badiou and Žižek, Frederiksen's contribution concludes:

> Yes, Badiou's Paul is our contemporary. And that is precisely how we know that Badiou [...] has presented us not with a study of Paul and his concerns, but with an oblique self-portrait, and an investigation of concerns and ideas that are irreducibly Badiou's.[20]

The term 'oblique' can mean 'indirect', but also 'ambiguous' and 'misleading'. Frederiksen herself notes that Badiou's reading of Paul does not present Paul, but rather an ambiguous and misleading *self-portrait*. This conclusion is mitigated by a previous remark that the same holds for the Paul staged by authors such as Origen and Augustine. Nevertheless, the title of her contribution is striking in light of her concluding sentence: 'Historical Integrity, Interpretive Freedom.'[21] Apparently, one can distinguish scientific historical research with its own integrity and objectivity from the interpretive freedom – read: arbitrariness – of philosophers who find their own thought reflected in the letters of Paul. It seems to me that such a dichotomy between objective science and subjective interpretation is not as clear as Frederiksen suggests, even if only because historical and New Testament scholarship is itself motivated by questions stemming from a particular historical context.

This last nuancing comment is, however, still too general. Moreover, Frederiksen is not the only author who has voiced criticism concerning contemporary philosophers' selective reading of Paul's letters. Their reading would be 'anachronistic' and 'ahistorical', as Blanton sums up a whole host of critics.[22] Frick, the editor of another volume examining the Pauline revival, suggests: 'In their philosophizing, they need Pauline thought only to the extent that it corroborates ideas already articulated in their systems of thought. This applies to more or less all the continental philosophers.'[23] Here, the marvel that Paul resonates so strongly with particular present-day philosophical commitments is skilfully stymied. Again, Frederiksen's powerful image comes to mind to capture Frick's reduction of the philosophical resonance of Paul. The thinkers turn out to be philosophical relatives of the Dutch painter Rembrandt van Rijn. Rather than painting a picture of Paul himself, they present us with a 'self-portrait as the apostle Paul'.[24]

Frick himself proposes another image, perhaps inspired by the identification of Paul with Hermes, the messenger and chief speaker for the gods (Acts 14:12). He argues that in these present-day readings, Paul's letters become the mouthpieces of these philosophers' own thoughts: 'Continental philosophy changes the voice of Paul to say things that Paul may not have been willing to say.'[25] In this context, he even compares Paul with a mute who depends on those who want to speak on behalf of the voiceless and who want to give him back a voice. I hold the image of the mute to whom a voice needs to be given quite dear and have elaborated this theme in several books, but it is unjustified to apply it to Paul.[26] The letters of Paul have had an unprecedented effect in Christian and Western culture and, through the ages, have proven a checkpoint in social and theological discussions, with a remarkable impact. To posit, as Frick does, that a handful of continental philosophers, who, at the end of twenty centuries of *Wirkungsgeschichte* (effective history) of Paul's letters, added their voice to the powerful and many-voiced chorus of Pauline interpretations, would have distorted and silenced Paul's own voice, is itself nothing short of an exaggeration and a distortion. Paul and his letters are certainly not voiceless, especially not compared with the plurality of voices and the multitude of texts that have simply disappeared and will therefore never be heard or read again. The image in Acts of Paul as Hermes can therefore perhaps be better explained in a different way. In fact, one should note that Paul's letters themselves are concerned with the voiceless who deserve a voice. In particular, 1 Corinthians comes to mind here, in which Paul identifies with the foolish and the weak, with those who cannot speak well and even with 'the scum of the world' and 'the refuse of all things'.[27] Thus, it is Paul who gives a voice to the voiceless and the powerless. In this study, I will extensively engage with this image. First, however, I want to try to rescue the amazement at the philosophical interest in Paul in the face of the questionable images of self-portrait and mouthpiece evoked by Frederiksen and Frick, respectively.

It is a crucial hermeneutic principle that texts can be read and understood in a different historical context than the one in which they originated. Originating from another cultural context, new readers are motivated by other questions and interests. These different perspectives may disclose meanings of a text that were not seen in other contexts and could perhaps never have been conceived before.[28] For some texts, this has led to a centuries-long interpretation history as they speak anew and differently to new readers in each new historical epoch. This applies to Homer. This applies to Plato. And it applies to Paul. When philosophers point out that the letters of Paul are primordial, foundational texts of Western culture, they demonstrate that Paul's age-long impact on this culture is itself a motivation to turn to these letters. The power of such texts is that they continue to appeal to readers throughout the centuries.

When Frederiksen claims that Origen, Augustine and Badiou find mainly themselves in Paul's letters, she has not yet explained why specifically *these* letters appeal. Frederiksen emphasises only one side of the hermeneutic coin. In *Truth and Method*, Gadamer comments that readers always read a text with their own prejudices in mind.[29] This means that readers are always motivated by questions and interests formed by the historical context to which they belong, even if the text itself comes from another one dominated by other prejudices. If one one-sidedly assumes this idea, one might be tempted to say, in the words of Ricœur, that readers *impose* their prejudices on the text when interpreting it. The image of the philosophical reading of Paul as a secret self-portrait tends towards this one-sided explanation of the part prejudices play in our interpretation of texts. When the meaning we find in texts only comes about in this way and only reflects our prejudices, it is good to meet such interpretations with a hermeneutics of suspicion à la Frederiksen and Frick, and to show that our prejudices and not the text itself (or its author) constitute the meaning we feigned to discern in it.

Yet, this 'hermeneutics of suspicion' necessarily remains one-sided.[30] It may be that readers bring along their own prejudices to the interpretation process, but in turn they are themselves *exposed* to the text. To be exposed to something means to undergo a foreign, different experience from which we cannot withdraw and which may fundamentally change us or even wound us. Readers of a text are exposed to what it says. What the text has to say may very well unmask the readers' self-image as ill-founded or illusory and force them to think differently about themselves and their world. When we say that we are touched by a text, we mean to say that it has something to say to us that we did not know before, that we were not aware of, and that does not confirm our prejudices and illusions but, rather, negates, corrects and criticises them. To express this, Gadamer introduced the striking term 'hermeneutic experience'.[31] When reading a text, we do not acquire any hermeneutic experience if it only confirms and reflects what we already know and what we already (think we) are. A hermeneutic experience is a proper experience when the text does not confirm us in our expectations but rather appears to be an 'opposite' of us contradicting our own ideas. In addition, a hermeneutic experience deserves to be called 'hermeneutic' because the confrontation with the text is not purely negative and does not only negate our own expectations and ideas. The text gives us to understand something else, and what it says about its subject matter inspires us to think differently about it. Only when this happens can we genuinely say that a text speaks to us.

Reading a text in light of our prejudices requires a hermeneutics of suspicion. Likewise, the text's claim on and appeal to us require a hermeneutics of trust, namely the trust that in an interpretation we not only paint our self-portrait but also take note of the meaning the text imparts to us. It is not a matter of choosing between the hermeneutics of suspicion and that of trust, because every interpretation is an interaction between, on the one hand, the prejudices we take along with us and which we impose on the text and, on the other hand, the power of the text itself to bring another perspective and another meaning into play and to expose us to it. Together they form the two conditions of every genuine interpretation because, in turning to a text, readers are motivated by their own questions. Posing a question to a text is therefore a dialectic movement of imposing prejudices on a text and exposing oneself to what the text is saying.

Consequently, the philosophical interpretations of Paul are only interesting when the apostle's letters bring into play something that cannot be retrieved, without remainder, from these philosophers' other works. Before concluding that philosophers when reading Paul are merely painting a self-portrait in their Pauline texts, we should first pose the question of what we can say about the point of view from which the philosophers read Paul and how this viewpoint allows Paul's letters to bring their own expressiveness into play. I will attempt to show this in the chapters that follow, but it is important to now first sketch in a few broad strokes three motifs that make Paul's letters philosophically productive today.

THREE LEITMOTIFS

Despite the important differences between philosophical approaches to Paul, it seems possible to distinguish at least three leitmotifs that return in many of them. These readings of Paul occur within the three-dimensional space spanned by the following leitmotifs. (a) Paul is seen as the announcer of a new beginning leading to a transformation of reality. (b) Paul presents a singular mode of living to the members of the different Christian congregations that they should adopt; to this mode of living corresponds a mode of being and a mode of thinking. (c) Paul's notion of the spirit (of God) introduces a principle of revivification and renewal that cannot be understood in terms of possibilities of change and transformation intrinsic to the order and dynamics of the world itself.

(a) Beginning and Transformation

'Saint Paul is trouble' – thus rings the first sentence of the chapter on Paul in Critchley's *The Faith of the Faithless*.[32] That Paul indeed is trouble is illustrated by the effect of his letters in church history. One thing is clear from this history, namely that these letters have a revolutionary potential actualised in several periods throughout that history. As soon as theology turns to Paul, something happens:

> As Adolph Von Harnack pointed out [...]: 'One might write the history of dogma as the history of the Pauline reactions in the Church, and in doing so would touch on all the turning points of the history.' This is true of

Marcion's opposition to the Apostolic Fathers, Augustine after the Church Fathers through to Luther after the Scholastics and Jansenism after the Council of Trent. Harnack continues, 'Everywhere it has been Paul ... who produced the Reformation.'[33]

Or, instead, as Monsignor Knox, who was less convinced of the desirability of all these transformations, writes when reflecting on the question of how Marcion's heresy was possible so shortly after Paul's absence:

> The mind of Paul has been misunderstood all down the centuries; there is no aberration of Christianity which does not point to him as the source of its inspiration, found as a rule, in his Epistle to the Romans.[34]

Whichever persuasion one endorses, it is clear from both Harnack's and Knox's citations that time and again the turn to Paul inspired and motivated a resistance to the status quo that marked the church at the time. As Welborn suggests, with Rom. 13:11, Paul is fundamentally issuing a wake-up call.[35] Wake-up call, resistance and reformation – each of the characterisations point to transformation and change.

The philosophers tap into this remarkable potential embraced in and proclaimed by Paul's letters. For them, Paul's letters signal a new beginning. Badiou, for instance, speaks of a 'pure beginning' (*pur commencement*) and Heidegger of 'only beginning' (*nur Anfang*).[36] Paul proclaims that something new has started, and through this, new distinctions come into play – or old distinctions with a new significance – such as between life and death, between spirit and flesh, and between faith and law, and a new sense of community is established. This idea of the new beginning raises questions concerning the status of the old, and these questions are answered differently by different authors. Yet, they all seem to agree that, according to Paul, nothing stays with the old.

With some of the philosophical reflections on Paul, and in particular of those scholars that work extensively with Badiou and Agamben, this focus on the proclamation of the new should be seen against the backdrop of a political reality that does not seem to allow any alternative. While, in Paul's time, the Roman Empire determined this reality, authors such as Badiou and Agamben translate it in the political constellation that took shape in the nineties. Following the fall of the Berlin Wall, it seemed the Western world had but one political-economic option left: that of capitalism. As bankrupt as communism was towards the end, it was still an alternative to the political reality to be found on the western side of the Wall. Today, capitalism and neoliberalism still seem to be the only option, tempting Žižek to posit that it is easier for us to imagine the end of the world than the end of capitalism. Especially in a world order that offers no alternative and in which history seems to be at its end, Badiou and Žižek turn to Paul as the one who knows how to herald a new beginning in a given socio-political and historical status quo.[37]

However, when assessing and furthering the importance of the new, it is important to recognise that the formal sense of the proclamation of a beginning has not been exhausted by this particular attention to the end of history in the 1990s. There are still structures in place today – of which capitalism has remained – that seem unchangeable when left to their own accord and logic and that therefore ask for a genuine new beginning.

In this more formal sense, Paul's proclamation of the new does not merely concern the unexpected – something truly new is, after all, always unexpected – but also the impossible or that which is not deemed possible. As Kearney argues, the image of the death and resurrection of Christ, the central focus of Paul's letters, is the ultimate paradigm of the impossible becoming possible: 'For Paul, the basic wager of Christian *dunamis* is the good news that it is now *possible* to overcome the *impossible* – to defy what Heidegger would call the impossibility of possibility, namely *death*.'[38] The Pauline God is thus also concerned with the gesture of giving up our sense of the possible and the impossible. The subsequent question is how this image should be understood and explained philosophically. One thing is clear: the new beginning has to be understood as exceptional and extraordinary. That is why, in conversation with Paul, philosophers turn to categories such as exception, remainder, event and excess – and my approach, if the reader will pardon the pun, is no exception to this rule. These terms refer to something in the order of reality that goes beyond the limits of the norm and of that which can be accounted for in the logic of the order that is in place.

(b) Mode of Living, Thinking and Being

If there is one theme in contemporary philosophy that expresses the revaluation of ancient culture, it is that of the *art of living* and the view that ancient philosophy is not concerned with knowing for the sake of knowing alone, but knowing for the sake of attaining the true *attitude to life* and the true *mode of living*. The revaluation of ancient philosophy as a mode of thinking that teaches us an art of living is introduced by Hadot and Foucault in contemporary philosophy.[39]

The true mode of living to which the ancient philosopher aspires can best be described as a 'life according to the spirit'.[40] This life demands turning one's soul to the spirit, which can only take place through spiritual exercises and techniques. These exercises are aimed at changing a person in such a way that they finally have the ability to receive or see the truth. Apparently, humans are at first not capable of doing so. The ability to see the truth is not a given but is, at best, something like a second nature's capacity, which can only be appropriated and nourished through meticulous exercise. Thus, a metamorphosis is required, a change of the form of the person and their mode of living.

In the Allegory of the Cave, Plato famously illustrates the strenuousness of the spiritual exercises required to realise such liberation in terms of the training and education – *paideia* – of the human souls in order to acquire insight into the truth.[41] Plato defines *paideia* as this art of *turning around*. Thus, education is not the carving of knowledge into the soul of pupils but the turning around of 'the entire soul'. Through this, the soul no longer focuses on the world of appearance and shadows but learns to behold the world of the true and the permanent.

In yet another normative text, the *Nicomachean Ethics*, Aristotle attributes the highest excellence and happiness to this state of beholding and contemplation – *theōria*. For this, Aristotle uses the formula of 'living according to the spirit'.[42] Yet, it is important to note here that 'spirit' renders the Greek *nous*, which also means 'reason' or 'intellect'. It does not translate *pneuma*, which plays a crucial part in Stoic and Pauline thought. Although for Stoicism, *nous* and *pneuma* are closely related, *pneuma* has a semantic field different from *nous*; like the Hebrew word *ruach*, it can also mean 'wind', 'gust of wind', 'breathing' or 'breathed air'.[43]

Aristotle distinguishes between mortality and immortality to indicate in which direction the human soul should turn. One should not listen to those who advise 'that a man should have man's thoughts and a mortal the thoughts of mortality', but 'we ought so far as possible to achieve immortality' and strain every nerve to live according to that best part of us.[44] Even if humans are not immortal according to Aristotle, they live immortally when they share in the most splendid and divine activity of the spirit, the *nous*.[45]

The present-day reappraisal of ancient philosophy is part of the context in which the turn to Paul takes place in the 1990s. We cannot fully understand the attention to Paul without considering the broader present-day philosophical focus on the art and mode of living in ancient philosophy and culture, and I will say more about this in Chapter 2. In this respect, Paul is a representative of ancient culture. So, it need not surprise that the mode of living Paul propagates is a central theme in philosophical readings. Yet, in the reflection on this theme, Paul's uniqueness also emerges. For Plato and Aristotle, spiritual life is in the first place a life that is aimed at contemplation of *theōria* and a life of the *nous*, the intellect. Paul's case is different.

The new beginning announced is always accompanied by an instruction to live differently, namely in accordance with the death and resurrection of Christ. While the death of Christ stands for disengagement from the way of life familiar to the world, the idea of life in accordance with the resurrection of Christ is a Pauline analogue of Aristotle's immortal life. Paul never presents the new beginning as a purely objective incident to which one can relate objectively. Rather, it requires human involvement and commitment. To obtain access to this new beginning, engagement and exercise are necessary. This mode of living is fundamentally nonconformist in the sense expressed in Romans: 'Do not be conformed to this world, but be transformed [*metamorphouste*] by the renewing of your minds [*nous*]' (Rom. 12:2). The Greek *nous*, translated here as mind, should be understood in the right way: it stands for the whole of our tendencies, moods, thoughts and so forth. How we are, how we see and experience the world and our relationship to the world – all of that needs to undergo a metamorphosis. Our mode of being, our mode of thinking and our mode of living must be renewed. The congruence between Paul's proclamation and the teaching of ancient philosophers seems apparent.

Yet, the citation from Rom. 12 also marks an important difference. The term *nous* does not only denote pure intellect, and the call to the new life is not in the first instance a call to contemplation or *theōria*. This does not mean that contemplation does not play any part for Paul, but rather that another term is at the heart of his analysis of mode of living. That term is *pistis*, which is usually rendered as 'faith' but which has a whole host of connotations in Greek, particularly centred on the word 'trust'. *Pistis* not only means 'trust', but can also refer to that in which trust is expressed, such as the faith put in something or someone, or to trustworthiness of something or someone, or to credit that is given us. Additionally, *pistis* can be used for that which inspires trust. A guarantee, an assurance or a solemn pledge inspire trust, but so does that which convinces us, such as evidence or arguments. Moreover, *pistis* can refer to that which is entrusted to us.[46] When Paul introduces *pistis*, and particularly the *pistis* of Jesus Christ, it is a concept fundamentally different from *theōria*. The relationship between God, Christ and believers is primarily understood in terms of *pistis* and not of *theōria*. At the same time, we should not mistakenly assume that this distinction between *pistis* and *theōria* implies that the latter term should be placed within the realm of reason and rationality and the former in the realm of the unreasonable and irrational. In the Greek, the word *pistis* is not set off against the notion of reason at all because the core meaning of trust does not exclude reasonableness: we may equally have a reasonable and an unreasonable trust in something or someone, but the former is held in higher esteem than the latter in ancient culture. The succinct sense of faith as that which does not follow the rules of reason, such as it emerges, for instance, in the work of Hume and Kierkegaard, is much rather a product of the modern age. Because contemporary philosophy is also exposed to the influence of Kierkegaard and related modern authors, it remains to be seen how to treat Paul's understanding of *pistis* in a present-day philosophical context. Nevertheless, it is clear that the analysis of the concept of faith must be central to a philosophical account because it is a core notion in the mode of living Paul propagates. Faith is in the first place the term for an *attitude to life* with which one relates to the new, and the way in which one enacts one's life in light of this new beginning. This mode of living is understood in different ways, but basic, shared predicates are: nonconformity, faithfulness and perseverance.

Žižek points out how this very theme of faith is crucial to Paul's letters and how it challenges Nietzsche's infamous analysis from *The Antichrist* that Paul would be only interested in life after death – that is, the afterlife – and as such would negate the life lived here and now. A contemporary reading of Paul's letters is, Žižek suggests, not led by the 'question "Is there (eternal) life after death?"' but by the 'question "Is there life before death?"' It is ultimately about the following concern: '[A]m I really alive here and now, or am I just vegetating, as a mere human animal bent on survival?'[47] Rather than the afterlife, such an intensified life is at stake in a philosopher's Paul.

This life is marked by an engagement that can pre-eminently be thought of in terms of Paul's notions of resurrection and faith. About the former, Žižek writes: 'Today we are like the anemic Greek philosophers who read Paul's words on the Resurrection with ironic laughter.'[48] About the latter, he writes:

> Recall the outrage when, two years ago, the Taliban forces in Afghanistan destroyed the ancient Buddhist statues at Bamiyan: although none of us enlightened Westerners believe in the divinity of the Buddha, we were outraged because the Taliban Muslims did not show the appropriate respect for the 'cultural heritage' of their own country and the entire world.[49]

The difference with the Western enlightened point of view is that the Taliban Muslims 'really believed in their own religion [...] to them, the Buddha statues were just fake idols, not "cultural treasures."' There is much to be said about this provocative example. Yet, it is clear that it is meant to demonstrate that faith and resurrection are untimely concepts (that have become) foreign to contemporary Western culture. For Žižek, Paul's letters can no longer simply be interpreted or appropriated in terms of present-day Western culture, even if they have been normative for and present in this culture for centuries. In this way, these letters form a cultural source of the West going beyond its current horizon of understanding.

Regardless of what one might think of Žižek and his examples, it is important to understand that the hermeneutic movement he makes here is not farfetched. Paul's letters indeed contain something non-contemporary, untimely, unprecedented and unthought-of (that has become) foreign to the very culture they originally (in)formed. To the extent that these letters are not completely foreign to this culture, it must be possible to make their content accessible again in present-day terms. For this reason, these letters must be reread and interpreted in light of today's cultural and social questions. It is a well-known hermeneutic principle that the start of an historical development is richer and more abundant than what follows from it, because it is marked by a multitude of possibilities, some of which are realised in time and some of which are not. The philosophical turn to Paul's letters may be understood in exactly this way. It is an attempt to broach the (philosophical) potential and expressiveness of these texts and its notions: what do faith and resurrection exactly say?

(c) Principle of the Spirit

For Paul, living according to the spirit is grafted on the Greek term *pneuma* rather than on *nous*. In a rather critical assessment of the turn to Paul, Stowers argues that the philosophical attention to the mode of living expressed in Paul's letters shows that the present-day readings are indebted to the reading of Bultmann, who focuses on the so-called *Existenz-Verständnis*, the understanding of human existence, expressed in these letters.[50] Others seem to subscribe to this argument as well: it can be found in Blanton and was quite significantly present in discussions I attended.[51]

Concerning this argument, the title of Stowers's essay is telling: 'Paul as a hero of subjectivity.' Today's philosophers, so he claims, are only concerned with the Paul who discovers new possibilities of existing for the human subject. However, such a strictly socio-ethical explanation of Paul is an anachronism, as he notes, because it completely conceals the specific ontological and cosmological commitments that allow

Paul to formulate these new possibilities. To reinforce his reproach, he cites Badiou's interpretation of the Pauline distinction between flesh and spirit: 'It makes perfect sense that Badiou treats flesh and spirit in the letters in a way similar to the Bultmann school's "understanding of existence."'[52] What 'makes perfect sense' is the following. For Badiou, *pneuma* is an ethical concept and perhaps a philosophical-anthropological concept, but not an ontological or cosmological one; this need not surprise us, according to Stowers, because there is not a single philosopher today who endorses Paul's cosmological concept of a divine *pneuma*.

This divine spirit is a 'heavenly substance', some material thing that not only gave way to Christ's resurrection but would also, in the resurrection of believers, replace the perishable and impermanent substance, so that they too could become divine, heavenly creatures. Stowers himself does not explain the exact nature of this substance, but he is referring to Paul's Stoic background as explored in the recent work of Engberg-Pedersen. The latter argues that Paul's concept of spirit is a thoroughly Stoic one that should therefore also be understood from this Stoic framework.[53] Indeed, Stowers is correct that Badiou does not mention this cosmology and does not transfer it to his own ontology. Nevertheless, it is incorrect to say that no ontological commitment can be found in the contemporary turn to Paul. I even dare say that this ontological commitment concerns exactly the notion of the spirit.

Let us briefly reflect on what it actually means that Paul uses a Stoic vocabulary.[54] A comparison might clarify this. Kierkegaard often uses a vocabulary derived from Hegel and the Hegelians of his time, but does that make him, the self-declared anti-Hegelian, a Hegelian? Or should we rather say the opposite, namely that we only get to discover the real Kierkegaard if we capture his idiomatic and idiosyncratic use of and deviations from Hegelian vocabulary? Keeping in mind this comparison, I want to recall, for the purpose of illustration and orientation, two examples of Paul's Stoic vocabulary.

First, when Paul draws a distinction between the spirit of the world (*to pneuma tou kosmou*) and the spirit of God (*to pneuma to ek tou theou*) in 1 Cor. 2:12, the question arises whether such a distinction between *kosmos* and God is at all conceivable in Stoicism. For the Stoics, the *pneuma* of the world is identical to the *pneuma* of God. There is no distinction here. For the philosopher interested in the historical effect of certain concepts, it will hardly come as a surprise that Hegel, who appropriates the Stoic *pneuma*-concept for his own philosophical project and develops a phenomenology of spirit, *Phänomenologie des Geistes*, can speak about the spirit of the world (*Weltgeist*), which means: the spirit that leads the historical and rational development of reality.⁵⁵ At this point, it is not inconceivable that Paul, by contrast, introduces an idiomatic use of *pneuma* and distinguishes a spirit of God that is not so easily inserted into a Stoic framework.⁵⁶ We shall see in Chapter 1 that, at this point, it is Taubes who suggests a fundamental difference between Hegel, as the heir of the Stoic *pneuma*, and Paul. Apparently, in contrast to what Stowers seems to think, serious attention *is* and *must be* paid to the ontological and cosmological dimension of the concept of spirit, albeit not in terms of identifying or interpreting the exact nature of the substance that the Stoics had in mind under this heading. The attention of a contemporary philosophical reading is rather drawn to those passages in which Paul does not appear to be an orthodox Stoic – if there ever was such a thing as an orthodox Stoic – but rather offers a creative variation of Stoicism that, by varying, also disengages from it.

Second, if this spirit of God is active in the resurrection of Christ, this resurrection is, both in the world and for the spirit of the world, undoubtedly an event in the strong sense that Badiou confers on the term. Here, the Stoic perspective on the relationship of *pneuma* and *cosmos* fails because we are no longer dealing with degrees of being but rather with two incomparable 'entities'. Interestingly, at the very moment that Stowers explains his basic thesis in discussion with Badiou's work and posits that contemporary philosophers understand the Pauline concept *pneuma* only as an ethical or philosophical anthropological category, he refers to the notion 'event', which is the pre-eminently metaphysical concept in Badiou's oeuvre. It is this very concept, notwithstanding all our possible questions about and objections to it (to which I will return in extenso later), that seems rather fitting in a reading of Paul that aims to locate the point at which the apostle starts negotiating with Stoic cosmology and draws a distinction between the spirit of the world and the spirit of God. In an astute remark, to which I shall return in the forthcoming chapters, Taubes essentially raises the same point, albeit in a different vocabulary: 'And it's a different matter whether one decides, in whatever way, to understand the cosmos as immanent and governed by laws, or whether one thinks the miracle is possible, the exception.'⁵⁷ The Stoic view of the cosmos is fundamentally immanent. By drawing a distinction between two spirits, it is all but evident that Paul would endorse such immanence.

OVERVIEW

In my discussion of the conception of the spirit, I probably exceeded the boundaries of what is properly included in an introduction. Nevertheless, I wanted to mention the complicated issues concerning the spirit and show that in this very first discussion a problem emerges regarding the tension between the *immanence* of the Stoic cosmos and its ultimately monist order, on the one hand, and the *transcendence* of the spirit of God and its corresponding *dualism*, on the other.

This tension derives from Paul's letters and their interpretations. The philosophical repercussions of this tension are discussed in Chapters 1 and 2, in which I address it in reference to two decisive names in the history of the reception of Paul who pose a challenge as well as a threat to a philosophical reinterpretation of Paul: Marcion of Sinope and Friedrich Nietzsche. While Marcion burdens the reception of Paul with the Gnostic temptation and the problem of dualism, Nietzsche accuses Paul of a nihilism affecting his thoughts about reality and about faith or *pistis*. These two chapters set the stage for the ontological issues discussed in Chapters 3 and 4 as well as for the ethical implications. It is, I argue, the attention to the particular attitude to life or ethos developed in ancient philosophy and in Paul that allows us to come to a better understanding of the political and philosophical stakes of the turn to Paul discussed in Chapters 5 and 6.

In Chapter 3, I examine in detail the charge of nihilism. In particular, I show that Paul's understanding of the world implies a certain 'meontology', but no nihilism. This reappraisal of Paul's meontology allows me to emphasise the motif of the outcast; this motif compares to what Bradley has recently introduced as 'unbearable life', that is, the life that 'is simply deemed to be ontologically or politically nonexistent'.[58] The acknowledgement of this 'scum of the world' is far from a nihilistic gesture because it allows the outcast to appear in the first place.

Chapter 4 examines the pre-eminent event in the letters of Paul and discusses which sense of temporality it implies. I show that these questions concerning the Pauline event can be posed in discussion with the thought of Hegel, who offers a modern, dynamic version of Stoic monism. Paul's version of the spirit offers an alternative take on Hegel's dialectic understanding of the spirit of the world. To flesh out this alternative, I turn to Kierkegaard and particularly to his notion of the exception. In the recent discussion on Paul, the Kierkegaardian legacy is usually limited to Schmitt's political philosophical reappraisal of this concept, but in Chapters 3 and 4, I show that there is more profound legacy of the Danish genius that helps us to understand Paul better in a modern context. Along these lines, Chapters 3 and 4 examine issues that already arise in Chapters 1 and 2, and a clear pattern emerges: Paul's reflections about world and time – and the modes of being, thinking and living that go with them – offer contemporary philosophy the means to navigate between the Scylla of monism and the Charybdis of dualism.

Chapters 5 and 6 examine Paul's political theology, another fundamental theme in contemporary philosophy. The background of this examination is a discussion with Schmitt, who provides a politico-philosophical (mis)interpretation of Kierkegaard's notion of 'exception'. In discussion with Schmitt, it is shown that Paul's analysis of the law, which is the central theme of Chapter 5, and the demand for a new community, discussed in Chapter 6, offer a fundamentally different political theology, one that is an extension of the true Kierkegaardian sense of exception. These chapters provide a practico-philosophical consequence of Paul's account of the principle of the spirit and furthermore show how the results of Chapters 3 and 4 also lead to other modes of thinking and living in politico-philosophical terms.

Finally, in the Epilogue I gather the results of the previous chapters by displaying a philosophical portrait of Paul that emphasises the features of a dialectic of exception. This allows us to assess whether and to which extent, when one adopts this portrayal of Paul, his 'serious words' have regained their breath and their inspiration so they can be heard to speak of another legacy.

NOTES

1. I have replaced 'newborn words' by 'firstfruits of the word' to render *Erstlinge des Wortes* in order to maintain the Pauline reference to *tēn aparchēn tou pneumatos*, 'the firstfruits of the spirit' (Rom. 8:23).
2. Throughout this study, unless indicated otherwise, I refer to originals and translations as #a/#b, where #a denotes the page number of the original and #b the page number of the translation.
3. See Van der Heiden, 'Witnessing the Uninhabitable Place'.
4. Unless otherwise stated, translations of biblical passages are taken from the New Revised Standard Version (NRSV). The specific phrasing 'the scum of the world', however, stems from the English Standard Version (ESV) and can also be found in the New International Version (NIV) as 'the scum of the earth'; the NRSV suggests 'the rubbish of the world'.
5. Blanton, *A Materialism for the Masses*; Jennings, *Outlaw Justice*; Crockett, *Radical Political Theology*, 126–44.
6. See, e.g., Jennings, *Outlaw Justice*, 69, 113.
7. Blanton, *A Materialism for the Masses*, 3–4.

8   In the framework of the philosophical positioning of relativism and particularism, Žižek argues in *The Puppet and the Dwarf*, 139–41, that we should return to the early Derrida and his concept of *différance* and not follow his later development since it could give way to forms of particularism as it would lead to a choice between either totalitarianism or otherness (read: a particularism in the making).
9   Badiou, *Saint Paul*, 10/9–10, 14/13.
10 See, e.g., ibid., 10–14; Žižek, *The Puppet and the Dwarf*, 130; Martin, 'The Promise of Teleology', 91; and Stowers, 'Paul as a Hero of Subjectivity', 160.
11 Blanton and De Vries, *Paul and the Philosophers*; Caputo and Alcoff, *St. Paul among the Philosophers*; Frick, *Paul in the Grip of the Philosophers*; and Van der Heiden, Van Kooten and Cimino, *Saint Paul and Philosophy*.
12 Bloechl, 'Love and Law according to Paul and Some Philosophers', 151. Note that Bloechl limits this remark to the Pauline understanding of community.
13 Muller, *Professor of Apocalypse*, 487.
14 See also Taubes, '"Frist"'.
15 Løland, *Pauline Ugliness*.
16 Critchley, *The Faith of the Faithless*, chap. 4.
17 Badiou, *Saint Paul*, 2/2.
18 Žižek, *On Belief*, 150.
19 Agamben, *Il tempo che resta*, 9/1.
20 Frederiksen, 'Historical Integrity, Interpretive Freedom', 72.
21 See also Løland, *Pauline Ugliness*, 14–15.
22 Blanton, 'Mad with the Love of Undead Life', 211.
23 Frick, *Paul in the Grip of the Philosophers*, 7.
24 Concerning the image of Saint Paul, see Benjamin, 'Reading, Seeing and the Logic of Abandonment'.
25 Frick, *Paul in the Grip of the Philosophers*, 8.
26 Van der Heiden, *The Voice of Misery*.
27 1 Cor. 4:13, English Standard Version.
28 This is noted, e.g., by Depoortere, 'Badiou's Paul', 163.
29 Gadamer, *Wahrheit und Methode*, 270–90/278–96.
30 Ricœur, *De l'interprétation*, 36–44/28–36.
31 Gadamer, *Wahrheit und Methode*, 356–64/359–66.
32 Critchley, *The Faith of the Faithless*, 155.
33 Ibid., 155; Harnack, *Lehrbuch der Dogmengeschichte*, 116.
34 Knox, *Enthusiasm*, 11. Quoted in Lilla, *The Shipwrecked Mind*, chap. 'From Mao to Saint Paul'.
35 Welborn, *Paul's Summons to Messianic Life*, 71.
36 Badiou, *Saint Paul*, 52/49; Heidegger, *Phänomenologie des religiösen Lebens*, 139/98.
37 Badiou, *Saint Paul*, 2/2.
38 Kearney, 'Paul's Notion of *Dunamis*', 148.

39 For more on Hadot's point of view, see Chase, Clark and McGhee, *Philosophy as a Way of Life*.
40 Hadot, *Qu'est-ce que la philosophie antique?*, 247/160. Hadot uses this expression several times.
41 Plato, *The Republic* VIII.518c–d.
42 Aristotle, *Nichomachean Ethics* X.7.1177b30–78a8.
43 See Liddell-Scott-Jones, *s.v. pneuma*. I use the Liddell-Scott-Jones version as included in the *Perseus Digital Library*; see http://www.perseus.tufts.edu/hopper/.
44 Aristotle, *Nichomachean Ethics* X.7.1177b30–78a1; for the translation, see LCL 73: 617.
45 See also Badiou, *Logiques des mondes*, 529/507.
46 See Liddell-Scott-Jones, *s.v. pistis*.
47 Žižek, 'The Necessity of a Dead Bird', 184.
48 Žižek, *The Puppet and the Dwarf*, 99.
49 Ibid., 7–8.
50 Stowers, 'Paul as a Hero of Subjectivity', 168–70.
51 Blanton, *A Materialism for the Masses*, 69, speaks of the Lutheran dimension of the readings of Boyarin, Badiou and Breton; this dimension refers also to Bultmann.
52 Stowers, 'Paul as a Hero of Subjectivity', 169.
53 Concerning the notion of *pneuma* as thoroughly material, see in particular Engberg-Pedersen, *Cosmology and Self in the Apostle Paul*. Also see Sellars, *Stoicism*, 91–9.
54 Engberg-Pedersen manoeuvres very carefully here when saying that Paul's ideas are 'Stoic-like', *Cosmology and Self in the Apostle Paul*, 98. See also Barclay, 'Stoic Physics and the Christ-event', 407.
55 Interestingly, the reappearance of the Stoic spirit in modern philosophy seems to elude Stowers. He offers an overview of modern philosophy, in which Descartes, Kant, Nietzsche, Schopenhauer, Heidegger, Marx, Althusser and Lacan are included, but Hegel is missing in an argument on the modern reception of the Stoic concept of *pneuma*. See 'Paul as a Hero of Subjectivity', 160–8.
56 See Engberg-Pedersen, *Cosmology and Self in the Apostle Paul*, 228–9; Barclay, 'Stoic Physics and the Christ-event', 411.
57 Taubes, *Die politische Theologie des Paulus*, 118/85.
58 Bradley, *Unbearable Life*, 5.

1. *The Dialectic Spirit of Paul*

Paul lived in the ancient world. New Testament research consistently shows how ancient philosophical language, vocabulary and notions permeate his letters. In these letters, one may, for instance, rediscover the cosmology of Stoicism but also an anthropology strongly inspired by Plato.[1] When realising this, one begins to understand why Paul's letters are not only missionary texts or occasional epistles addressing questions relevant to the communities with which the apostle corresponded. They also contain a specific philosophical potential and evoke particular philosophical questions, allowing for the discovery of something universal in them, beyond the confines of the specific situation in which, and occasion for which, they were originally written.

At the end of the previous chapter, I briefly discussed the Stoic background of Paul's use of the terms *pneuma* and *cosmos*. In 1 Cor. 15, there is an even stronger presence of the Stoic vocabulary and cosmology, as Engberg-Pedersen has argued.[2] The presence of this cosmology is philosophically interesting because it seems to imply that Paul, just like the Stoics, opts for a cosmological *monism*. At the same time, this monism seems difficult to reconcile with his distinction between a spirit of the world and a spirit of God, as found in 1 Cor. 2:12.

Interestingly, such a tension with Stoic ideas can also be traced in 1 Cor. 15. In the rhetoric of this chapter, Paul draws a distinction several times between what is rendered as natural or sensuous – the Greek terms are *psuchē* and *psuchikon*, which refer to the principle of animal life – and the spiritual – *pneuma* and *pneumatikon*. Whether it concerns the description of the first Adam as the living being and the last Adam as the life-giving spirit (Cor. 15:45), or the contrast between the natural body (*sōma psuchikon*) and the spiritual body (*sōma pneumatikon*, 1 Cor. 15:44), these distinctions play a crucial role. From the perspective of Stoicism – a 'standard' or 'average' Stoicism, if there is such a thing – this is a rather strange distinction, because Stoics usually understand *psuchē* as one of the lower gradations – or tensions, *tonos* – of *pneuma*.³ Hence, these two terms are not seen as opposites: *psuchē* rather describes a particular degree of complexity in reality, higher than those expressed by the terms *hexis*, referring to physical cohesion, and *phusis*, referring to life in general; yet, all are degrees of complexity of *pneuma*. In Paul's vocabulary, however, we do see a juxtaposition that seems to challenge Stoics monism. He alludes to two principles, natural or animal *versus* pneumatic life, thereby rather suggesting a dualism.⁴

To be precise, the distinction as such between the transitory and the permanent is generally Stoic. Within Stoicism, the cosmos is presented as a developing whole with a particular life cycle that ends in a return through a conflagration, *ekpurōsis*, to pure *pneuma*. Yet, this still amounts to a monism because the life cycle is nothing other than *pneuma* ordering and organising itself in degrees of complexity and returning to itself. This organisation is so perfect that, once completed, the cycle starts afresh from the beginning and repeats itself in the exact same way, in an eternal repetition of the same. Within such a strict monistic view, there is no reason to *oppose* the transitory to the permanent, because the transitory is but a moment in the life cycle of the permanent – a life cycle that is affirmed by *pneuma* time and again in endless repetition. Paul's rhetoric, however, rather emphasises an opposition between natural and spiritual, transitory and permanent, earthly and heavenly, and so forth.⁵

This raises the following question. Are Paul's views to be characterised as a monism à la Stoicism or rather as a dualism, which might point to a more Platonic legacy itself clearly discernible in his anthropology? This question on monism or dualism has direct consequences for the leitmotif of transformation. In the Stoic view of the cosmos, there is development, but there is no transformation in the strong sense of the word because all development is that of one spirit, which, moreover, endlessly repeats itself in the same way. If there is something missing from the Stoic universe, it is what contemporary philosophy calls 'event', which refers to a transformation in the strongest sense of the word, as well as to a genuine sense of history. While absent from Stoicism, the present-day readers of Paul do find proper events in Paul's letters, for instance under the heading of the resurrection of Christ. In Rom. 8, the transience of creation is described as a form of servitude from which the spirit should liberate creation. Yet, why would this reference to a liberation of creation be necessary if the cycle comprising creation is merely the rational development of *pneuma* itself, as Stoicism contends? Why would this spirit have to plead on our behalf 'with sighs too deep for words' (Rom. 8:26), and what is the urgency of suffering or the senselessness of the transitory if it has always already been part of the natural self-deployment of the cosmic spirit?[6] In such passages, Paul is negotiating with and displacing the Stoic meaning of the term *pneuma*. He even seems to be engaged in a polemic with Stoicism when he suggests that another spirit, that of God, is to be considered beside the spirit of the world (*to pneuma tou kosmou*).

Should the conclusion of these considerations be that Paul is rather a dualist? A long reception history that emphasises Paul's dualism supports an affirmative answer to this question. Among philosophers, this dualistic reception is linked to two names in particular, one from antiquity and one from the more recent past: Marcion of Sinope and Friedrich Nietzsche. The importance of these two figures as a (negative) benchmark for reading Paul is strikingly present in Critchley's *The Faith of the Faithless*. He argues that, for instance, Heidegger, Badiou and Agamben are not capable of overcoming a dualist Paul and, in fact, present a Marcionite Paul – and that is hardly a compliment.[7] Critchley's argumentation is characteristic for the particular, twofold task assigned to a renewed reading of Paul. The name of Marcion serves as a litmus test to determine whether or not a philosophical interpretation of Paul is capable of radically transforming the Pauline legacy. Therefore, we need to consider in more detail later why Critchley charges the authors who themselves emphatically reject the Marcionite Paul, of Marcionism; and whether he is justified in doing this. For now, however, we first need to be aware that the name of Marcion does not only represent a particular interpretation of Paul but also a temptation intrinsic to Paul's letters. With respect to an interpretation of Paul, one of the guiding questions is whether and to what extent it is capable of resisting this temptation.

The attempts to reveal the Stoic quality of Paul's letters can be read – and that is why they are so important – as attempts to overcome this temptation. Yet, the overall picture that arises from this multiplicity of approaches to Paul – emphasising either monism or dualism – is a Paul marked by a specific tension between monism and dualism. Perhaps – such is the suggestion I aim to develop in the next chapters – this tension is intentional in order to pave a way out of this alternative. Whether this suggestion makes sense needs to be examined. The first step in this examination is understanding why Marcionite dualism needs to be rejected as a framing of Paul. This is the task of this chapter. The next chapter will raise similar questions with respect to Nietzsche's conception of a Pauline nihilism.

PAUL, A DUALIST?

According to Taubes, the reception history of Paul is thoroughly coloured by Marcion of Sinope, the first interpreter of Paul. The father of Marcionism, a form of Gnosticism that played a significant role in early Christianity, was excommunicated in 144 CE because of his theological views. He is the first person to have declared a canon of Bible books, which comprised his own version of the Gospel – a revised version of Luke's, as Irenaeus suggests – as well as rewritten versions of Paul's letters, but not a single book from the Tanakh, the collection of Jewish religious scriptures that in Christianity is sometimes referred to as the Old Testament.[8]

Paul, one gathers from the canon proposed by Marcion, played an important role for him in formulating the viewpoints that led to his excommunication. Of crucial importance for Marcion is the distinction between two gods, and the two realities corresponding to these two gods. The God of the world or of creation is the source of evil. This is the God of the Old Testament of which the Jewish Tanakh would speak. The true God is the father of Jesus Christ, who represents the principle of the spirit (*pneuma*) and the good, but has nothing to do with the first God. With these two respective gods, Marcion introduces a form of dualism: reality splits into two and is determined by two mutually exclusive principles.

This Gnostic dualism was strongly influenced by Platonic dualism, in which a purely intelligible world is pitted against the sensory world and in which the body is described as a cage and prison of the soul, which denies the soul the true view of the highest and shackles it to physical desire; in the famous image of Plato's *Phaedrus*:

> [The soul] is forced to examine other things through it as through a cage and not by itself, and that it wallows in every kind of ignorance. Philosophy sees that the worst feature of this imprisonment is that it is due to desires, so that the prisoner himself is contributing to his own incarceration most of all.[9]

The father of Jesus Christ is a god who is foreign to this world of creation and does not belong in it.[10] Likewise, the human soul is a stranger in the physical, created world. Because this body, as we see in the citation above, is inclined to mislead and corrupt the soul, making it even complicit in its own imprisonment, one should actively cultivate this foreignness and also actively focus on the other, uncreated reality of this other god. This dualistic worldview therefore prompts us to turn away from our bodies and this world, and place the centre of gravity of our existence in that other world and in our soul liberated from the shackles of our body.

This rejection of the world in which we live had significant consequences for the nature and practices of the Christian communities Marcion founded. The heretic from Sinope founded a church of ascetics in which celibacy was generally propagated and in which intercourse was to be waived, even in matrimony.[11] It goes without saying that such a mode of living results in communities that cannot maintain themselves through the birth of children. That is why new members constantly need to be recruited. For no other church is missionary work as vital as for this Gnostic one.

How does this Marcionism relate to Paul and to the influence of Paul's letters on our cultural history? To answer this question, Taubes may point the way. He notes that in certain respects, Marcion is closely aligned to Paul:

> It's easy to read the story of Paul one-sidedly and to overlook latent elements within him. No one understood him, one might say, but then no one completely misunderstood him either. It's not a question of showing, pedantically, where Marcion diverges from Paul; that's easily done. The question is where does he capture an intention [...].[12]

Indeed, Paul's letters do have a substantially 'Gnostic trait' and harbour a Gnostic temptation, to which Marcion succumbed.[13] For instance, the preoccupation of the Old Testament with lineage – such as in the stories about 'Sarah, Rebecca, Rachel and Hannah, the mother of Samuel' – is absent from Paul's letters, because lineage refers to the order of the 'flesh', which may easily be confused for that of the body. For Paul, Christ is the offspring of David, but only in spirit and not in flesh (Rom. 1:3–4).[14] Furthermore, it seems that the idea of creation plays only a supporting role for Paul, because the central motifs seem to be salvation and reconciliation. The passing away of the present figure of the world referred to in 1 Cor. 7, which I will discuss at length in especially Chapter 3, also seems perfectly connected with a Gnostic rejection of the world – at least at first sight. Moreover, passages exist in which Paul seems to make a direct link to a Gnostic experience of *sophia*, wisdom.[15] Finally, is Paul's use of the contrasts between flesh and spirit, law and religion, and death and life not a perfect illustration of a dualism on which Marcion could easily graft his own?

GNOSTIC TEMPTATION AND PAULINE SPIRIT

It is important, for the contemporary philosophical interpretation of Paul, to raise the issue of the Gnostic temptation, because the Gnostic version of Paul strongly influenced nineteenth- and early twentieth-century German liberal theology.[16] The eminent example is Von Harnack, who hails Marcion as the first reformer of the Church, as the citation in the previous chapter showed, rather than as the first one of a whole series of misunderstandings of Paul, as Knox proposes. Von Harnack emphatically agrees with Marcion's rejection of the Old Testament by stating that the upholding of these texts in the canon was a *Lähmung*, a paralysis that crippled Protestantism.[17] Marcion's legacy, with its rejection of Judaism, made Christianity receptive to anti-Semitism. This anti-Semitic orientation, as Taubes argues, helped to ensure that Protestant German liberal theology was not able to offer an intellectual counterbalance to Nazism in 1933.[18] For Taubes, as we shall discuss later, Paul's relationship with Judaism and the Old Testament is a core question in his discussion with Schmitt, who supported the Nazi regime for a substantial period of time.

Marcion's emphasis on the great dispute between Judaism and Christianity is also grounded in Paul's letters. In Romans, for instance, Paul laments the unbelief of Israel and speaks about the fall, rejection, and obscuration of Israel, calling Israel a branch that has 'broken off'.[19] In this regard, Marcion discerns a definite intent in Paul's letters. Nevertheless, one cannot limit oneself to these passages, since Paul writes more. Marcion's one-sided emphasis marks an important tradition of interpretation, but if one follows this emphasis, one forgets to read carefully, as Taubes claims Schmitt did: 'he did not take over a text but a tradition.'[20] In his own reading of Rom. 8–13, Taubes therefore indicates to what extent Paul refuses to let the above-mentioned rejection of Israel result in a mere juxtaposition or dualism between Judaism and Christianity; rather, Paul takes it up in a dialectic of salvation in which rejection not only contributes to the reconciliation of the heathens but in the final analysis also results in the salvation of Israel as a whole. In Chapter 6, which examines the theme of a Pauline community, this element is explored in detail. Requiring our attention at the moment, however, is the alternative to the dualism that Taubes finds in Rom. 8–13 and in which he sees an antidote to Gnostic temptation. This alternative gives us a first sense of Paul's *dialectic* method of reading, a procedure that is also followed elsewhere in his letters and that can be retrieved in what I would like to call his pneumatic hermeneutics.[21]

Rather than defining dialectic at this point as a technical philosophical concept, let me provide a Pauline example. In the above-mentioned context of Rom. 8–13, Paul's argumentation unfolds according to a dialectic movement. Besides the statement that Israel is a branch that has broken off, Paul also brings into play a contradistinction that negates and relativises the first statement, thus requiring us to read it in a different sense and to relate it to its contradistinction. Marcion may try to detach Paul from the Old Testament, but this does not change the fact that Paul himself, for instance in Romans, amply cites from texts from the Jewish tradition and, hence, resumes and reinterprets this tradition rather than rejecting or erasing it. This is part of a *dialectic* operation.

This brings us to a crucial point in the argument that aims to read Paul as offering a dialectic alternative to both monism and dualism. In order to explain how Paul reappropriates texts from the Jewish tradition in this dialectic operation, let us recall, with Taubes and Breton, a well-known distinction between two ways of reading and interpreting. Compared to the emphasis on the *sensus historicus*, the historical meaning of a text, or the *sensus nudus*, the naked meaning of a text, which both provide points of departure for the modern critique of the Bible, Paul's letters use another method of interpretation when speaking about Jewish writing.[22] When Paul cites texts, he rather aims at the *sensus allegoricus*, the allegorical meaning. The texts from the Old Testament point forward to that which is still to come, the crucifixion and resurrection of the Messiah that Paul proclaims. This allegorical interpretation raises important questions, certainly when viewed from the modern perspective.[23] How could the history of the people of Israel, centuries before the birth of Christ, point ahead to the vicissitudes of Jesus' death and resurrection? Is such a spiritualising reading of the Old Testament not eminently a denial of the Jewish histories? Nevertheless, this allegorical hermeneutics has a long history in the ancient world and thereafter.[24]

Nietzsche, for whom such an allegorical reading displays nothing but intellectual dishonesty, posits in his characteristic, sardonic way: 'wherever reference was made to wood, a rod, a ladder, a twig, a tree, [...] or a staff, such a reference could not but be a prophecy relating to the wood of the Cross.' To punctuate his suspicion of the intellectual dishonesty of this reading, he then asks rhetorically: 'Has anyone who asserted this ever *believed* it?'[25] Rhetorical or not, Taubes answers Nietzsche's question: 'Yes, Paul the Apostle.'[26] For Paul, the allegoric interpretation is not the product of a runaway, intellectually corrupt imagination that aims to reduce everything to the same – so that a piece of wood, a rod, a ladder, a twig, a tree and a staff all stand for the wood of the Cross – and that cannot do justice to the historical or literal meanings of the stories. For Paul, this interpretation is founded on a distinction between flesh (*sarx*) and spirit (*pneuma*), between a natural and a pneumatic order. This distinction is crucial for Paul. For this reason, it might be better not only to insert Paul's way of reading in a list of comparable allegorical readings, as Breton suggests, but also to call his hermeneutics a *pneumatic* hermeneutics, indicating that this hermeneutics can only be allegorical *because of* and *founded in* the principle of the spirit or *pneuma*.

At this point, it is important to note that, at first sight, this distinction between flesh and spirit may seem to fit perfectly into the Marcionite framework. Yet, there is a subtle, but crucially different interpretation possible. For Paul, the contrast between the natural and the pneumatic order is not the contrast between two *ontologically separated* worlds. Instead of a dualistic conception of the world, Paul offers a dialectic one. The interpretation that seeks the allegorical meaning does not exclude or erase the literal, historical or natural meaning but includes them in another, higher interpretation and in this way reveals a pneumatic meaning and significance.

Thus, apparently, there is a principle in reality, which Paul calls *pneuma* or spirit, by which the history of the Jewish people is not only this history but also the prehistory of something else.[27] Marcion's dualism postulates and hierarchises two realities and two gods in order to erase one of the two. The pneumatic interpretation does something entirely different. The histories related in the Jewish texts are not alien to the proclamation of Paul but form its prelude and are repeated at a different level in this proclamation. For this reason, we may understand the principle of the spirit or *pneuma* as the maxim of *transformation*. Paul does not wish to leave this world, but he does contemplate that the existing order of this world is characterised by a fundamental bankruptcy, as he so persuasively describes: 'For the creation was subjected to futility' and 'the whole creation has been groaning together' under this futility (Rom. 8:20, 22). Yet, this does not mean that creation should be destroyed but rather that creation eagerly looks out for the principle of the spirit, that is, to a principle that can transform this futility and meaninglessness, and *elevate creation itself to a higher, pneumatic meaning*.[28]

DIALECTIC BETWEEN MONISM AND DUALISM

When modern philosophy refers to dialectic, the name of Hegel invariably comes up. With respect to Hegel, Taubes's analysis offers another important ingredient for understanding the precise nature and stakes of a Pauline dialectic, which I will elaborate in Chapters 3 and 4. Earlier, reference was made to the distinction between the spirit of the world and the spirit of God (Cor. 2:12). This reference was made to show that Paul cannot simply be taken for a Stoic monist. Taubes refers to the same distinction to clarify that Paul's spirit of transformation and the corresponding dialectic he develops in his hermeneutics of Jewish texts should not be understood in terms of Hegel's introduction of the *Geist* as *Weltgeist* or 'spirit of the world'.[29] In modern times, Hegel is the preeminent heir of Stoicism who breathes new life into the Stoic concept of *pneuma* under the title of spirit of the world. He uses the term 'dialectic' to refer to the working of the spirit, and his understanding of dialectic is quite similar to my description above.

In order to position this dialectic and to prepare the ongoing discussion with Hegel in Chapters 3 and 4, let me emphasise the following features of Hegel's version of dialectic movement. For Hegel, dialectic movement is in the first place a movement from abstractness to concreteness, which can be clarified by the following example. We depart from a universal concept of the world and we hold this concept to be true, that is, in it we comprehend what the world is in itself. However, subsequently, we encounter or experience something in the world that contradicts our understanding of the world and confronts us with the fact that this concept does not capture the world in itself, but is rather how the world *appeared to be* for us. In this sense, our experience of the world negates our view or concept of (something in) the world. This negation, however, is not a negative result, because it inspires us to integrate the new experience of the world in a new conception of the world that preserves the truth of the old concept but also relativises it and allows the new experience of the world to become part of it. In this process, our universal concept of the world has become more concrete – and, hence, more universal, if it makes sense to speak of degrees of universality – since it now includes our own particular, concrete experience of the world.

This dialectic movement is, consequently, a movement of assimilation and appropriation. A concept is not a petrified or fixed entity, but is rather dynamic, capable of integrating and appropriating new concrete experiences. *Aufhebung*, or sublation, is the term that Hegel develops to describe the result of the confrontation of the concept with new experiences of the world. It is important to note – and I will return to this later – that this pivotal notion in Hegel's dialectics seems to be of Pauline descent itself. In this sense, Hegel's thought offers yet another interpretation of Paul. Important, however, is that the movement of *Aufhebung* is here understood as a rational and unifying movement of appropriation of all particulars that are encountered in and by an improved universal concept that has become more concrete in this process. Consequently, this movement is a teleological movement towards *totalisation*: it aims to include each and every concrete experience in its conceptuality. It is this particular goal that allows us to describe Hegel's dialectic thought as basically a form of monism. Moreover, it shows that the rational and absolute totality that is the goal of this movement, is related to only by *mediation*. These different characteristics of Hegelian dialectics – *Aufhebung* as appropriation, the productivity of negativity, its quality as mediation, and the absolute rational totality that unifies the different moments of negativity as the goal of the dialectic movement – need to be highlighted if one wants to understand in which sense and to what end the dialectic of Paul needs to be distinguished from that of Hegel. Yet, as we shall see again and again in the course of this study, this difference between forms of dialectic remains subtle and complicated – complicated because, as soon as one emphasises the difference with a Hegelian dialectics, one runs the risk of joining forces with a Marcionite, dualist account of Paul.

Hegel's concept of the *Weltgeist*, the spirit of the world, is nothing but this immanent, rational and organising process through which the world changes and through which our conception of it changes. For Hegel, spirit should therefore be understood as a principle of dialectic development that is *inherent* in the world itself and that will therefore take place necessarily and in a strictly rational manner. This dialectic development is thus a possibility and capacity of the spirit *intrinsic* to the world itself. This description of a spirit of the world, a *pneuma*, as an ordering principle of the development of the world or cosmos, allows one to call Hegel a truly modern heir of Stoicism.

Exactly at this point, however, we may discern an important difference with Paul and his principle of the spirit. Paul's pneumatic interpretation and the principle of transformation in which this mode of interpretation is grounded are not anchored in a *necessary* development. The principle of the spirit (of God) is no purely immanent or rational one that naturally occurs and unfolds in the world. Paul's pneumatic principle is not the principle of the spirit of the world, but rather that of the spirit of God. This latter principle brings something new and something different into play that does not allow itself to be understood from the existing world order and its intrinsic possibilities or potentialities. The pneumatic principle is active in the world, according to Paul, but is anchored and grounded in an event – that of the coming of the Messiah – that does not belong to the world and through which the working power of this principle really *began* for the first time.

Even in 1 Cor. 15:40–3, in which Paul so clearly uses Stoic vocabulary, the transformation that the resurrection of Christ brings about is central for him, and *pneuma* articulates the principle of this transformation. Completely in line with Stoic cosmology, he begins by speaking about the different *doxai* of earthly and heavenly bodies. *Doxa* is usually translated as 'glory', 'brilliance' or 'magnificence', but given the rhetoric with which Paul uses the term here, it could also be rendered somewhat poetically as 'esteem': the heavenly bodies are held in high esteem and the earthly in low esteem. There is also a difference between the esteem in which the heavenly bodies themselves are held, between the moon, the sun and the stars. Subsequently, Paul draws a parallel with the resurrection. The resurrection is, however, not so much something that is held in a certain esteem but is rather the term that describes that the esteem of bodies is not fixed or permanent, because this esteem can be transformed through the spirit: the mortal body is sown in insignificance or low esteem, as Paul writes, but is raised in the highest significance, esteem or glory of the spirit. Where Stoicism argues that degrees of esteem exist in reality and that the cycle of life culminates in pure *pneuma*, Paul argues in Stoic vocabulary that a transformation transpires through which that which is nothing and is totally insignificant is elevated to the status of pure *pneuma*. An interesting additional point is that Paul writes: 'But it is not the spiritual that is first, but the physical, and then the spiritual' (Cor. 15:46). As humans, we – and, according to Rom. 8:20–2, the whole creation – are naturally mortal and at the mercy of futility and insignificance but are transformed through the spirit into a new creation. At the end of this chapter, in discussion with Žižek, I will return to this specific order of natural and pneumatic to which Paul refers here.

Let us consider in this context Taubes's striking observation that the philosopher Walter Benjamin and the theologian Karl Barth share one basic Pauline trait: they resist the *immanentism* that characterises the thought of both the Stoics and Hegel. We use the term 'immanentism' if a principle is present in reality itself that causes the process of transformation. Benjamin and Barth are Pauline in so far as they deny the existence of only one natural principle or process of reality. The latter would imply that the cosmos does save or rationalise itself, as Hegel suggests in his variation of the spirit of the world. Benjamin and Barth, on the other hand, are of the view that salvation does not come from within: 'You have to be told from the other side that you're liberated.'[30] Thus something comes from outside the existing order through which *something other* begins and through which the world can be changed. At the same time, this beginning is not disconnected from the past; it rather brings this past to its fulfilment.

In philosophical terms, one would say that this 'other(ness)' transcends the immanent order of reality. Transcendence is up against immanence. Yet, one is, at the same time, faced with a challenge here. It does not suffice to simply call this transcendence 'other', because the latter term may suggest the existence of another, transcendent reality in addition to this reality. The contrast with both Marcion and Hegel reveals the Scylla and Charybdis that Paul tries to avoid. To avoid this Scylla and Charybdis is also the task of every study that aims to reveal the Pauline legacy of a dialectic of exception.

With the understanding of the spirit, Paul resists a strict immanentism in which there is nothing but the world order and its given laws or principles, but he also resists a strict dualism of two worlds. The distinction between spirit of the world and spirit of God therefore concerns the question of the nature of the cosmos itself. In the cosmos, is everything purely what it is, ruled by immanent principles – read: through the movement and self-development of the spirit of the world? Or is the cosmos of such nature that everything that is can also be *other(wise)*, and that there could be a principle, *pneuma*, that can really *begin* something? Taubes quite strikingly formulates this juxtaposition as follows, which is yet another crucial ingredient that needs to be reflected on when considering the Pauline legacy for philosophy today: 'And it's a different matter whether one decides, in whatever way, to understand the cosmos as immanent and governed by laws, or whether one thinks the miracle is possible, the exception.'[31] *Pneuma* is the name for the principle of this *possibility*. An exception can present itself in the existing order, and this exception forms a new beginning in the world, through which the world can be transformed.

In more metaphysical terms, one may understand this as follows. In philosophy, the terms for beginning and principle – both translating the Greek *archē* – usually refer to the basic presuppositions of the order of thinking and of being. So, for instance, the principle of sufficient reason holds that, for any being, sufficient grounds or reasons for its existence can be provided. This means that for every being we encounter in reality, we have the prior knowledge that reasons and grounds exist for its existence and that it therefore makes sense for us to try to find them. Thus, this principle expresses that which is always *presupposed*: that there are sufficient grounds for every being that exists is the presupposition of our scientific quest to find these reasons and grounds; this presupposition renders this quest meaningful in advance.

When *pneuma* is called a principle here, however, we should not understand it in this classic metaphysical way but rather as the term that expresses for Paul the possibility of a new beginning and a new principle. One might phrase it as follows. The pneumatic principle breaks away from the thought that a principle is always that which is presupposed. It posits, on the contrary, that an *archē* is a beginning; that *archē* concerns the enactment of this new beginning. This new beginning does not imply any dualism, because it changes something fundamental in the world in which it begins; at the same time, it resists monism because it resists the thought that the course of the world is characterised by a lawful, rational and organising continuity that is *always already* inscribed into reality. *Pneuma* is not so much the name for a transcendence – in the sense of another reality behind the reality in which we live – but the name for the exception that is always related to the rule or order to which it is an exception; it is a name for that which is not assimilated into the order of the cosmos and its laws. Differently put, it is a difference of the order with itself. As principle of exception, it interrupts the existing order and its regularities.

This reflection on the twofold meaning of *archē* is also part of other discussions in present-day thought. In her reading of *City of God*, Arendt notes how this difference between two forms of *archē* is reflected in Augustine's account of creation and how he uses two different words in Latin for these two forms of *archē*: *principium* and *initium*.[32] *Principium* concerns the beginning of creation. The divine act of creation is placed 'in the beginning', *in principio*, as a presupposition of the order of creation in which all creatures always already exist and behind – or before – which the creature can never reach.[33] *Initium*, on the other hand, concerns beginning as an intervention and interruption in the midst of a given order in creation, such as Arendt's example of birth makes perfectly clear: where there was nobody and nothing before, there is a human being to whom all present now must relate.[34] While Arendt emphasises the political meaning of this distinction, it also has a metaphysical bearing; her comments on the aforementioned passage from *De Civitate Dei* immediately show their implications for a Stoic monist cosmology and its eternal return of the same: 'Moreover, the beginning that was created with man prevented time and the created universe as a whole from turning eternally in cycles about itself in a purposeless way and without anything new ever happening.'[35] This Augustinian conception of the human, however, is based on a more encompassing notion of the Pauline spirit as the interruption of the eternal return of the same.

WHICH DIALECTIC?

To get a better sense of this dialectic alternative to dualism and monism, let us examine the dialectic movement that Žižek discerns in the apostle's letters. He introduces his own version of a Pauline pneumatic hermeneutics by referring to the notion of repetition. According to Žižek, a direct, concurrent choice between the spiritual and the natural or physical (as in 1 Cor. 15:46) is impossible for Paul, because such a concurrent choice implies that both worlds or principles have always and simultaneously been a given – which implies, in short, a dualism.[36] The non-dualistic meaning of Paul's remark in 1 Cor. 15:46 is that the natural or the earthly body is first. Only then, in second place, and as repetition of the first, earthly body, does the possibility of the spiritual body occur. Hence, repetition is also here repetition at a pneumatic level.

Žižek notes that a literal interpretation of, for instance, passages from the holy Jewish scriptures concerns their first, 'natural' meaning: 'the true speculative meaning emerges only through repeated reading, as the aftereffect (or byproduct) of the first, "wrong" reading.'[37] He places 'wrong' between quotation marks here because the difference between literal and speculative or spiritual only becomes meaningful in and through the repetition, when the spiritual meaning is announced and understood. Thus, the spiritual meaning or dimension is not always already available, in another reality or world, before being juxtaposed with the literal or figurative meaning. Rather, it exists only at the moment of the spiritual rereading or repetition of the first meaning.

Because the earthly or natural body comes first for Paul, and the human is first and foremost Adam – a living, earthly creature – Žižek emphasises that detachment or, in more dialectic terms, negativity play a fundamental role in the principle of the spirit because disengagement and negativity are adaptations of the human reality through which this reality no longer coincides with the living, earthly creature that the human being has been from the start. This detachment does not imply that there is another reality, ready and prepared, alongside the reality we inhabit, but it produces or creates a difference that is expressed, at first, in the negative judgement of a non-identity: humans are *not* merely living, earthly creatures. Let us phrase this in the proper Pauline terminology going beyond Žižek's concerns. In Stoic philosophy, the Greek term that Paul uses in 1 Cor. 15:45, *psuchē*, expresses the *pneuma* of the living creature that not only vegetates but also observes and has rational capacities. As repetition of the first Adam, Paul speaks about the last Adam. This Adam is no longer a living, earthly being – determined by the gradation of the *pneuma* that is specific to the human being in the Stoic view of nature and the cosmos – but a vivifying spirit. Vivification or quickening (*zōopoieō*) points to a new life (*zōē*) being created (*poieō*) in light of which the old life is no longer normative for what being human *can* include (Cor. 15:22).[38]

Playing with the meaning of spirit as ghost, Žižek writes that, through Paul's prose, the ordinary, everyday life of the human being, which is purely focused on its own survival, is haunted by the difference Paul announces here: '[Is it] not that, in such a case, the promise of real life haunts us in a ghostlike form?'[39] This circumscription expresses the positive experience of detachment or negativity: by introducing this difference, ordinary life is haunted by the thought of a real life escaping from ordinary life, by the thought of a remainder or excess of life that cannot be assimilated into or lived in ordinary life.

Recall Žižek's notable description of God as 'the name for the purely negative gesture [...] of giving up what matters most to us'.[40] In light of the considerations above, this description sounds less strange. After all, which concern weighs heavier than ensuring one's own earthly, living existence? As the name that introduces a change to the nature of human existence and with that brings about the non-identity of the human being with this nature, God is also the name for the creation of the space in which the possibility of another life could occur. The God of Žižek is therefore perhaps best compared to the God whom Jacob met at Jabbok and who, in a bout of wrestling, dislocated his hip and disrupted his existence, giving him a new name: Israel (Gen. 32:23–9). This experience of intervention, interruption and disruption expresses the central motif of detachment and negativity with which Žižek characterises Paul's dialectic. Between Gnosticism, which holds that another world, not this one, is our true home, and humanism, which holds that we are completely at home in this world, Žižek positions the perspective of not being at home anywhere and always living a detached life in the world.[41] Using Heidegger's notion of thrownness, he explains this alternative:

> What both these positions [Gnosticism and humanism, GJH] share is the notion that there is a home, a 'natural' place for man: either this world of the 'noosphere' from which we fell into this world and for which our souls long, or Earth itself. Heidegger shows the way out of this predicament: what if we are effectively 'thrown' into this world, never fully at home in it, always dislocated, 'out of joint,' and what if this dislocation is our constitutive, primordial condition, the very horizon of our being?[42]

Žižek supplements Heidegger's view with the Pauline insight that this interruption, not-being-at-home, is not purely negative but should be understood dialectically. One should add that a Pauline reinterpretation of this quotation would emphasise that being 'out of joint' is not only a social-anthropological characteristic, but also concerns the world, both in the sense of *kosmos* or creation, where its out-of-jointness unsettles each and every being (Rom. 8:20-21), and also in the sense of the social world, in which justice has been disrupted.

At these points, Žižek's dialectic proposal is close to my own. There is, however, one element in Žižek's explication of the Pauline dialectic that brings him too close to a Hegelian variation thereof, namely that which he calls 'the perverse core of Christianity'.[43] This perverse core concerns precisely the negative moments in Paul's history of salvation, without which salvation cannot take place. For instance, the Fall is necessary so that the resurrection can bring salvation; Judas's betrayal of Jesus is necessary, so that the crucifixion can take place; and the unbelief of Israel is necessary, so that the other people too can count themselves among God's people. As Žižek writes: 'the Fall is *in itself* already its own self-sublation, the wound is *in itself* already its own healing.'[44] The reason why I believe this comes very close to a Hegelian form of dialectic – and perhaps a Stoic form of providence – is the following. One could only allege that the above-mentioned moments are 'necessary' if one adopts the point of view of the absolute; if one judges these different moments from the perspective of a complete, rational and dialectic ordering, in which these moments have found – by dialectic development – their necessary place. That is, however, the point of view in which the spirit of the world is identified with the spirit of God; consequently, this dialectic is, in the end, nothing but a philosophy of immanence and a strict monism.

Interestingly, this idea is fundamentally at odds with the claim that we are not at home in the world. When the natural body already necessarily includes its own sublation – read: salvation – as potentiality, the reference to the human experience of not-being-at-home as the genuine point of departure for such a sublation is reduced to a mere moment in a necessary movement leading to sublation. It seems to me that Paul can also be read differently at this point. The possibility of a pneumatic repetition is not already a given in the natural body – if it is indeed already *in itself* its own self-sublation – it is not a potentiality or real possibility *of* the body, but rather its impossibility. The possibility is begotten by the principle of the spirit as gift and grace. In a given cosmological order in which everything has its own esteem or glory, this principle introduces the *real* possibility of transforming this esteem or glory.

Paul's point of view is not that of the spirit of the world. Rather, for him, the issue seems to be that creation groans under the insignificance and futility that comes with the natural and the earthly. This insignificance does not imply that creation has the innate capacity or power for a new sense and meaning, waiting to be unfolded; rather, it leads to the insight of the necessity of disengagement and interruption. Rom. 8 suggests that not only humankind but also creation itself is interrupted and dislocated. The natural order of creation itself has become powerless. For Paul, this weakness (*astheneia*) is not in itself a power, but only becomes a power through the spirit; this frailty can be raised in power (*dunamis*), as he writes in 1 Cor. 15:43. The dialectic principle of the spirit of God can procure such a reversal of the order.

Yet, the relation between Hegel and Paul is a complicated and subtle one. As soon as the modern variety of Stoic monism, in the form of the thoughts of Hegel or Žižek, is placed *opposite to* Paul's thoughts on the spirit, the Gnostic temptation reinstates itself. If creation's own order is weak according to Paul, does that not mean that creation is insufficient and suffers from a privation of the good, which should come from elsewhere? In order to resist this temptation, it has to be noted that it makes more sense to say that creation is not *in itself* flawed or powerless, but that the natural order has *become* powerless. This crisis is a *historical* catastrophe, and as such it elicits a cry for salvation, which is not exactly the same as stating that it is the perverse core of salvation. Paul does not take an absolute point of view but rather a historical one: through a given (de)generation, creation begins to suffer and starts groaning for salvation. Earlier, I noted that Žižek understands 'the true speculative meaning' as 'repeated reading, as the aftereffect (or byproduct) of the first, 'wrong' reading'.[45] In light of the absolute position that Žižek occupies, the quotation-mark-ensconced 'wrong', which I highlighted before, becomes substantially less innocent, because it suggests that the first is always and has always already been the 'wrong'. However, such a suggestion can only be made from an absolute point of view – or from the point of view of looking back on what happened – but not from the point of view of the moment of crisis itself, in which Paul finds himself, his fellow humans and the whole of creation. It is, however, very well possible that the first and the natural, and the corresponding literal interpretation, is simply nothing more and nothing less than the first, the merely presupposed beginning, the *archē* as *principium*. Only when the natural order *becomes* powerless or appears in its powerlessness, the need for salvation arises. Paul writes against the backdrop of *this* type of necessity, namely necessity as need. Yet, strictly speaking, this is a historical – and by no means an absolute – position *between* the first, natural beginning and the completion of the working of the spirit. The latter statement can also be read in a Hegelian vein – and how could it not? Yet, the subtle difference with the Pauline form of dialectic should not be lost sight of. Therefore, more of this needs to be discussed in the following chapters.

Paul introduces a dialectic, pneumatic hermeneutics that attempts to find a fragile balance between monism and dualism. If this dialectic is not that of the Hegelian absolute spirit of the world, which develops purely out of necessity, how then are this dialectic and the role of the principle of the spirit in dialectic to be understood? It is a dialectic *of exception*, as I will argue. The spirit is the exception to the first, natural order and can, for this reason, transform the weakness of this order into a power. In the next chapters, we need to hone our understanding of such a dialectic. In the foregoing, it also became clear that in this context the distinction between Paul and Marcion is as decisive as it is subtle – and the same could be said for the distinction between Paul and Hegel. To gather all the contemporary philosophers together under the heading of a (crypto-)Marcionism, as Critchley does, is confusing, because it precludes Paul's own dialectic position from ever coming into sharp focus – and exactly the determination of this dialectic position comprises an important part of the philosophical discussion on Paul.[46] Breton's description of Paul's position is much more helpful at this point. Paul's hermeneutics, which indicates how the spiritual order arises from necessity and how Christ derives from a preceding history, presents an equilibrium that is 'delicate, so difficult to maintain that there frequently results a hesitation between a necessity that imposes itself and a gratuity that challenges it'.[47] A simple embrace of necessity would pull us back into the trajectory of the Stoic-Hegelian dialectic of cosmic or divine self-development. In Paul, however, the spirit also presents a form of unfounded and absurd gratuity. Such a spirit is truly exorbitant, pulling us out of the orbit of Hegelian dialectic thought and forming an exception to the Stoic eternal return of the same.

NOTES

1 See, e.g., Van Kooten, *Paul's Anthropology in Context*.
2 See Engberg-Pedersen, *Cosmology and Self in the Apostle Paul*, 26–37. This Stoic vocabulary eludes many contemporary scholars; see, e.g., Boyarin, *A Radical Jew*, 61.
3 See Sellars, *Stoicism*, 91–9.
4 Boyarin's analysis in *A Radical Jew* departs from this dualism.

5   These questions also emerge in New Testamentary scholarship; see, e.g., Barclay, 'Stoic Physics and the Christ-event', 410–13.
6   There seems no mention of this when Rom. 8 is referred to in Engberg-Pedersen, *Cosmology and Self in the Apostle Paul*, 53.
7   Critchley, *The Faith of the Faithless*, 195; also see 200–1.
8   Also see Breton, *Saint Paul*, 66–7/47.
9   Plato, *Phaedrus* 82e. Translation taken from Cooper, *Plato*, 72.
10 Taubes, *Die politische Theologie des Paulus*, 80/57.
11 Ibid., 81–2/58–9.
12 Ibid., 80/57.
13 See Terpstra, 'The Management of Distinctions', 263–7.
14 Taubes, *Die politische Theologie des Paulus*, 83/59.
15 Taubes, for instance, points to 1 Cor. 2:6–10 in *Vom Kult zur Kultur*, 124–5/86–7.
16 In this context, Heidegger mentions 'the deep opposition' between Christians – and hereby he alludes to those living according to the 'early Christianity' Paul advocated – and the mystics: compared to the Christian, the mystic is 'through manipulation, removed from the life-complex' of early Christianity. See *Phänomenologie des religiösen Lebens*, 124/88–9.
17 Taubes, *Die politische Theologie des Paulus*, 84–5/60–1.
18 Ibid., 77–86/55–62, and Taubes, *Vom Kult zur Kultur*, 173–81/137–46.
19 See Rom. 9–11.
20 Taubes, *Die politische Theologie des Paulus*, 72/51.
21 The account of Paul's hermeneutics proposed here thus differs significantly from that of Boyarin, *A Radical Jew*, 14, who argues that Paul's hermeneutics is *dualistic*.
22 Taubes traces this modern critique of the Bible back to Spinoza, for whom all interpretations other than the historical and the literal meanings are 'ideology and swindle' (Taubes, *Die politische Theologie des Paulus*, 63/44). Nietzsche's account of these other interpretations is similar to that of Spinoza, as we shall see in the next chapter.
23 Breton, *Saint Paul*, 27/55–6.
24 For those interested in a more contextualised analysis of this allegoric hermeneutics of Paul and the extent to which this way of interpreting can also be found elsewhere in the ancient world, see, e.g., ibid., 26–44/55–73; for an analysis more integrated in a contemporary cultural-theoretical framework, see Boyarin, *A Radical Jew*, 13–38.
25 Nietzsche, *Morgenröthe*, 76/85 [= Book I, § 84].
26 Taubes, *Die politische Theologie des Paulus*, 64/45.
27 Ibid., 65/46.
28 In the Epilogue, this statement is elucidated.
29 Ibid., 59–62/41–3.
30 Ibid., 105/76.
31 Ibid., 118/85.

32. Arendt, *The Human Condition*, 177; and Arendt, *Love and Saint Augustine*, 55. See Yazıcıoğlu, 'Arendtian Beginning under the Threat of Violence', 80–3.
33. Augustine, *De Civitate Dei* XI.32.
34. Ibid. XII.21.
35. Arendt, *Love and Saint Augustine*, 55.
36. Žižek, *The Fragile Absolute*, XVI.
37. Ibid., XVII. Also see Žižek, *On Belief*, 163, and Žižek, *The Puppet and the Dwarf*, 81.
38. I borrow this notion of quickening, which I will invoke several times, esp. in the Epilogue, from Dennis J. Schmidt; see, e.g., Schmidt, 'Hermeneutics as Original Ethics', 45–6.
39. Žižek, *The Puppet and the Dwarf*, 99.
40. Žižek, *On Belief*, 150.
41. Gnosticism and humanism are Žižek's anthropologised versions of dualism and monism, respectively.
42. Ibid., 9.
43. Subtitle of Žižek, *The Puppet and the Dwarf*.
44. Ibid., 86; emphasis added. Also see 81–7.
45. Žižek, *The Fragile Absolute*, XVII.
46. Badiou explicitly rejects Marcion's ontological dualism in *Saint Paul*, 36–7/34–5. Yet, his is a borderline case: his systematic distinction between being and event has all the signs of a new type of dualism, even if, in his own terminology, it is not ontological.
47. Breton, *Saint Paul*, 37/66.

2. *The Ghost of Nihilism*

To further clarify why dualism poses a particular problem for any present-day philosophical attempt to renew the legacy of Paul, it is imperative to discuss Nietzsche, for whom the problem of dualism is, ultimately, a problem of nihilism. Given the German philosopher's influence on European thought, it is hardly surprising that his reflections on the apostle are often referred to and are object of separate study.[1] In the turn to Paul, Nietzsche's remarks on the founder of Christianity tend to serve as a counterpoint to clarify which version of Paul philosophers would like to bring to the fore. In the introduction, I already referred to Blanton writing that Nietzsche 'failed radically to transform [...] the ongoing cultural and political functions of the Pauline legacy'. This remark basically captures the mood of the present-day philosophical assessment of Nietzsche's Paul. Let me begin this chapter by admitting that my own approach also uses – or abuses? – Nietzsche in this way. Yet, I do think that, at particular points, Nietzsche did portray the apostle quite accurately. Let us therefore consider what he captured and what he distorted in his portrayal of Paul. This chapter is devoted to this consideration by addressing, first, Nietzsche's judgement on the ontological dualism he perceives in the apostle; second, the peculiar polemic in which he is engaged with the founder of Christianity; and, third, the particular implications of these two issues for his interpretation of *pistis* or faith. The last section of this chapter is devoted to Foucault's reappraisal of ancient philosophy in contemporary European thought, in order to show how this facilitated a reappreciation of Paul after Nietzsche's devastating critique. The details of this reappreciation are explored in the following chapters.

DEVALUATIONS OF LIFE

In the preface of *Beyond Good and Evil*, we find Nietzsche's famous verdict that Christianity is Platonism for the masses, implying that Christianity defends a democratised form of dualism.[2] In this sense, Nietzsche's Paul belongs to the tradition of the Marcionite Paul, even though Nietzsche values this dualism completely differently than the heretic from Sinope. The Platonic contrast between the sensuous and the intelligible world is judged in the following terms: 'The "apparent" world is the only world: the "true world" is just a *lie added on to it*.'[3] This lie is detrimental, not so much for depriving us of the correct theoretical view of the world and for burdening us with a false ontology or cosmology, but rather for having an exceptionally negative influence on our appreciation of life and the world we live in. With the lie of the 'beyond' or the 'afterlife', Platonism and Christianity equally aim to deprive our world of all value:

> The concept of the 'beyond,' the 'true world,' invented to devalue the *only world* there is, – to deprive our earthly reality of any goal, reason or task! The concept 'soul,' 'spirit,' finally even 'immortal soul' invented in order to make the body despised, to make it sick – 'holy' –, to treat as frivolous all the things about life that deserve to be taken very seriously – questions of nutrition, residence, spiritual diet, treatment of the sick, cleanliness, weather.[4]

Everything in life that deserves our attention is neglected and considered to be worthless in light of another, true world or the afterlife. Thus, the thought of a true world and a 'beyond' influences our morality and our attitude to life. When everything is seen in light of this other world, we approach earthly matters 'frivolously' and with indifference. It is precisely because of this devaluation of everything that is valuable in life that Nietzsche qualifies Platonism and Christianity as forms of *nihilism*, as propagating ways of living that find *nothing* in this world worthy to value; and because for Nietzsche there is no other world than the one in which we live, Platonism and Christianity propagate an attitude to life that affirms *nothing* at all. Paul is one of the main figures in Western culture to have invigorated this particular form of nihilism: 'When the emphasis of life is put on the "beyond" rather than on life itself – when it is put on nothingness –, then the emphasis has been completely removed from life.'[5]

Strictly speaking, however, this does not mean that the dualism found in Paul, Plato or Christianity can simply be qualified as a genuine form of nihilism. As Nietzsche himself defines it, nihilism should be understood in the following terms: 'A nihilist is someone who is of the judgement that the world as it is, ought *not* to be, and that the world as it ought to be, does not exist.'⁶ Strictly speaking, the second part of this definition does not apply to the dualist, because dualists are of the opinion that the world 'as it ought to be' is the only one that exists truly and completely. It is only from Nietzsche's perspective, namely that the second world is a world of fiction, that this dualism can be interpreted as a form of nihilism. Nevertheless, this Nietzschean assessment follows more or less naturally from Platonism, because the latter is driven by a will to truth. Due to this will to truth and the forms of science and knowledge which it has inspired, this mode of thinking will eventually turn on itself and reveal the claim that the 'beyond' exists as lie and fiction.⁷

Given the analyses from the previous chapter, it could be argued that Nietzsche's emphasis on dualism is too blunt, and that therefore also his analysis of this form of nihilism goes a little too fast. Let us, however, take a step back and first note that, with his focus on the *negation* of the importance of life on earth, Nietzsche most definitely does find a pertinent motif in Paul's letters that also affects my considerations concerning the role of dialectic in these letters. Dialectic, whichever modern shape it adopts, always implies a form of negation and negativity. The question, however, is whether or not this negation leaves us indeed with nothing – such as the 'nothingness' Nietzsche discerns in 'the 'beyond'' of life – or whether it opens up a space for *creation* in the form of a genuinely life-giving power – *zōopoieō*, as 1 Cor. 15:45 says. The motif of creation is, of course, much closer to Nietzsche's own philosophical heart and understanding of the human. Thus, this motif might lead to a more complicated relation between Nietzsche and Paul than is usually accounted for. However, let us begin by exploring the basics of this relation.

Nietzsche's judgement of Paul in *The Anti-Christ* coincides, to a large extent, with the line of argumentation just pointed out. He argues that Christianity, in its morality and perspective on humankind and reality, does not have a single 'point of contact with reality'. Christianity exists in the domain of the purely imaginary:

> Once the concept of 'nature' had been invented as a counter to the idea of 'God,' 'natural' had to mean 'reprehensible,' – that whole fictitious world is rooted in a *hatred* of the natural (– of reality! –), it is the expression of a profound sense of unease concerning reality … *But this explains everything*. Who are the only people motivated to *lie their way out of* reality? People who *suffer* from it. But to suffer from reality means that you are a piece of reality that has *gone wrong* … The preponderance of feelings of displeasure over feelings of pleasure is the *cause* of that fictitious morality and religion.⁸

This citation repeats the dualist reading of Christianity. The fabrications of this religion opposed God to the world in which we live, which has led to the world being viewed as reprehensible and abject. Judging by what follows in this passage, Nietzsche is particularly interested in the psychological dimension and origin of this judgement of the world in which we live. According to him, the 'hatred' and 'profound sense of unease concerning reality' that emanates from this rejection of the world in which we live issues from a psychological life that suffers from this world and that, for this reason, wants to withdraw from it. Thus, he analyses the specific life *pathos*, affect or, in Heideggerian terms, mood or attunement – *Stimmung* – that motivates this dualism behind the scenes. Poignant is that he understands suffering from reality as the basic affect from which Christianity is born. If Paul is in fact the founder of this Christianity, it means that his argument, in Rom. 8, that the whole of creation is subject to senselessness, is interpreted by Nietzsche as a claim by someone who is himself a reality '*gone wrong*' and who subsequently transfers and projects this failure to reality as a whole. This is a striking example of a hermeneutics of suspicion: Rom. 8 is then not read as a text that has something to say about reality and which therefore should be taken seriously in this claim. Rather, Nietzsche reduces it to an underlying psychology: the claim is produced by the troubled psyche of someone who is suffering and who does not fit in reality as it is.

What interests me here, though, goes in another direction. By focusing on the life pathos from which Christianity is born, Nietzsche argues that the dualist illusion is the theoretical expression of such pathos as well as of the associated *attitude to life*. The life that suffers – too much or significantly more than it enjoys – does not want to affirm this suffering but seeks a mode of living that allows it to withdraw from this suffering. With this pathos a cosmology, ontology, anthropology and psychology are subsequently *invented*: the concepts to think about the world, the reality, the human being and the soul all serve to support this attitude to life. Even if Nietzsche speaks with unmistakable disdain about Christianity – 'the Christianity of *Paul*', as he emphasises – the following can surely not escape the meticulous reader.[9] On the one hand, the suffering is apparently so unbearable that the Christian psyche refuses to concur with this life and this world, while, on the other hand, this suffering mental life is capable of *creating* something unheard-of. This psyche creates an illusion that allows it to negotiate with life on its own terms and thus invents its own way of dealing with the world. The imagination and its creativity are truly in charge here.[10] Paul, the founder of Christianity, is the one who propagated

NIETZSCHE'S POLEMIC

Despite Nietzsche's sharp critique of the founder of Christianity, he acknowledges that Paul knew how to accomplish at least one aspect of that at which Nietzsche himself aimed. The founder of Christianity knew how to create new values in the ancient world and to effectively bring about a transvaluation of all values.[11] This leads to descriptions of Paul unlike the ones from *The Anti-Christ*. In *Daybreak*, Paul is described as struggling with the Jewish value of the law *and* as someone capable of destroying this value, replacing it with that of the resurrection of Christ.[12] According to *Daybreak*, the climax of Paul's rhetoric is to be found in what he says about becoming one with Christ, rising from the dead with Christ, and partaking of the divine glory with Christ. Interestingly enough, these are the very passages in which the principle of the spirit plays a crucial role. Through the divine *pneuma* in us, this unification, resurrection and participation in the divine glory become possible. For the sardonic Nietzsche, it is this 'anticipatory revelling in *divine* glories' with which Paul conquers the value of the law and expresses an 'intractable lust for power'.[13] Hence, a powerful will works in Paul with an unprecedented, 'life-giving', creative force: his new values made history. It was Paul, and no one else, who split history in two, into a before Christ and an after Christ.

In turn, it is Nietzsche who wants to break Paul's values that have prevailed for many centuries.[14] His harsh, ruthless rhetoric should be understood in the context of such a struggle, as also Badiou suggests: 'If Nietzsche is so violent toward Paul, it is because he is his rival far more than his opponent.'[15] Nietzsche is not Paul's opponent, as if they are contenders in a game with set rules by which they have to play. Rather, Nietzsche is Paul's rival: he does not want to play by the 'rules of the game' Paul has drawn up; in fact, he wants to change them.

In Greek, the two terms used for battle are *polemos* and *agōn*. While *agōn* expresses the fight at stake in a competitive game governed by rules, *polemos* names the wars the Greek city-state fought against the barbarians, the non-Greeks who did not speak the Greek language. Nietzsche is not embroiled in an *agōn* with Paul but in a *polemos*, in a battle in which he neither speaks Paul's language nor shares his vocabulary or values. The struggle of Nietzsche with Paul is a polemic and one might call their difference a 'differend' (*différend*) in the strong sense Lyotard affords this term.

The terms Nietzsche brings into play to describe Paul's ethos and mode of living, such as nihilism, decadence and resentment, arise in the context of such a polemic. Referring back to *On the Genealogy of Morality*, Nietzsche writes in *The Anti-Christ* that resentment is a reactive attitude that does not affirm or create anything; it only negates a '*noble* morality'.[16] In order to say no to this latter morality, the morality of resentment has to 'invent [...] *another* world, a world that viewed the *affirmation of life* as evil, as intrinsically reprehensible'.[17] Polemically, Nietzsche thus presents the Pauline values as nihilistic, reactive and life negating.

When it can, however, be questioned whether Paul should be seen as a dualist and when Nietzsche's writings on Paul may be characterised as polemic,[18] the following question imposes itself. Is it indeed justified to call Paul nihilistic? Taubes and Badiou provide different answers to this question. Even if these answers seem to contradict each other at first sight, they might rather be complementary. Taubes writes that Nietzsche correctly pointed out nihilistic tendencies in Paul. At work in Paul's letters is a 'profound nihilism' that is specifically focused on the destruction of the Roman Empire. Not only does Paul resist the Jewish value of the law, he also resists its Roman value, according to Taubes.[19] Moreover, nature and creation are seen in light of their futility or 'vanity'. Nature groans under this futility and senselessness (Rom. 8:20–2). Yet, one should add – and in this way also object – to Taubes's comments that this nihilistic judgement is only part of Paul's assessment of creation. For Paul, these groans are not just groaning of vanity: creation groans 'as in the pains of childbirth'. Thus, futility is reinterpreted as expectation and birth. Hence, Taubes's attention to Paul's nihilism should be qualified. When Paul indeed is in a polemic with the world in which he lives and aims to revalue all values, a moment of negation is inevitable, because the old values and the old world ought to be presented as nothing. Nietzsche, in turn, does the same with regard to Paul: he presents the values Paul created as nihilistic ones. Such a negation – Paul versus the Roman and Jewish values and Nietzsche versus the Pauline and Christian values – is specific to each *creation* of new values. Precisely for this reason, this negation should be meticulously distinguished from nihilism in a strong sense of the word. For the founder of new values, the old values are insignificant in light of the new ones. Creation groans in worthlessness and futility, as new values and a new spirit are about to be born that will cast everything that is in a new light.

Badiou emphasises this aspect in his comments on Nietzsche's interpretation of Paul as nihilist. For him, Paul's affirmation and creation of new values precede the negation of the values of the Roman Empire. There is a well-known passage in one of Heidegger's texts about Aristotle from which one could conclude that the German philosopher is not interested in the lives of the thinkers he wrote about, or the circumstances in which they found themselves. About Aristotle's life, Heidegger only writes: 'our only interest is that he was born at a certain time, that he worked, and that he died.'[20] Paul is even worse in this regard, as is often observed. His letters indeed proclaim Jesus Christ but are not interested in any way in the vicissitudes of the life of Jesus of Nazareth.[21] For Nietzsche, this confirms Paul's hostility to life:

> Paul simply shifted the emphasis of this whole being, putting it *behind* this being, – into the *lie* of Jesus' 'resurrection.' Basically, he had no use whatsoever for the life of the redeemer, – he needed the death on the cross, *and something else besides* ...[22]

In stark contrast to his attack on Paul, who would only focus on the death and resurrection of Jesus, is Nietzsche's appreciation of the life of Jesus. If there is one tender comment found about Christianity in *The Anti-Christ*, it is about Jesus' *mode of living*, which is still an option for Christians today according to Nietzsche: 'only the *practice* of Christianity is really Christian, *living* like the man who died on the cross ... A life like this is *still* possible today, for *certain* people it is even necessary: true, original Christianity will always be possible ...'[23] Paul's negation of the life of Jesus thus serves, Nietzsche argues, to solely and wholly encompass the death of Jesus as well as the lie of the resurrection.

At this point, Badiou contradicts Nietzsche. Although Badiou explicitly judges the resurrection to be a fable – numerous times even, as if he fears being seen as a believer[24] – he is nevertheless of the opinion that the resurrection in Paul's discourse cannot be properly understood as lie or aversion to life. Paul does not speak of the life of Jesus of Nazareth because, more than anyone, he wants to limit his proclamation to its very core: the resurrection. As Badiou emphasises, this resurrection is the opposite of an aversion to life. For Paul, the resurrection is not the 'death of life' or what is 'used to *kill life*', as Nietzsche is at pains to emphasise, but concerns the 'death of death'.[25] Moreover, Paul's discourse lacks a reactionary moment. To invalidate Nietzsche's suggestion that Paul's teaching departs from denying or saying no to a prominent existing morality, Badiou points to a passage from 2 Corinthians in which Paul writes about the Messiah: 'In Him it has always been "Yes"' (2 Cor. 1:19). Paul thus understands his own proclamation as an affirmation. The resurrection is the new value, the new beginning, and the event in light of which Paul sees the world. Thus, Paul does not leave life behind him, but rather introduces a principle of *sur-existence*, a principle of a higher or more intensified existence, 'on the basis of which life, affirmative life, was restored and re-founded for all'.[26] Paul is, therefore, not concerned about having to face illness, suffering and death any longer; rather, he is concerned with an attitude to life that is not deathly but alive, a *sur-existence*. With the prefix *sur-* Badiou is undoubtedly mirroring Nietzsche's own use of the prefix *Über-* in the term *Übermensch*, which wants to express a higher or intensified mode of human existence, or a mode of existence that goes beyond the existence we know as human. Thus, Badiou suggests that Nietzsche's emphasis on such an intensified existence resonates with Paul's.

To explain the difference between his and Nietzsche's judgement of Paul, Badiou refers back to the polemic between Paul and Nietzsche. Every true transvaluation of all values is 'an intervention within [h]istory': Paul as well as Nietzsche strives to split history in two: the new values propagated are the beginning of a new era.[27] In Nietzsche's case, this requires the breaking of Pauline values. When Nietzsche laughs at Paul and his values in *The Anti-Christ*, it is not an expression of opposition, but rather of a 'disjunction', of an unbridgeable separation of spirits, where the one, filled with incomprehension, listens to the language of the other, as if it were gibberish, only to then involuntarily burst into laughter.[28]

Taubes, in turn, gives a striking example of this unbridgeable divide. For him, the principle of the spirit and its accompanying pneumatic hermeneutics are proof that Paul does not propagate dualism but rather shows how the Jewish past and the Jewish stories and prophecies are fulfilled in his proclamation of the Messiah. When we return, in light of Nietzsche's Pauline critique, to these passages in Taubes's book, we are immediately struck by Taubes bringing the notion of the spirit to the fore *in reaction* to Nietzsche's sharp judgement of the notion of the spirit as a lie and an illusion. Taubes argues that Paul's principle of the spirit should not be understood as referring to something ethereal, intellectual or eternal that has nothing to do with the world in which we live, but as a principle of transformation that is able to cast *that which is* in another light.[29] The difference between Nietzsche's interpretation of the spirit in Paul's letters as a life-threatening principle that rejects and negates the world in which we life and Paul's attempt to emphasise the transformative power of the spirit, through which the world appears in a different light, is powerfully expressed in Nietzsche's judgement on Paul's pneumatic hermeneutics. In *Daybreak*, under the title 'The Philology of Christianity', Nietzsche describes Paul's tendency to read everything in the Old Testament in light of Christ in following terms: 'the Old Testament was supposed to speak of Christ and only of Christ.'[30] Nietzsche bursts out laughing when speaking about the resurrection; he is overcome by laughter and indignation when reflecting on Paul's pneumatic hermeneutics: '[A] philologist who hears it is caught between rage and laughter and asks himself: is it possible?' At this precise point we see the conflict between Paul and Nietzsche *in optima forma*. For the latter, even the way in which the former *reads* is dishonest, untrue and objectionable. In *The Anti-Christ*, this can be seen when Nietzsche qualifies Paul's spiritualisation of the Jewish past as a forgery and fraud (and what else to expect from the author who, in *On the Genealogy of Morality*, appears so sensitive to the fickle ways of the history of interpretation?): 'he falsified the history of Israel once again, to make it look like the prehistory of his *own* actions: all the prophets have talked about *his* "redeemer"....'[31]

At the end of 'The Philology of Christianity', Nietzsche concludes that one should not be surprised at Paul's pneumatic hermeneutics: the apostle was, after all, in 'a *war* and paid more heed to [his] opponents than to the need to stay honest'.[32] Yet, Nietzsche's assessment of Paul could *mutatis mutandis* be the judgement on his own interpretation of the founder of Christianity: Nietzsche is at war with him.

We can now come to the following twofold conclusion:[33]

(1) It is exactly Nietzsche who is aware that Paul is involved in a struggle for a new beginning, a new value and a new event. He links this beginning to the proclamation of the Messiah. Focusing on this struggle for other values, Nietzsche also argues that Paul's nihilism does not, in the first place, allow itself to be led by an ontological or cosmological interest; Paul's views about reality and cosmos are, for Nietzsche, derivative of his pathos, ethos and attitude to life, particularly that of resentment and hostility to life. Even if a contemporary reappreciation of the philosophical legacy of Paul cannot endorse Nietzsche's characterisation of Paul's ethos, it does take Nietzsche's lead seriously that there is something substantial to be found in the mode of living proclaimed by Paul. However, in contrast to Nietzsche's assessment, such a reappreciation does not claim that this ethos is the ground or foundation for the invention of an ontology or cosmology; rather, as I will argue in the next chapter, one needs to be aware that Paul's ethos and ontology mirror one another and that one cannot be had without the other.

(2) Concerning the question of ethos, the present-day philosophical turn to Paul opposes Nietzsche's qualification of Paul's attitude to life as vindictive, life threatening and nihilist. I showed that the understanding

of nihilism is, in the final instance, dependent on the dualism for which Nietzsche blames Paul: he invents another world to devalue the world in which we actually live. At this stage, Nietzsche fails to appreciate (and even denies) the critical and affirmative power of Paul's letters, which Taubes traces in the principle of the spirit and which Badiou perceives in Paul's proclamation of the resurrection. For this very reason, one may find in Paul a potential to *resist* the all-too-easy affirmation of the already existing order.

Perhaps the fact that Nietzsche appropriates one of the characteristic themes from Stoic cosmology, the eternal return of the same, for his own use is indeed distinctive of the difference or difficulty with Paul. Nietzsche embraces this idea to tear down the pathos of resentment he detects in Paul's Christianity. Only when we learn to embrace and affirm what has happened as something that we truly want, we no longer run the risk of lapsing into vindictiveness towards reality.[34] We have seen, however, that Paul's principle of the spirit *does* break with the Stoic eternal return, but not to embrace resentment. It breaks with it because Paul, negatively formulated, affirms the non-coincidence of reality with itself, as argued in the next chapters. This non-coincidence effects a difference in reality itself, opening up another possibility for and in reality. For this reason, the rejection of the principle of eternal return harbours a basic resistance against every all-too-easy affirmation of the existing order, whether it be a social or ontological one. In technical terms, to be examined in later chapters, Paul offers present-day philosophy an alternative to ontotheology, of which a Platonic-Marcionite dualism is a striking exponent.[35] Before exploring the meaning of this alternative, the discussion of Nietzsche needs to be extended. There is one more important concept that Nietzsche links with Paul in *The Anti-Christ*, and that I consider to be a key concept in the examination of the attitude to life Paul propagates, namely that of faith.

FAITH AS HOLDING-TO-BE-TRUE

In his lectures on Paul, Heidegger makes only one brief remark about Nietzsche's interpretation. He argues that the themes Paul raises in his letters 'should *not* be ethically understood' and Nietzsche's misinterpretation of Paul's resentment indicates that he 'has understood nothing'.[36] One could wonder what precisely Heidegger means by 'ethical' in this all-too-concise rejection of Nietzsche. If ethical is understood in the sense of ethos and mode of living – in line with what is set out above – then Heidegger seems to deny the kinship between his own project and that of Nietzsche. Yet, Heidegger's interpretation of the apostle's letters also centres on a certain mode of living or, more precisely, on what he calls the enactment of life. With this notion, which will be discussed later, he expresses a specific attitude of believers to life and the world in which they live. Despite this potential misunderstanding concerning the kinship between these two thinkers, Heidegger's rejection quite clearly indicates where his disagreement with Nietzsche concerning the role of the attitude to life must be situated. I want to reconstruct this disagreement on the basis of Nietzsche's use of the concept of faith and Heidegger's interpretation thereof.[37]

Nietzsche's rhetoric concerning Paul's understanding of faith continuously revolves around the peculiar contradiction inherent in the nihilism of Paul. How could his attitude to life, if it really deserves the title attitude *to life*, proclaim *hostility* to life? Living a life-hating life seems a performative contradiction: to the extent to which Paul's resentment strives for power and dominion in the enactment of life, this resentment actually confirms the dynamic that is characteristic of life. Here, Nietzsche discovers the intrinsic untruthfulness of Paul, and he traces it in the notion of faith. The importance Nietzsche attaches to Paul's untruthfulness is not to be underestimated in light of the central theme of his reading, namely Paul's nihilism. For Nietzsche, it is the will to truth in philosophy and Christianity which this mode of thinking will eventually turn on itself, as Van Tongeren argues.[38] By continuing to implement the ethos of truthfulness, both philosophy and Christianity would finally see their idea of the true world revealed as a lie resulting in a more mature nihilism. By calling Paul untruthful, Nietzsche suggests that the will to truth is not very strong in the founder of Christianity.

In *The Anti-Christ*, Paul's hostility to life firstly comes to the fore in the contradiction Nietzsche discerns between a mode of living and a religion. Nietzsche runs this contradiction parallel to the difference between Jesus and Paul. We have seen that Nietzsche argues that Paul 'had no use whatsoever for the life of the redeemer'. If there has been one meaning of the word 'Christian' that Nietzsche could appreciate, it concerns Jesus' life: 'only the *practice* of Christianity is really Christian, *living* like the man who died on the cross ...'[39] After noting that this is '*still* possible today, for *certain* people [...] even necessary', Nietzsche explicitly opposes Jesus' mode of living to Paul's faith: '*Not* a believing but a doing, above all a *not*-doing-much, a different *being* ...'[40] If Jesus brought something into the world, it is, Nietzsche argues, '[a] new way of life, *not* a new faith ...'.[41]

Why is Nietzsche so insistent upon the distinction between a 'new way of life' and a 'new faith'? Does believing not entail its own mode of living? Why then does he deny faith this mode of life in these passages? To obtain an answer to these questions, we need to take a closer look at Nietzsche's interpretation of the term 'faith'. But first, let us consider how he describes the Pauline or Christian conception of faith in *The Anti-Christ*.

In his interpretation of the famous passage in which Paul writes that God made foolish the wisdom of the world (Cor. 1:20), Nietzsche argues that the believer denies that which is true in favour of holding that which is deceitful to be true. For him, notions such as the afterlife, the spirit and the resurrection are as many lies, and the Pauline faith is nothing but 'taking' these lies 'to be true' – a holding-to-be-true, *ein Für-wahr-halten*.[42] Even if these notions are untrue, the believer holds them to be true. As Nietzsche writes at the beginning of *The Anti-Christ*, believers are those who shut their eyes to their own lies. '[S]eeing-*wrong* is given a *good* conscience' by the believers, and '*other* types of optic are not allowed to have value any more now that this one has been sanctified with names like "God," "redemption," and "eternity."'[43] The call to faith, for this reason, does nothing but '*veto* [...] science'.[44] Along these lines, Nietzsche declares that faith, in his definition of holding the lie to be true, is opposed to truth and the will to truth. The attitude of faith is thereby based on the absence of a basic honesty and will to face the truth. For this reason, Nietzsche very purposefully writes: '"Faith" means not *wanting* to know the truth.'[45]

In each of these considerations, Nietzsche juxtaposes believing with knowing, and considers the latter to be superior to the former. In philosophy, faith – in Greek: *pistis* – is also – *but not only* – an epistemological category expressing our convictions about the world in which we live, but one that falls short in terms of genuine knowledge (*epistēmē*).[46] When we do not know for sure – and that constantly happens to us in our daily life – we take refuge in our convictions, even if they cannot be fully underpinned. As epistemological category, faith is understood against the background of the supremacy of genuine knowledge. As epistemological category, faith also aims for knowledge and truth; hence, it is led, in Nietzschean terms, by a will to truth, even if it cannot reach genuine knowledge. At this point, Nietzsche argues that *Paul's* faith radicalises its subordinate epistemological role up to the point of transforming it into its opposite. Paul's faith is not simply marked by an inability to truly know; it is rather led by a will that is opposed to the will to truth: faith is not *wanting* to know what is true. Plato's *pistis* is a lower form of knowledge than *epistēmē*. Nietzsche places Paul's *pistis* also against the epistemic measuring stick, but on the opposite side of knowledge: it is the total privation or absence of knowledge. It ends up there as the expression of a particular will: faith is nothing but a *not*-wanting-to-know.

Despite the rhetorical verve with which Nietzsche propagates the untruth and dishonesty of Paul's faith, we must not let down our guard but rather consider carefully what is happening here. In his rhetorical attempt to discredit Pauline *pistis*, Nietzsche points to a performative contradiction: faith claims to proclaim the truth but appears to misunderstand and deny in every way possible the will to truth, which guides every scientific practice. Therefore, in *The Anti-Christ*, Nietzsche conceives of faith in a contradiction to knowledge and science: faith does not want to know what science has to offer, does not in any way respect the will to know expressed in science, and clings to illusions.

All of this, however, does not mean that Nietzsche simply embraces the will to truth in his resistance to Paul. In fact, he subjects the idea of truth to a *comparable* critique as he does the notion of faith. This has important implications for the relationship between faith, knowledge and truth. Let us recall some of the strategies Nietzsche employs to problematise the idea of truth.

In a famous passage from *On Truth and Lies*, Nietzsche depicts truth as an arrested and now canonical army of metaphors that were previously mobile and dynamic.[47] A metaphor is a mobile and dynamic expression of language – '*a poem in miniature*', as Paul Ricœur suggests – that creates and establishes new meanings.[48] The vitality, inventiveness and dynamic of language can be found in a metaphor. A concept, on the other hand, Nietzsche argues, is a metaphor worn out: an expression of language that has lost its original creative power and vitality. The same applies to the concepts of reality and truth. These concepts also only arise when the mobile, changing nature of reality is fixed and has come to a standstill. Truth thus denies the character of reality as becoming. This analysis is part of Nietzsche's rejection of Platonic dualism. For Nietzsche, the intelligible world of permanent, stable ideas is the product and creation of the knowers who *fix* the original dynamic, changing and creative character of reality, so that it could become a *hold* for them.[49]

This motif of a hold is of great importance, because it shows that metaphors wearing out is not only a 'natural' process of wear to which everything new is subjected – every creative metaphor eventually becomes commonplace and, similarly, we eventually become accustomed to everything new – but also that this process of wear is *desirable*. Those who are led by the will to know are those who are looking to secure the world and create an order in the world, so that the world can be held in the knower's grip of understanding. Yet, this requires the denial and misjudgement of reality as sheer becoming.

In *The Anti-Christ*, Nietzsche uses the concept of truth to show that the Pauline religious beliefs are lies. Yet, elsewhere he notes that truth and reality are also illusions.[50] When Nietzsche so strongly juxtaposes faith and knowledge, and (religious) lie and truth, he exposes the reader to a rhetorical violence – he is after all engaged in a 'a *war* and paid more heed to [his] opponents than to the need to stay honest' – ensuring that the intrinsic connection between faith, knowledge and truth that Nietzsche observes elsewhere is obscured in *The Anti-Christ*.

Nevertheless, Nietzsche reveals this connection in his description of believing as holding-to-be-true. In his judgement of the Pauline faith, he juxtaposes holding-to-be-true with the will to know. Yet, a more complex understanding of faith – *Glaube* – emerges in other texts. In the *Posthumous Fragments*, the same definition of faith can be found: 'What is a *faith*? How does it originate? Every faith is a *holding-to-be-true*.'[51] In the context of these posthumous fragments, however, Nietzsche does not limit this determination of faith to religious convictions; he rather argues that human knowledge as such is founded on a fundamental act of faith:

> The original acts of thought, confirming and denying, holding-to-be-true and not-holding-to-be-true, are, insofar as they assume not just a custom but also a right to hold to-be-true or hold not-to-be-true, already dominated by a faith *that there is knowledge for us*, that *judgments could really reach the truth*.[52]

While Nietzsche suggests that the Pauline faith as holding-to-be-true is opposed to knowledge, it appears here that the structure of holding-to-be-true itself is the presupposition and *archē* of every knowledge: from sheer necessity, every knowledge assumes one faith, namely the conviction that our judgements could reach the truth and take the world as it is. What we tend to forget, according to Nietzsche, is that in the process of knowing, we depart from structures we first created ourselves – such as, for instance, mathematics, geometry and logic – and impose these structures as 'a scheme of being posited by us' on the truth, thus making the world '*formulate-able, calculable for us*'.

The parallelism with the argumentation in *The Anti-Christ* is striking: this faith preceding knowledge creates fictions that we subsequently deploy to shape our view on and orientation to reality. It is only based on this faith that we can speak of knowledge, which is thus neither based in itself nor in reality. The transcendental illusion of a true, real world plays tricks on us, and this fiction is the a priori, the presupposed faith that makes knowledge possible in the first place. In the above, we saw that Nietzsche uses the term 'nihilism' to characterise every attitude to life that employs the illusory, fictitious idea of a true world, to deny the importance of the world in which we live. In the context of his reflections on faith, he even speaks about 'the most extreme form of nihilism' that judges that '*every* faith, every holding-to-be-true is necessarily false: *because there is no true world*'.[53] This extreme nihilism, '*as denial of a true world*', according to Nietzsche, '*could be a divine way of thinking*'. We now also understand why Nietzsche introduces this extreme nihilism: only this nihilism can reveal the extent to which we operate, in believing as well as knowing, on the basis of a holding-to-be-true. Nietzsche's extreme nihilism, which suspends this foundational faith, thus clears the way for another understanding, namely the understanding that humans apparently have the ability *to create* other perspectives and new values, and with that can assume new attitudes to life.

Much more distinct than the contrast between faith and knowledge that Nietzsche develops in *The Anti-Christ*, these considerations of believing *as holding-to-be-true* touch a core problem that occupies Nietzsche in his reflections on faith and knowledge. We can now interpret Nietzsche's understanding of faith as follows.[54] There is an intrinsic connection between faith and truth for Nietzsche. Faith as holding-to-be-true is 'holding firm in the "truth" and holding fast to the true', as Heidegger writes.[55] Believing is holding on to the idea of the true world and staying within the boundaries of this truth. It moreover refers back to the specific *attitude* of those who believe. Living in a world characterised by change, the believer seeks a hold in the true (world). The true is, for Nietzsche, nothing other than that which has been secured and fixed, and has become stable and come to a standstill so as to provide a hold. For this reason, *the religious-philosophical attitude to life aims to consolidate itself in the stability provided by what has been thus secured*. It is this attitude to life that Nietzsche resists. In this context, Heidegger refers to the following significant citation: '"I no longer believe in anything" – that is the correct way for a *creative* human being to think.'[56] Interpreted as the attempt to find an ever stronger and firmer hold in the stability that the idea of the true world offers, *faith is no longer at odds with truth and the will to know, but rather with creating and with the attitude to life of the creative person*.

Consequently, the real struggle between attitudes to life is for Nietzsche not that between believing and knowing, *but between believing and creating*. The believer and the knower fix, but the creator and the artist destroy everything that has come to a standstill.[57] Nietzsche puts the two relevant wills opposite (or actually: below) each other in the following way: '"Will to *truth*" – *as impotence of the will to create*.'[58] The creator is, in short, the person who wants to put into motion, who wants to bring about other values, other interpretations, other ways of thinking, other ways of being, other ways of living and other histories. In this way, the creator breaks away (from) that which for the believer is secured.

This last consideration about the conflict between believing and creating brings us back us to a theme discussed before. As the one fighting against that which has become solidified in many centuries of Christianity, Nietzsche adopts the creative position and wages war against the believer who holds on to what is petrified. As the founder and inventor of Christianity, however, Paul can hardly be called a believer in Nietzsche's sense of the word. In the analysis of Paul's concept of *pneuma* or spirit, a genuine principle of transformation is recognised. Against the background of Nietzsche's contrast between believing and creating, it hardly seems bold to claim that such a principle is linked to creating – recall once more the Greek verb *zōopoieō*, to quicken and to give life to what is dead, which Paul uses in this regard – rather than to stabilising and securing. Under the heading of this *pneuma*, another history and another attitude to life announce themselves, along with the passing of the present order of the world. Thus, in Nietzsche's vocabulary, Paul is a creator rather than a believer. It is therefore imperative to distinguish the passages in which Nietzsche introduces Paul as the *pars pro toto* of petrified Christianity from the passages, such as those in *Daybreak*, in which he paints a picture of Paul as the founder of Christianity and as the creator of new values. We can, perhaps, in the passages in *The Anti-Christ* in which Nietzsche characterises Paul's faith as the total absence of the will to truth and knowledge, discern another significance of this faith. If Paul's *pistis* is truly marked by a total absence of the will to truth, does this not imply that the characteristics of Paul's faith *cannot* be found in the basic pathos of philosophy, that is, the will to truth? The following question arises anew. If not the will to truth, which *pathos*, then, leads the Pauline faith? Is it resentment, as Nietzsche sometimes suggests? Or is it another *pathos* inspiring *creation*, namely the longing for transformation?

With these questions in mind, it becomes clear why Nietzsche's version of Paul as a man driven by resentment and as an exponent of dualism is less interesting. Rather, Nietzsche's fundamental dispute with Paul should not hide the *other* alternative Paul may offer to a philosophical dualism and its emphasis on stability and security as well as to a concept of faith that is not opposed to creation. As Heidegger notes: 'The *pistis* is not a holding-to-be-true.'⁵⁹

RETRIEVING ANCIENT THOUGHT

Let me conclude this chapter by bringing Paul back to the context of ancient thought and showing how changes in its present-day reception have created a context for the retrieval of the apostle and his letters. This reception, led by Hadot and Foucault, presents ancient philosophy as an art of living. The philosophical turn to ancient culture offers a number of interesting indications that the question of the art of living is related to the problems of dualism, nihilism and Paul's understanding of faith as discussed before. I take my point of departure from Foucault's last lecture-series at the Collège de France, a couple of months before his death in 1984, published under the title *The Courage of Truth*. In these lectures, Paul does not really play a role, although he makes a brief appearance as a representative of ancient culture and its practice of *parrēsia*, that is, of courageously speaking the truth in dangerous circumstances.⁶⁰

Foucault argues that the questions of dualism and faith discussed above actually belong to a much wider context of ancient philosophy and its genuine stakes:

> Maybe [...] it could be said that with Platonism, and through Platonism, Greek philosophy since Socrates basically posed the question of the other world (*l'autre monde*). But, starting with Socrates, or from the Socratic model [...] it also posed another question. Not the question of the other world, but that of an *other* life (*vie autre*). It seems to me that the other world and other life have basically been the two great themes, the two great forms, the great limits within which Western philosophy has constantly developed.⁶¹

The Platonic question of the other, true world is indeed of great importance in antiquity. Yet, at least as important is the question of another mode of living – and that concerns a life lived in *this* world. This second question complicates the first question of the other world, and it forms the origin of the well-known theme of the art of living. How can we live differently from the prevailing ways recommended by our (social) environment?⁶² Foucault finds this search for another life in an exemplary way in the ancient Cynics, who live an uncompromising life. The lifestyle of the Cynics was a scandal – a *skandalon* – for their immediate environment, because they flouted all social mores, as is clear from the example of Diogenes, who allegedly lived in a large ceramic jar and masturbated in public. Paul might have propagated a different kind of life, yet the motif of *skandalon* is embraced in his letters.[63] His proclamation is fundamentally at odds with the modes of living and thinking his environment expects of him. For Foucault the distinction between the question of another world – in Christianity: the afterlife – and the other life implies a caesura in ancient philosophy, and two alternatives emerge on the horizon.

In the first alternative, primacy is granted to the affirmation of the other, true world and the other life – Foucault writes: 'une autre vie' – becomes nothing but living in this other world, that is, the perfect life in the afterlife, the life after death.[64] This first alternative is, in Nietzsche's terminology, the nihilism par excellence of Christianity, characterised by an animosity towards earthly existence. Given Nietzsche's influence on Foucault, it is hardly surprising that the latter also finds the ultimate example of this alternative in Christianity.

The second alternative is represented in an exemplary fashion by ancient Cynicism. At the centre of this alternative, we do not find the question of the other world but that of the other life. To mark the distinction with the first alternative, Foucault now writes 'la vie autre' and notes that this theme is the fundamental contribution of Cynicism to the history of Western ethics.[65] This other life is nothing but the true life in *this* world. Even if Foucault agrees with Nietzsche that this alternative is not to be found in Christianity, there is nevertheless a striking similarity with a remark on Christianity made by Žižek. For the latter, the true legacy and stakes of Paul's letters are not to be found in the question of whether there is an eternal life after death, but rather of whether true life before death is possible.[66] Thus, it is the theme of the other life – *la vie autre* – that Foucault uncovers in ancient philosophy and that since then, despite Nietzsche's and Foucault's analyses of Christianity, philosophy has been able to (re)discover in Paul's letters as well.

This theme of the other life makes itself felt in two ways. First, in connection with the first emphasis on the true, higher world, the transformation of one's life is a precondition for obtaining access to this true world. The practices of asceticism in Christianity and Gnosticism are, for Foucault, important examples thereof. For Foucault, it was even a stroke of genius of Christianity, because this invention allowed Christianity to connect the two basic questions of ancient philosophy. The emphasis on the other world – *un autre monde* – can, however, reduce the other life in this world to the other life in the other world and found the former in the latter.[67] In this case, *la vie autre* is reduced to and founded in *l'autre vie*, thus erasing the specificity and unicity of the theme of *la vie autre*, the other life in this world.

Second, the other life in this world – *la vie autre* – need not be conceived as an attempt to purify and change one's own life in light of the hereafter; it can also be understood as a basic struggle for and in *this* world, that is, a struggle to change this world, so that another world – *un monde autre* – becomes possible. Foucault again finds this exemplified in the life of the ancient Cynics, the true heroes of *The Courage of Truth*:

> [T]he Cynic is someone who, taking up the traditional themes of the true life in ancient philosophy, transposes them and turns them round into the demand and assertion of the need for an *other* life [*vie autre*]. And then [...] he transposes anew the idea of *an other* life into the theme of a life whose otherness must lead to the change of the world. An *other* life [*vie autre*] for an *other* world [*monde autre*].[68]

A transformation of the world is announced here, brought about by those who lead their life according to this other mode of living. So, the ethics of the other life is not founded on the ontological primacy of a true, unchangeable world but rather takes place in and as the socio-political transformation of the world we inhabit. The spiritual exercises and self-techniques that ancient philosophy developed to be able to live a life according to the spirit therefore form the ingredients of an art of living that in some versions of Cynicism is also a political art and struggle for another social world. This implies that this other life adopts a revolutionary and militant guise; this is the basic legacy of Cynic philosophy:

> The principle of militantism constantly [recurs] in these movements, an open militantism which is the critique of real life and of men's behavior, and which, in personal renunciation and destitution, conducts the battle which must lead to the change of the whole world.[69]

Foucault limits his analysis to the political dimension of this ethical turn to the other life in Cynicism and has little regard for the ontological implications thereof. That does not mean, however, that the attention to ontology (or cosmology) can be left aside in favour of a specifically activist, militant political programme. It does mean that, if we wish to draw the ontological implications thereof, we need to understand, in the first place, that we have to let go of the perspective of a true, *unchangeable* world. The basic insight of this other life – *la vie autre* – is, after all, that the world or the cosmos, the natural and the earthly, *can be changed*. The power of Paul's focus on the principle of the spirit is that it simultaneously speaks about a *mode of living* – namely living according to the spirit, a variation of the other life – about a *mode of thinking*, as we saw in his pneumatic hermeneutics, and about a *mode of being*, a reality that does not get absorbed in the first, natural, cosmic order, but can be changed. By paying attention to this ontological dimension of the spirit, we may see how, for Paul, the perspective of the mode of living must always be embedded in a mode of being and accompanied by a mode of thinking.

At the same time, this implies a departure from Foucault's analysis of ancient philosophy when turning to Paul. Foucault fully emphasises the spiritual exercises and techniques that ancient philosophy developed and perfected into an art of living. Yet, when we only focus on the art of living and its techniques, the impression could arise that the transformation of human existence can happen through these techniques alone – thus reinvigorating Stowers's objections discussed in the introduction – as if ancient philosophy advocates a form of self-malleability and as if the life-giving character, *zōopoieō* from 1 Cor. 15:45, sprouts from the spiritual exercises instead of from the spirit, which *lends* and *grants* these exercises their spiritual character. For Paul, this perspective would be unthinkable. Transformation is of the order of the spirit. A life according to the spirit is a mode of living that ultimately depends on grace; despite all exercises and techniques, it depends on being made alive by something that comes from outside, something which Paul addresses under the heading of *charis*, grace.[70] Along these lines, we will be able to retrieve the triad of Paul's principle of the spirit in the chapters that follow: mode of living, mode of thinking and mode of being.

NOTES

1 Also see Frick, *Paul in the Grip of the Philosophers*, 6.
2 Nietzsche, *Jenseits von Gut und Böse*, 4/4 [= Vorrede].
3 Nietzsche, *Götzen-Dämmerung*, 69/168 [= 'Die "Vernunft" in die Philosophie', § 2].
4 Nietzsche, *Ecce Homo*, 372/150 [= 'Warum ich ein Schicksal bin', § 8].
5 Nietzsche, *Der Antichrist*, 215/39 [= § 43].
6 Nietzsche, *Nachgelassene Fragmente Herbst 1887*, 30 [= 9[60]]; translation taken from Van Tongeren, *Friedrich Nietzsche and European Nihilism*, 167.
7 Nihilism is a complex problem that can be found in many manifestations and variations in Nietzsche's work. See, among others, Van Tongeren, *Nietzsche and European Nihilism*, who analyses the form of nihilism I discuss here on 57–62. He links this form of nihilism to the will to truth that characterises philosophy and the sciences, but that forms an important theme in Christianity as well: 'It turns out that the search for truth can itself be called nihilistic, even in its earlier shape, to the extent that it

is a negation of the "world in which we live": it is as if it says that "this world of ours ought not to exist" [...] For this reason Nietzsche may at times label philosophy (as well as morality and religion, with which it forms an alliance [...]) "nihilistic"' (ibid., 59). Concerning the relation of Christianity and nihilism, Nietzsche sardonically notes: 'Nihilist and Christian [*Nihilist und Christ*]: this rhymes, it does more than just rhyme ...' (Nietzsche, *Der Antichrist*, 245/62 [= § 58]).

8   Ibid., 179–80/13 [= § 15].
9   Ibid., 190–1/21 [= § 24].
10 Nietzsche is aware of this particular role played by creation in the constitution of this cosmology, ontology and anthropology and already makes a similar point in *Die Geburt der Tragödie*, 111/85 [= § 18] concerning the illusions created by three types of noble souls.
11 Taubes noted exactly this point, see *Die politische Theologie des Paulus*, 40/26, 109/78–9.
12 Nietzsche, *Morgenröthe*, 60–4/39–42 [= Book 1, § 68]. Along the lines of Taubes's interpretation, as set out in the previous chapter, this is also a clear example of the dualist, Marcionite version of Paul that Nietzsche offers.
13 Ibid., 64/42 [= Book 1, § 68].
14 Taubes, *Die politische Theologie des Paulus*, 113–14/82.
15 Badiou, *Saint Paul*, 65/61.
16 Nietzsche, *Der Antichrist*, 190/21 [= § 24].
17 Ibid.
18 Rather than being engaged in a polemic with Paul, some literature suggests that Nietzsche portrays himself as a 'dialectical resemblance' or 'dialectical overcoming' of Paul; see Salaquarda, 'Dionysus versus the Crucified One', 120, 116. Based on this characterisation, one can ask whether this dialectical relation is Hegelian or not, that is, an 'overcoming-preservation' or not; see Azzam, *Nietzsche versus Paul*, xvi–xvii, 88–9. Yet, when the conclusion of this analysis turns out to be that Paul is not preserved but only overcome by Nietzsche, it seems that we are simply dealing with a polemic.
19 Taubes, *Die politische Theologie des Paulus*, 100–3/72–4.
20 Heidegger, *Grundbegriffe der aristotelischen Philosophie*, 5/4.
21 Badiou, *Saint Paul*, 66–7/62–3.
22 Nietzsche, *Der Antichrist*, 214/39 [= § 42].
23 Ibid., 209/35 [= § 39].
24 See, e.g., Badiou, *Saint Paul*, 5/4, 62/58, 116/108.
25 Nietzsche, *Der Antichrist*, 245/62 [= § 58].
26 Badiou, *Saint Paul*, 65/61.
27 Ibid., 46/43.
28 Ibid., 62/58. Laughing rather than wrath kills, see Nietzsche, *Also sprach Zarathustra*, I. 'Vom Lesen und Schreiben' and IV. 'Das Eselsfest', § 1.
29 That indeed Nietzsche's sharp judgement of the spirit motivates Taubes to

provide another interpretation of Paul's notion of the spirit is also the conclusion of the editors of Taubes's book; Taubes, *Die politische Theologie des Paulus*, 160-1/128.
30 Nietzsche, *Morgenröthe*, 75-6/49-50 [= Book 1, § 84].
31 Nietzsche, *Der Antichrist*, 214/38 [= § 42].
32 Nietzsche, *Morgenröthe*, 76/50 [= Book 1, § 84].
33 The same insight can be found in Nietzsche studies; see, e.g., Salaquarda, 'Dionysus versus the Crucified One', 103.
34 See Nietzsche, *Also sprach Zarathustra*, II. 'Von der Erlösung'.
35 For the concept of ontotheology, see Van der Heiden, *Ontology after Ontotheology*, 1-21, and *Metafysica*, 229-41.
36 Heidegger, *Phänomenologie des religiösen Lebens*, 120/86.
37 I focus on Heidegger, *Nietzsche I*, 341-54; see also *Nietzsches metaphysische Grundstellung*, 131-42.
38 Van Tongeren, *Friedrich Nietzsche and European Nihilism*, 57-62.
39 Nietzsche, *Der Antichrist*, 209/35 [= § 39].
40 Ibid.
41 Ibid., 204/31 [= § 33].
42 Ibid., 210/35 [= § 39].
43 Ibid., 173/8 [= § 9].
44 Ibid., 223/46 [= § 47].
45 Ibid., 231/51 [= § 52].
46 This use of terminology can already be found in Plato whose account of the divided line in *The Republic* VI, 509d-11e is characteristic of this: *pistis* is a mode of knowing that belongs to the realm of the sensible things and concerns our convictions about physical things; *epistēmē* is genuine knowledge that belongs to the realm of intelligible things.
47 Nietzsche, *Über Wahrheit und Lüge in aussermoralischen Sinne*, 375/117 [= § 1].
48 Ricœur, *La Métaphore vive*, 121/109.
49 For Aristotle, *Metaphysics*, Book VI, theoretical sciences such as first philosophy are characterised by the fact that they leave the beings they aim to know *untouched*; unlike practical and technical knowledge, theoretical knowledge does not aim to change beings or circumstances, but simply wants to know.
50 Nietzsche, *Über Wahrheit und Lüge in aussermoralischen Sinne*, 375/117 [= § 1].
51 Nietzsche, *Nachgelassene Fragmente Herbst 1887*, 18 [= 9[41]]. Translation: Joey Kok. Heidegger also refers to this citation in *Nietzsche I*, 345; our translation slightly deviates from the one offered in Heidegger, *Nietzsche*, 2:124.
52 Nietzsche, *Nachgelassene Fragmente Herbst 1887*, 54 [= 9[97]]. Translation: Joey Kok.
53 Ibid., 18 [= 9[41]]. Translation: Joey Kok.
54 See Heidegger, *Nietzsche I*, 341-54.

55 Heidegger, *Nietzsche 1*, 346; Heidegger, *Nietzsche*, 2:124.
56 Nietzsche, *Nachgelassene Fragmente Sommer-Herbst 1882*, 67 [= 3[1], 119]. Heidegger, *Nietzsche I*, 346; Heidegger, *Nietzsche*, 2:125.
57 Heidegger. *Nietzsche I*, 347.
58 Nietzsche, *Nachgelassene Fragmente Herbst 1887*, 29 [= 9[60]]. Translation taken from Van Tongeren, *Friedrich Nietzsche and European Nihilism*, 167.
59 Heidegger, *Phänomenologie des religiösen Lebens*, 108/76. Translation adapted.
60 Foucault, *Le Courage de la vérité*, 301/329–30. Here we indeed find 'Paul among the Parrhesiasts', as Blanton, *A Materialism for the Masses*, 97, suggests.
61 Foucault, *Le Courage de la vérité*, 262/245.
62 Agamben, 'Where is Science Going?', 109, affirms the importance of this Socratic discovery for philosophy today: 'Philosophy is always about ethics. It always implies a form of life.'
63 In the Epilogue, I return to this motif and show based on considerations to be developed in the next chapters, how and why the Pauline *skandalon* is not exactly the Cynical one.
64 Foucault, *Le Courage de la vérité*, 292–3/319–20.
65 Ibid., 226/245.
66 Žižek, 'The Necessity of a Dead Bird', 184.
67 Foucault, *Le Courage de la vérité*, 293/320.
68 Ibid., 264/287.
69 Ibid., 264/286.
70 Also see Ruin, 'Faith, Grace, and the Destruction of Tradition', 31.

3. Meontology

A new legacy of Paul, as I argued in the previous chapters, can only be found if his letters are read beyond dualist and nihilist interpretations. However, with the rejection of the Marcionite and Nietzschean version of the apostle, the ghosts of dualism and especially nihilism have not yet been fully exorcised in favour of a dialectic of exception. This is due to one of the foci of the present-day debate. The apostle's understanding of the world, *kosmos*, is often approached by focusing on what one might call the nihilistic passages in the letters. In them, Paul announces for instance the end of the world, evoking in some of his readers images of the apocalypse; and in them, he claims there is a divine partiality for non-beings over beings (Cor. 1:27–8).

When a legacy of Paul is based on such passages, does this not irrevocably lead to a nihilistic Paul? This seems to be Critchley's argument, among others. He concludes that such readings end up being 'crypto-Marcionite'. Incapable of finding a positive ontology, these passages advocate a Pauline *meontology*, a doctrine of nothingness and of non-beings.[1] Yet, rather than removing these 'nihilistic' passages from my reading, I will argue that they actually offer important building blocks for a Pauline dialectic of exception. Therefore, let us address these passages, and confront the possible problems they produce, head-on.

As I turn now to these 'nihilistic' passages I note that they play a twofold role in my examination of Paul's ontology and ethics. The second role concerns the question of time and event and is taken up in the next chapter. The first is developed in this chapter by approaching Paul's cosmology and ontology in light of the relevant meontological statements and by demonstrating how they are mirrored in a particular Pauline ethos. Throughout this chapter, I will provide an argument showing why it is wrong to understand the Pauline meontology that arises in our reading as a nihilism.

NOTHING IN THE WORLD

The letter pivotal to Paul's understanding of the world is 1 Corinthians, and exactly this letter contains important meontological passages. I agree with Critchley that these passages are of the utmost importance for a renewed philosophical legacy of Paul, even though I deny that, for this reason, this legacy is doomed to be (crypto-)Marcionite. The meontological passages are connected by the famous *tou kosmou*-formulas, 'of the world', woven through 1 Corinthians as its chorus. In the sections that follow, some of these passages are discussed. First, however, let me outline in more broader terms the specific ontology or order of being corresponding to these *tou kosmou*-formulas. Exemplary in this regard is 1 Cor. 1:27–8:

> But God chose what is foolish in the world [*ta mōra tou kosmou*] to shame the wise; God chose what is weak in the world [*ta asthenē tou kosmou*] to shame the strong; God chose what is low[born in the world; *ta agenē tou kosmou*] and despised, things that are not [*ta mē onta*], to reduce to nothing [*katargēsē*] things that are [*ta onta*].

Paul identifies both the members of the community in Corinth and himself with those who are considered 'foolish', 'weak', 'low(born)' and 'despised' in and by the world.[2] By this particular rhetoric, the concept of the world is assigned an antagonistic role characteristic of this letter. Since this antagonism is clearly reminiscent of a dualism, a dialectic reappraisal of the letters needs to face up to these formulas and discover their significance.

The last sentence of the fragment cited above explicitly suggests and concisely expresses a Pauline doctrine of non-beings, especially if we slightly adapt its translation: 'God chose the non-beings [*ta mē onta*] to suspend and deactivate [*katargēsē*] the beings [*ta onta*].' The expression *ta onta*, the beings, refers to that which exists or that which is considered to be of value in the world. Similarly, the expression *ta mē onta*, the non-beings, refers to that which does not exist, which is not(hing) in the world or which is considered to be of no value in the world. Consequently, in this passage, the God of Paul is not presented as affirming beings, but rather as preferring non-beings.

What does this mean? Is this meontology indeed a nihilism in which God embraces non-being(s) or nothingness at the expense of that which exists? Or does it concern something else? Let me address these questions by making three consecutive comments on this verse the aim of which is to explicate what the notion of meontology might mean in a Pauline context, calibrated on 1 Cor. 1:28, and how it corresponds to related conceptions of non-being in the context of both ancient and modern philosophy.

(1) In the first place, it is important to refrain from the impulse to read the preference for non-beings in a merely socio-political way. The non-beings, *ta mē onta*, refer to that which *was not assigned a place in the current world order* or does not fit into this order. The term 'world' has to be read in its ambiguity. Its order can refer both to the ontologico-cosmological category of the *kosmos* as well as to the socio-ethico-political reality of the social world, including social morality and political order. Paul often addresses these two dimensions, the ethical or political life in a social world and the ontological status of beings in the *kosmos*, at the same time, and they mirror each other. Therefore, we should always keep this ambiguity in mind.

This warning applies especially to the passage we are reading here. When *tou kosmou* is translated as 'in the world', it seems only natural to view 1 Cor. 1:27–8 as a *merely* socio-ethical commentary: God is not the God of worldly morality but rather represents another mode of living. This verse, however, also concerns the *mode of being*. Mode of being, mode of thinking and mode of living are not separately available in ancient culture, as we have seen in Foucault's analysis of ancient thought. The questions about mode of being and mode of living should always be considered together, because the true perception of reality is only given through and in a life according to the spirit. The same interwovenness of living, thinking and being applies to Paul.

Moreover, as soon as we are willing to hear the divine partiality for non-beings expressed in 1 Cor. 1:28 in an ontological and cosmological key, we also get a better sense of the conception of being for which a Pauline meontology is supposed to offer an alternative. In the context of the readings of Paul, Heidegger's characterisation of metaphysics as ontotheology – or more precisely of the ontotheological constitution of metaphysics – often returns. It seems to me that there are good reasons for this. Metaphysics offers a conception of being that is determined by a particular conception of God and by a particular conception of the *kosmos* as the order in which each being is awarded its own proper place, role and position. In ontotheology, being is understood in terms of a highest being, God, which in turn is the measure and the norm of all other beings as well as the goal to which all other beings strive. In this metaphysical theology and cosmology, God is the highest being that merits all the properties that are understood as perfect in classical – medieval – metaphysics: almighty, omniscient, pure reality, pure intelligibility and so on. In ontotheology, *everything that is* is grounded in and caused by this highest being, either as final cause in the form of Aristotle's unmoved mover or as effective cause in the form of the medieval, Christian conception of the creator. This highest being is thus the very principle of the *cosmos* and its order.[3] A crucial consequence of this description of reality is that a being that is closer to God, that is, that resembles God more, thereby also *is* more. For this reason, the beings that are truly powerful, truly wise and so forth, are more perfect than the beings that lack these properties.

Reference to ontotheology can often be found in the discussion of Paul because Paul resists this logic. Paul's God is not a God of being in this ontotheological sense.[4] Paul's God prefers the lowly, the long-suffering, the foolish and the weak and is thus marked by partiality for non-beings rather than for beings, as expressed by 1 Cor. 1:28. Paul's God has more to do with the creation that suffers than the created beings that are victorious in the eyes of the world. In fact, Paul's God deactivates the reign of these victorious beings that in the ontotheological model are positioned as higher and as closer to the metaphysical God. In this sense, the issue of meontology concerns nothing less than the quest for an alternative to ontotheology. If we adopt Heidegger's claim that Aristotle and Plato are the first philosophers who have contributed to this ontotheological constitution of metaphysics, it becomes clear why another source and another ontology – or, rather, a meontology – is needed to reinterpret and recalibrate our conceptions of God, *kosmos* and being.[5]

(2) Second, 1 Cor. 1:28 is not about the simple destruction of the current world order and its beings. Regarding his issue, translations matter much. The NRSV proposes to translate the verb *katargeō* as 'to reduce to nothing'. However, this verb does not exactly mean to destroy or to reduce to nothing. As authors such as Marion and Agamben have pointed out, *katargeō* rather means 'to suspend' or 'to deactivate'.[6] Let us recall Agamben's etymological argument. If this verb were the antonym of *poieō*, to make or to create, it could indeed have meant 'to destroy', but it is rather the antonym of *energeō* – to be operational or to be at work – and hence means 'to suspend', 'to deactivate' or 'to defer the operativity of' the order of this world.[7]

With these notions in mind, we enter the philosophical arena. In the last verb, *energeō*, the Greek *energeia* is heard. Aristotle coins this term in his *Metaphysics* as the Greek understanding of actuality. As the antonym of *energeia*, *katargēsis* is Paul's term for the deactivation what is actual as well as for the suspension of the actual operative or working order of what is. This is different from destruction. When a machine is out of order, it does not mean that is has been destroyed, but rather that it does not function properly and needs to be repaired or replaced.

Similarly, we can deactivate a machine. We do so when we notice that it does not function properly anymore. The machine is deactivated in order to create an opportunity and a leeway for operators to repair it, to alter it or to replace (parts of) it. This particular explication of *katargēsis* is highly suggestive. Are the non-beings in the context of 1 Cor. 1:28 not precisely the motivation for Paul's God to suspend the working of the current world order and the beings supporting it because this order cannot award a place to those non-beings?

The confrontation between Paul's *katargēsis* and Aristotle's *energeia* is not only important in an attempt to trace the meaning of the Greek term but also because it includes a fundamental philosophical issue. In Aristotle's *Metaphysics*, the notion of *energeia*, actuality, is raised in conjunction with the notion of *dunamis*, power, potentiality or possibility. One of the most important reasons for Aristotle to introduce the pair of *energeia* and *dunamis* is to solve a particular problem *concerning non-being*. The pair allows him to understand how qualitative movement is possible, how something can change or become something else. Ancient thought is dominated by the conviction that it is impossible for something to originate out of nothing: a *creatio ex nihilo* is unthinkable.[8] How then is it possible, for example, that from the unreasonable, new-born child who is not yet able to speak ultimately may come an adult with a language ability and a capacity to reason? Does this not imply that something – linguistic competence and rationality – originates from nothing? To solve this riddle, Aristotle suggests that the not-being-there of the linguistic competence of the child is not simply nothing. The child's linguistic competence is potentially there, the ability to speak is not *simply not* in the child. There is much to be said for this solution. After all, other than a dog, for instance, that cannot speak and will also never acquire the ability to speak, the new-born child can indeed *not yet* speak but may activate this capacity after some time. In the child, non-speaking is not pure negativity; it is speaking-in-potential. However, to actualise this potential, the child does need to *undergo a change*. The child is passive in this transformation. For Aristotle, this change the child undergoes is, therefore, understood as the actualisation of this potential. At the same time, this potentiality does not actualise itself necessarily or automatically. Only if the circumstances are favourable, the child is changed in such a way that it acquires the ability to speak – the child cannot complete this actualization by itself alone; it needs, for instance, proper education and nourishment. When circumstances are unfavourable, this potential will perish unactualised in the given reality. This squandering of possibilities receives particular significance in Paul's ontology.

Two conclusions may be drawn concerning Aristotle's notion of *dunamis*. First, placed side by side, Aristotle's *dunamis* and Paul's *katargēsis* are notions developed to confront problems posed by forms of non-being that are *not* simply nothing. Aristotle is not the only one to address this ambiguity of negativity and nothingness. Plato's account of non-being in terms of that which is other or different, *to heteron*, as developed in the *Sophist* is another important example of this. In both cases, the ontological status of those non-beings that are not merely nothing poses a particular problem.[9] This insight motivates my explication of the term 'meontology': a doctrine of non-being needs to be developed to deal with these forms of non-being that are not simply nothing. Paul's *katargēsis* belongs in the same range of notions as Aristotle's *dunamis* and Plato's *to heteron*, in which the ontological status of a specific category of non-being is at stake.

Second, the confrontation with the Aristotelian pair of actuality and potentiality may also orient the further clarification of *katargēsis*. Specifically, the question of the 'result' of the suspension of *katargēsis* is aided by a confrontation with the Aristotelian pair, demonstrating the specificity of the Pauline notion. The suspension of a given reality does not open an empty space of the purely unreal or the mere non-being but *a well-defined space of possibilities that have* not *been actualised in a given reality*. As an unfavourable fate can deny the child the ability to speak or even the gift of life itself in the stillborn children, actuality is rich in possibilities that are and remain unactualised. These precluded, wasted possibilities are the non-beings that are not merely nothing.

My imposition of Aristotle's conceptuality on Paul might give cause for certain hesitations, even if, for instance, Agamben argues that Paul had to have been aware of this pair.[10] Yet, this interpretation of *katargēsis* seems to fit in the context of 1 Cor. 1:28, in which Paul aligns being with power, wisdom, knowledge, strength and authority. By contrast, he and the members of the community in Corinth he addresses are presented as insignificant, foolish, weak and despised. Each of these terms refer to possibilities of existence that have not been actualised in the current order of the world; they refer to what stays behind with that part of the world that flourishes and tingles with great power and dazzling wealth. For Agamben, it is therefore obvious to refer, in this context, to another, famous fragment from Paul: '*dunamis* is made perfect in weakness' (2 Cor. 12:9).[11] The eventual fulfilment of this *dunamis*, then, does not lie in actuality, in what is powerfully and orderly operative and at work in the world, but exactly in what is characterised by *weakness*, by what appears, in actuality, to be a lack of effective, operative power. At this point, Paul disengages from Aristotle's metaphysics and uses *dunamis* in a definite non-Aristotelian way. The potentiality of speech is the child's, which under normal, favourable circumstances will be actualised. Paul, however, is concerned with impotent beings that are nothing and have lost their potential to flourish in the given order of the world. It is in this sense that something is needed that does not simply belong to the given order of the world.

Moreover, if *katargēsis* indeed concerns the suspension rather than the destruction of this world, there is every reason to assume that this notion implies a dialectic alternative to the nihilism attributed to Paul and his readers. If the current world is not destroyed, there is no other world on the horizon, but only this *kosmos*, albeit in another way. Here, we confront a conceptual difficulty. On the one hand, *kosmos* is the very name in ancient thought for the world and its given order. It remains to be seen in which sense we can still refer to the suspension of this order as 'world'.

What is clear at this point, though, is the relation of Paul to dialectic thought, which is especially manifest in the modern reception of Paul. There are good reasons to assume an intrinsic connection between the central concept of Hegel's dialectic, *Aufhebung*, and Paul's *katargēsis*.[12] Even though my aim is to argue that Paul's dialectic is not exactly Hegelian, it is important to note that the basic concept of *Aufhebung* by which Hegel overcomes every *mere* negation – as well as the forms of dualism and nihilism to which such a negation would lead – is of Pauline origin. Hegel's *Aufhebung* is itself a concept that shows that the status of non-being or negation is much more complex than one could surmise and that it definitely cannot be equated with mere nothingness. If the term 'meontology' is used to indicate what Paul says in 1 Cor. 1:28 about non-beings and the *katargēsis* of beings, how does this further help us in the discussion on nihilism?

(3) There is only one other fragment in the letters of Paul in which the expression *ta mē onta* is used, namely in Rom. 4:17.[13] What Paul writes there is closely connected to 1 Cor. 1:28, and it is moreover linked to two other important motifs: 'God [...] who gives life to the dead [again: *zōopoieō*] and calls into existence the things that do not exist [*kalountas ta mē onta hōs onta*].' Here, the phrase *ta mē onta* is used in relation to the creative, life-endowing power of the spirit capable of transforming the mode of being of non-beings. The second part of this citation could also be rendered as 'that calls non-beings as beings' or, less literally, as 'that calls non-beings into existence'. By anticipating the motif of the call or the vocation, discussed in the next section, we can say that God's call does not confirm or affirm the order of reality but rather recalls the first call and word – that of the creative word in

the beginning, *in principio* – by which the world received this order: it calls non-beings into existence, granting them a place *despite* the order of the world, which grants them no place. This pneumatic possibility is opened up by the suspension of this order of the world and it is fulfilled in the enactment of the divine power to create life and existence. Here we see most clear how the Pauline possibility or potential of non-beings to be revivified and quickened is not simply always already inscribed in them or in the order in which they exist; thus, this possibility is fundamentally non-Aristotelian. The privileged Pauline expression for this possibility released by *katargēsis* and fulfilled in the call to faith is 'the new creation'. This expression does not point to another, higher world substituting the old one, but to another, pneumatic mode of being of the world.

The phrase 'the current order of the world' additionally reveals the philosophical impact of this passage. Philosophical thought is traditionally one of order, in which God is in the first place the being and principle that enables the order of actuality. When Paul's comment is read not only socio-ethically but also metaphysically, it becomes clear that, for Paul, God is not only the God of creation where creation is understood as the order in which everything is assigned its own place but, importantly, also the God who suspends this order because somehow it is in a crisis: not everything is assigned a proper place; some things are out of place. The things that are not – *ta mē onta* – are thus those things that, and those people who, are the *symptoms* of this crisis; they are not simply non-beings but rather symptomatic *problematic cases* exposing the crisis of actuality. They cry out for the necessity of change and call for a repetition of the divine, creative powers on another, pneumatic level.

When understanding meontology along these lines, we see why and in which sense it cannot be qualified as nihilistic. As further support of this conclusion, let me point out that this is consistent with a particular, modern reception of the Greek *mē on*. According to Schelling, a distinction needs to be drawn between two forms of non-being: *mē on* and *ouk on*.[14] Non-being as *ouk on* neither is (actual) nor has the possibility to be. *Mē on* is also subject to not being actual but has the possibility of becoming actual: '*mē on* can *become being*.'[15] *Mē on* is thus exactly recognised as the term for the forms of non-being that are not merely nothing. In this way, Schelling's interpretation of *mē on* closely approximates Paul's use of the term *ta mē onta*. For Paul, the non-beings are pneumatically filled with the possibility of another existence, of a materialisation of which they have been deprived in the given reality. The realisation of this possibility is, for Paul, not natural

– *psuchikon* – but is attributed to the principle of the spirit that repeats the impeded and squandered potential for existence in this other power that grants existence.

Heidegger mentions the same distinction between *mē on* and *ouk on*, even though he interprets it in light of Platonic dualism: while *ouk on* is what purely does not exist, *mē on* is the not-truly-being that nevertheless exists in one way or another.[16] The standard Platonic-dualist example uses *mē on* to describe the mode of existence of the sensory, changeable being: it should indeed be awarded some form of existence, even though it is not true, intelligible, immutable being. By using the model of dualism, Heidegger basically understands *to mē on* as a privative mode of being.[17] Yet, this interpretation is not the only option explored in present-day thought. Deleuze equally links the distinction between *mē on* and *ouk on* to Plato, specifically to the *Sophist*, which focuses on the question of the status of the being of non-being.[18] For Deleuze, *to mē on* is not 'the being of the negative'. Rather, it is 'the being of the problematic'. *To mē on* is a symptomatic case that does not fit in the prescribed order of being – of a Platonic dualism, in this case – thus confronting this order of being with a problem it cannot solve. This is an important correction of Heidegger's version: *to mē on* does not follow the paradigm of Platonic dualism. Only when we are confronted with what withdraws itself from this dualism do we encounter the non-being that after all *is* in an undetermined sense.[19] Reading Plato's *Sophist* against itself, Deleuze argues that *to mē on* is not privative and is certainly not nothing, but rather what is other or what is different. Thus, for Plato, *to mē on* is the being that is not part of the given order of being determined by the intelligible. Consequently, this non-being is the pre-eminent symptom of the (intellectual) crisis of Plato's dualism. It is precisely this not-merely-negative meaning of non-being that resonates with the meaning encountered in 1 Cor. 1:28. *Ta mē onta*, the non-beings, represent the problematic cases pushing the given ontological order to its limits and simultaneously calling for another order. For Paul, this call is echoed by the principle of the spirit that harbours the possibility for non-beings to be, that is, their quickening and revivification.

Against the background of the accounts of *to mē on* by Schelling and Deleuze, it becomes plainly clear that the term 'meontology' has no nihilistic meaning in a philosophical context. Not-being in the sense of *to mē on* rather points to an original difference and an original possibility of being that constitutes an exception to the actual order of being; for this reason, the non-beings constitute a question to and a symptomatic problem in and for this order. Only once this order of being is suspended and disabled, these possibilities and differences can manifest themselves as possibilities and differences in being, in the world, and in actuality itself. In this way, the non-being of meontology obtains a double sense. First, non-being means the difference or the alterity that as such constitutes a problem for the order of being and the actual order of the world. Second, non-being means the possible in which a true change of that which is actual, is announced. Suspending the current world order is the very thing that shows the non-beings in their difference with this order, and in light of the possibility established by Paul's pneumatic principle. It is this fundamental experience and pathos that may be gleaned from Paul's meontological fragments in 1 Corinthians. Let us consider these fragments in more detail.

SENSE OF AN ENDING

According to Paul, the current figure or the cosmos (*to schēma tou kosmou toutou*) is not permanent but passes away: 'For the present form of this world is passing away' (Cor. 7:31); in the less literal translation of the Contemporary English Version (CEV): 'This world as we know it is now passing away.' At first sight, it seems that it can hardly get more nihilistic than this. Paul sees the world in light of its imminent ending; the Greek verbal form he uses even suggests that this ending is already taking place.

The Greek word *schēma* expresses the figure or form of the world. We do not know the cosmos itself, only the form and the figure by which it appears. When we mean this in the sense of how the world appears to our senses and that we only know the world thanks to its appearance, this passage suggests a reference to empirical knowledge in which different facets of the world can become known through experiments and sensory observations. This is the world as we know it. Where one might be inclined to read 1 Cor. 1 on a strictly sociopolitical level, the passage from 1 Cor. 7 rather seems to call for an ontological reading. This suggestion is reinforced when taking the Stoic background of Paul into account. Stoicism offers an account of the end of the cosmos as *ekpurōsis*, and Paul seems to have his own conception of such an ending.

Yet, the Greek word *schēma* also refers to another semantic field. *Schēma* can also mean habit or custom. Your *schēma* concerns your behaviour, your habits, your way of life. When the CEV translates *to schēma tou kosmou toutou* as 'the world as we know it', then 'know' does not only include the somewhat narrow meaning of knowing the world through the senses or knowing the cosmos through reason, but also the sense we intend when we want to 'get to know' someone. When we get to know someone, we know how someone behaves, their habits and their attitude to life. If we were to apply this to the world, we would perhaps be allowed to somewhat freely translate the Pauline formula *to schēma tou kosmou toutou* as 'the present way of the world', that is, the way in which things are done in the social world, the way of our dealings with the world and with each other. Hence, also *to schēma tou kosmou toutou* should be understood in a double ontologico-ethical sense; it concerns a mode of being as well as a mode of living.

I emphasise this ethical dimension because, without it, one would fail to understand the connection between 1 Cor. 7:31 and Rom. 12:2, which is often made, for instance by Barth in his famous *The Epistle to the Romans* as well as by Heidegger. The latter firstly interprets Paul's understanding of the cosmos in terms of 'this condition and this situation of human beings [...] and way of their Dasein [*Weise ihres Daseins*]' and only to a lesser extent in terms of 'nature or the "cosmic"'.[20] To support this reading he points out that *schēma* in 1 Cor. 7:31 mirrors Rom. 12:2: 'Do not be conformed to this world.'[21] The Greek *suschēmatisesthē*, to be of equal form, uniform, or conform, includes the word *schēma*. In Rom. 12:2, Paul calls on the members of his Roman community not to conform to the world in their way of life. He calls them to nonconformism.[22] 1 Cor. 7:31 underpins this call from Rom. 12:2 by an argument: do not behave like the world behaves because the common way of the world is passing away. There is an attunement to life that allows itself to be guided by a practical wisdom that is worldly wise and knows the ways of the world. Yet, there is also another prudence that departs from the sense of an ending. The ways of the world are not permanent and do not grant the certainty they purported to offer. This passing character of the world – as mode of being and as mode of living – is crucial because it alludes to the *contingency* of the world. That which is necessary exists and cannot not exist; that which is contingent, by contrast, exists but could just as well not be. 1 Cor. 7:31 is a prime expression of this contingency. The sense of an ending attunes one to the world *as contingent*; yet, with this sense, a space or a leeway for the spirit of God and its life-endowing power is opened up. Hence, this sense of an ending suspends the necessity of the world, discloses the world in its contingency, and opens up the possibility of another, life-endowing divine power.[23]

The conflict between conformism and nonconformism to the way of the world is supported by the *tou kosmou*-formulas that express the same polemic or differend between the *schēma tou kosmou*, the way of the world, and Paul's self-identification as *perikatharmata tou kosmou*, the scum of the world (Cor. 4:13). He opposes divine wisdom to *tēn sophian tou kosmou*, the wisdom of the world (Cor. 1:20) and uses the *tou kosmou*-formulas in 1 Cor. 1:27–8 to describe similar oppositions. These other *tou kosmou*-formulas contextualise the *schēma tou kosmou*-formula from 1 Cor. 7. On its own, the latter formula might be read as a rejection of the world, an expectation of its destruction, or an announcement of the apocalypse. Yet, the other formulas show that the original inspiration of Paul's use of the *tou kosmou*-formula is not grounded in his – or his God's – rejection *of* the world but rather in the rejection of the scum of the earth *by* the world; that is to say, it is founded in the inability of the present order of the world to actualise the possibilities of the weak, foolish and despised. In the world, a variety of beings appear as weak, foolish, garbage, scum, lowborn and despised, but none of these is nothing: they are only nothing in (the eyes of) the world. They have no value in and for the way of the world and they are obstructed by the world in the actualisation of their potential to flourish.

Hence, the nonconformism Paul calls for is aimed at disclosing the non-beings as the symptoms of a world in crisis. Yet, such a disclosure cannot be obtained 'theoretically'. It requires practice, exercise and ascesis to become an exception to the way of the world and to learn to see the world's crisis. The possibility of this exception is anchored in the *schēma tou kosmou*-formula, and the iron logic that it implies: there is either nothing but this order of the world or an exception is possible.

The passage about the present form of the world is not so much a rejection of everyday existence or of the world as such, but only of the world in as far as it has no eye for or is incapable of valuing differently the outcasts of the world. For this reason, it is not necessary to discern apocalyptic visions in Paul's conviction that the current form of the world is passing. After all, the appearance and the look of the world change just as easily and frequently as the appearance and the look of people. Agamben and Heidegger, for instance, read 1 Cor. 7:31 in light of such a change. Calling these readings nihilistic seems to miss the crucial import of these *tou kosmou*-passages: they stress the great effort that is demanded of the believers who want to embrace the alternative to the way of the world. As simple as it may seem to theoretically accept the changeability of morals and habits, as difficult it is to develop an attitude of constantly taking into account this changeability and allowing the sense of an ending to resonate in everything we do. That is why Paul constantly repeats his call. If his proclamation concerned an already fixed end of the world, nothing would have to be repeated. However, because he calls for a particular mode of living that we do not naturally have or develop, unremitting encouragement is required. A permanent summons reawakening the sense of an ending is needed when human habit and human inclination to conformity with the world constantly draw one back in the world's way.

Before taking a closer look at this moral difficulty, let us add one more consideration concerning the end of the world announced in 1 Cor. 7:31. The Greek verb *paragō* is translated as 'to pass away'. 'To pass away' can be interpreted as 'to die' and the Greek verb indeed suggests a form of decay. This sense of decay might lead one back to the aforementioned apocalyptic visions. Yet, Paul does not seem to understand the end of the world so much as a destruction but rather as a change, as 1 Cor. 15:52 suggests;[24] in fact, the verb *paragō* itself can be used in the sense of 'to change'. Used metaphorically, *paragō* means 'to disappear'. Considering these different meanings together, we see that *paragō* expresses a dimension of reality often lost sight of. Everything that lives will perish one day. Everything that was ever embraced and propagated in a culture or a society will disappear at some point in time. Everything that was laboured for and everything that was invested in will lose its meaning and value. A genuine sense of an ending, if there ever was one.

This tone is not so much apocalyptic as reminiscent of the tenor of Ecclesiastes and the famous verdict 'vanity of vanities! All is vanity' (Ecc. 1:2) that it pronounces on human toil in this world. Marion, for instance, hears this tone in 1 Cor. 7, because Paul's description of the passing of the world is in the same key as Rom. 8:20, in which it is written that creation is subject to vanity and futility.[25] In an exemplary and symptomatic way, this vanity can be observed in those who are not allocated a part in the world, that is, in the non-beings Paul has in mind in 1 Cor. 1:28, as well as in the outcast with which he identifies himself in 1 Cor. 4:13.

Even though the non-beings are symptoms, Žižek emphasises that as symptoms they somehow represent the whole and, therefore, have a universal meaning.[26] This may sound strange. Do these symptoms not form the part banished from the order, and are they therefore not precisely the *exception* to the order and its totality of beings? In light of 1 Cor. 7:31, however, this part that is granted no part in the world is a genuine *pars pro toto* for Paul because it represents par excellence futility and transience; yet, these qualifications apply not only to this part, but extend to the whole as soon as we are attuned to the whole by the sense of an ending. This is precisely why the meaning of *to mē on* as a symptomatic problematic case, is important. A symptom manifests a hidden sickness or crisis of the present order of world as a whole.

Yet, we should not misunderstand this verdict as a form of nihilism. In this sense, the connections Marion draws between Ecclesiastes and Rom. 8 are problematic. The sigh of creation is the sigh of the expectant; and the passing of this figure of the world does not imply the destruction of the world as such, but rather implies that the current order of the world is not necessary and can be transformed. The sigh of creation in Rom. 8 is also the announcement of something at the point of being born – not the *in principio* of creation but the *initium* of the new-born is the *archē* at stake here, as Arendt's Augustine suggests.[27] In light of this prospect, one should not identify with and conform to what is, because that would mean conforming to what is transitory and not being attuned to the *potentiality-of-being-otherwise* of the world.[28] The sense of an ending is not one of destruction, but is rather dialectically reflected in the attunement to this potentiality-of-being-otherwise. This latter notion connects possibility – 'potentiality-of-being' – and difference – 'otherwise' – which reflect the two dimensions of the Greek *mē on* we discovered in the previous section. Paul's meontology, then, is not about nihilism but about the potentiality-of-being-otherwise of the world that refuses to affirm and embrace, with a misunderstood *amor fati*, the present form of the world, but also refuses to foolishly destroy the world. Paul's keyword *katargēsis* opens up this very space between affirmation and negation, between *amor fati* and nihilism – this space is the latitude for the use and the play of the spirit.

AS NOT

1 Cor. 7 also offers a more detailed, albeit enigmatic description of the mode of living associated with this potentiality-of-being-otherwise. The related texts comprise the next meontological fragments. In 1 Cor. 7:29–31, Paul uses the expression *hōs mē* – 'as not' or 'as if not' – as a chorus to articulate the mode of living corresponding with the passing of the world. This local chorus of *hōs mē* offers us another basic ingredient of what I consider to be the Pauline dialectic of exception.

The use of the Greek *mē* again raises the presumption of a meontology. Taubes even calls it a nihilistic passage.[29] The King James Version (KJV), in which this chorus resounds clearly, renders it as follows:

> But this I say, brethren, the time is short: it remaineth, that both they that have wives be as though they had none [*hōs mē*]; And they that weep, as though they wept not [*hōs mē*]; and they that rejoice, as though they rejoiced not [*hōs mē*]; and they that buy, as though they possessed not [*hōs mē*]; And they that use this world, as not abusing it [*hōs mē*]: for the fashion of this world passeth away.

In the translation of this passage in Agamben's *The Time That Remains*, the 'as not'-chorus is retained even more strictly:

> even those having wives may be as not [*hōs mē*] having, and those weeping as not [*hōs mē*] weeping, and those rejoicing as not [*hōs mē*] rejoicing, and those buying as not [*hōs mē*] possessing, and those using the world as not [*hōs mē*] using it up. For passing away is the figure of this world.[30]

What does it mean to live in this mode of *hōs mē*? Shortly before this passage, Paul reminds his fellow believers that, when they were called to faith, they found themselves in a specific situation or position in the world: they were married, were circumcised, were slaves or masters, were joyful or distressed. These are the significant relations in which they find themselves in their everyday lives. Paul does not advise them to leave these relations; they are part of their worldly vocation, which can remain intact. Those who are married should remain married, and slaves can remain slaves. 'Let each of you remain in the condition in which you were called' (Cor. 7:20). To be called to faith is thus not another vocation, *klēsis*, in the world; the worldly vocation can remain, as Paul emphasises as many as four times, as if he fears that his readers would otherwise try to change their positions in life.[31]

This non-worldly, second call – also: *klēsis* – raises several questions. Does being called to faith – or the believers' 'having-become', as Paul describes their changed state due to the second call in 1 Thessalonians – not suggest that everything has to be different in the world and in the believer's life? Should believers not change everything, including their worldly vocation, and align it with their being called to faith? Yes and no. Or, as Heidegger writes enigmatically, the life of believers 'remains unchanged, and yet it is radically changed'.[32] The worldly callings remain, but one lives or enacts these old vocations in a fundamentally different way. The everyday relations of significance are placed in the light of the dichotomy of the spirit of the world and the spirit of, God and the parallel bifurcation of flesh and spirit introduces a double mode of living these significant relations – according to either the flesh or the spirit.

The formula *hōs mē* thus truly aims to express a mode of living, a new way of enacting a particular vocation; it is not another worldly – nor otherworldly – vocation replacing and destroying the previous one. Rather, *hōs mē* duplicates the first vocation; Paul's proclamation of this mode of life discloses that the worldly vocation can be enacted in two different ways. Mindful of the Greek distinction between *mē on* and *ouk on*, Heidegger stresses that the expression is '*hōs mē*, not *ou*', indicating that it is indeed about another *enactment* of a worldly vocation and not about its destruction or replacement.³³ Following up on these Heideggerian concerns, Agamben points to a dialectic tension in Paul's use of the term 'vocation'. Paul introduces the 'messianic vocation' as a '*revocation of every vocation*'.³⁴

Inspired by these Heideggerian and Agambenian lines of thought, we can conclude that Paul's understanding of the second calling does not refer to another calling, separate from the worldly one, but rather concerns a *dialectic repetition* of the worldly, first vocation. Therefore, it does not call the believer to another, fictional world, and it also does not establish any vocations cultivating a specific hostility to life. Rather, the dialectic repetition calls to a different enactment of the worldly calling. The formula 'as not' expresses and articulates exactly this tension: the enactment of the first vocation no longer follows the prescriptions of the way of the world.

In Rom. 4:17, Paul also uses the verb *kaleō*, 'to call', to which *klēsis*, 'vocation', is related: God is the one who 'calls non-beings into being [*kalountas ta mē onta hōs onta*]'. The verbal act of creation from Genesis is thus *dialectically repeated* here – from *principium* to *initium* – with respect to the beings that are nothing in the present order of the world. This passage thus describes, in meontological terms, how something that is not can be called into existence by the divine call. This is a radical example of the potentiality-of-being-otherwise, the actualisation of which requires the divine call and, hence, the principle of the spirit.³⁵ 1 Cor. 7 offers a characterisation of the attitude to life that accompanies this vocation. It does not confirm the old vocation; on the contrary, it dialectically repeats, or re-calls it, issuing a call to enact the worldly calling differently.

To get a sense of what it means to enact a calling in the mode of the 'as not', one should first understand what it means to enact one's calling in the worldly mode, let us say in the mode of 'as'. To live in this mode is to *identify* oneself with this vocation, to be totally wrapped up or be absorbed in the place that is assigned to one in this worldly order. To be called to live in the mode of 'as not' is then, by contrast, to live one's vocations in such a way that one experiences oneself as someone who is more than or different from the identities that the worldly order has to offer.

How does this interpretation relate to the one that argues that the mode of 'as not' propagates *indifference* to one's vocations? Paul seems to present, in his own, idiomatic way, a variation on Stoic *adiaphora*: the first vocation, which was significant to the earlier lives of the believers, becomes indifferent through the new, second vocation.³⁶ This indifference expresses in Stoicism that the positions in which we find ourselves are simply what they are. They are neither good nor bad. While, in the world, vocations are valued in different ways, there are no worldly callings that would privilege people or grant them a greater entitlement to the second call. It seems to me that this indifference is indeed expressed by *hōs mē*, 'as not'. To live 'as not' means to not lose oneself in one's worldly vocations, relationships and positions. This is something entirely different from rejecting them. To be married 'as not', as Paul encourages, is quite different from rejecting marriage and encouraging celibacy, as Marcion and his disciples proposed.

A more problematic sense of indifference, however, comes into view when we consider Taubes's account of the nihilistic sense of the *hōs mē* passage.[37] Taubes notes that Paul is *not* calling for actively changing the world, because the end of the world is fast approaching, thus positioning 1 Cor. 7:29–31 in light of an imminent apocalypse: 'under this time pressure, if tomorrow the whole palaver, the entire swindle were going to be over – in that case there's no point in any revolution!'[38] For Taubes, Paul preaches indifference with regard to this form of the world and the positions in which we stand, *because* these do not matter in light of the imminent ending of it all: the relation(ship) of believers to the world and their positions therein are characterised by a resignation regarding worldly affairs.[39] Such an quietist interpretation of the indifference Paul proclaims, however, is essentially a version of world avoidance and hostility to life. Thus, it runs contrary to the interpretation of *hōs mē* that I propose here. It is remarkable that Taubes does not mention the principle of the spirit in his discussion of the *hōs mē*-passage. This principle is central elsewhere in his reading of Paul, as discussed in Chapter 1, and one wonders whether this spirit of transformation should not also have also been given a part in the interpretation of this passage and the implied 'loosening of one's relations to the world'.[40] How would that have changed Taubes's verdict of *hōs mē* as a mode of living? What would a truly dialectic interpretation of the *hōs mē*-passages look like, which avoids Stoic indifference?

Agamben seems to refer implicitly and critically to Taubes's reading when he argues that in 1 Cor. 7 'there is no mention of an eschatological indifference'.[41] Instead, he suggests that we read *hōs mē* as expressing a dialectic tension. I concur with that suggestion. The sentence 'she weeps as not weeping' is not identical to 'she is not weeping' or 'she should stop weeping'. Rather, if we understand the injunction to live 'as not-weeping' as a 'weeping-otherwise', we hear this sentence saying that being-married should be enacted in light of its potentiality-of-being-otherwise, in light of the possibility to enact it according to the flesh or to the spirit.

This simple example also demonstrates how the *hōs mē*-formula expresses a contradiction – being-married and not-being-married. Yet, a static contradiction is impossible. Something cannot simultaneously be the case and, in the same respect, not be the case. Therefore, the negation expressed by the *hōs mē*-formula should be understood dialectically. Paul's 'as not'-formula links two opposites, thus precisely expressing this dialectic relationship. Yet, he does so *without removing the tension* between these contradictions; and he does not even reconcile them in a Hegelian fashion. Paul is thus not so much interested in the formal contradiction – married versus not married – as in the unmistakable dialectic tension the 'as not'-formula evokes. The life of believers unfolds against this tension, and this life should provoke the expression of this tension again and again because it cannot be solved or removed. The believers find themselves in a particular worldly position, which is their actuality or 'thrownness', as we might say with Heidegger. Yet, they are called to enact this actuality in light of its potentiality-of-being-otherwise. In this way, Paul does not call believers to an eschatological indifference with regard to positions in the world *tout court*. Rather, he calls upon them to make a difference between, on the one hand, the way in which these positions are usually lived in the ways of the world and, on the other hand, the potentiality-of-being-otherwise that inhabits the existence of the believers as well as the present order of the world, when pneumatically repeated.[42]

At this point, another question arises regarding the issue of nihilism. If the second vocation is not a new vocation, does not call for anything, and does not call anywhere, does that not indeed mean that we are dealing with a crypto-nihilism? If the second vocation only exists in terms of revoking every vocation that orients us in our way of living, to what then does it contribute? Does it not result in indifference and disorientation in life? What is the life that remains in this world?

Yet, these questions miss the quintessence of this dialectic reading when another concept from Paul's vocabulary is not taken into account. This brings us to what I consider to be the true discovery of Agamben's reading of Paul, namely the importance of the notion of *chrēsis*, use or dealing with, in the *hōs mē*-passages. To capture the semantic field and plural senses of the noun *chrēsis* and the verb *chraomai* in Greek, the German *Umgang* might offer us a better orientation than 'use'.[43] Like all dialectic interpretations, that of *hōs mē* has a negative and a positive side. The negative side, however, does not exist in the destruction of worldly vocations; these continue to exist. Yet, the dialectic repetition of the calling disables and deactivates the way of the world and the normal valuation of worldly vocations. Consequently, *hōs mē* has a deactivating result. The believers do not comply with the demand for conformism, so the space opens up for another way of living. The existing nexus of the meaning of human relationships – that Paul so strikingly expresses in his *tou kosmou*-formulas – is suspended to create space for another way of living these relationships and, with that, for bestowing upon them another significance.

At first sight, this suspension seems to leave the vocation empty. There is indeed no specific new vocation to be found. Yet, there is a positive side to this dialectic at the heart of living in the mode of 'as not'. The radical suspension of every vocation opens up an entirely unique mode of living, found in Paul's notion of *chrēsis*, use. Agamben's reading of Paul is unique in having uncovered the importance of this notion.[44] No other reading has seen so clearly that this concept ensures that the *hōs mē*-attitude is not described in merely negative or indifferent terms. *Chrēsis* is not the unification, appropriation or suspension of the tension between two opposing terms. Rather, it is the way in which this contradiction provides an alternative for possession, ownership, property and individuality.

Paul uses *chrēsis* in 1 Cor. 7, and he does so first in the following prelude to the *hōs mē*-passages: 'Were you a slave when called? Do not be concerned about it. Even if you can gain your freedom, make use of your present condition now more than ever [*chrēsai*]' (Cor. 7:21).[45] Following Agamben, we may point out that the Greek contains an ambiguity, which is maintained in the American Standard Version (ASV): 'Wast thou called being a bondservant? Care not for *it*: [a] nay, even if thou canst become free, use *it* rather.' What is this '*it*' that the chosen ones should rather use? According to the NRSV, it is the opportunity to gain freedom, as we can see in the translation above. In this way, however, this translation makes a rather strong interpretive choice. Yet, it is doubtful whether this rendition does justice to Paul's commitment. To wit, the apostle often insists on the fact that, in faith, the distinction between slave and master has no meaning and has become indifferent. Would it not be particularly strange that he who is so emphatic about the indifference of slave and master and he who, moreover, always calls himself 'slave' (*doulos*) – and never master – because he regards himself as the slave of Christ, is actually saying here that one is better off if one is *not* a slave?[46] Consequently, it is also possible to read this verse as follows: 'But if thou mayest be made free, use your *klēsis* [vocation] as slave.' Hence, the '*it*' that can be found in the ASV refers to the vocation as a slave, as Agamben concludes: '*Use*: this is the definition Paul gives to messianic life in the form of *as not*.

To live messianically means 'to use' *klēsis*; conversely, messianic *klēsis* is something to use, not to possess.'[47]

This last citation is crucial for an explanation of the dialectic status of the 'as not'-formulas in Paul. The opposition between master and slave returns here in the contrast between possession and use. The master is the one who *possesses*, slaves in particular. Slaves are those who possess nothing, who cannot appropriate anything for themselves, and who do not even possess the right to use. Yet, the slave has the freedom to use the possessions of the master. Considered in terms of this contrast between possessing and using, as reinterpretation of the distinction between master and slave, Paul's *hōs mē* means that every believer has been called to be a slave or servant of Christ. This is the vocation that revokes every other vocation; revocation here means that no single vocation or position is our possession, can be genuinely appropriated, or is an essential characteristic of us: none of these vocations identify us. By finding the positive meaning of the attitude of 'as not' in free use, even by them who have no right to possession,[48] it becomes clear that the 'as not' has suspended and deactivated possession, right to possession, ownership, property and socio-cultural identity. In short, everything that is one's own or is owned by someone.

Let me extend this reading beyond Agamben's considerations. The crucial importance of the concepts of use and possession can also be traced in the rhetorical crescendo of the *hōs mē*-passage that culminates in the following two forms of 'as not': 'and those buying as not [*hōs mē*] possessing, and those using [*chrōmenoi*] the world as not [*hōs mē*] abusing [*katachrōmenoi*] it' (Cor. 7:30–1). Even buying, which is nothing but taking possession of, should be done in such a way that it does not take possession of us. The passage culminates in the use of the world, but here use is not contrasted with non-use; rather, *chrōmenoi* is placed in tension with *katachrōmenoi*, abusing, misusing, using up or using excessively: the Greek prefix *kata-* denotes here reversal, opposition or degeneration. This change in rhetoric displays the special role awarded to *chrēsis*. Use is the name for the mode of living that is aimed for, but it has to be distinguished from abusing, misusing, using up or using excessively. It concerns 'using as not abusing' or as not 'using up': use apparently has to be distinguished from abusing, misusing or using up because *use carries its tension* – its reversal, opposition or degeneration – *within itself*. To use is always also to struggle with – or simply to be abandoned to – the possibilities of abuse, misuse or using up, which inhabit every use. This latter element is absent from Agamben, who is too preoccupied with the distinction between possession and use.[49]

Nevertheless, this element is essential. Free use is the use that carries its tension within itself; it is the use that is always exposed to its own degeneration and thus always confronts the one who lives according to the second vocation with the continuous and strenuous task *to use as not abusing* – this task is always assigned anew with every use and in every present.

This interpretation of the *hōs mē*-passages, it seems to me, is capable of doing justice to Paul's 'variations of *hōs mē*'.[50] It demonstrates why the *hōs mē*-chorus has to culminate in a reference to a use of the world that does not abuse the worldly and does not misuse or use up the world. Yet, as I agree with Van Kooten, such a reading no longer follows a strictly Stoic logic, despite the implicit, often invoked reference to 'indifference' derived from the Stoic *adiaphora*. In fact, it seems as if a certain *Sceptic* logic is brought in by Paul, which places a significantly different emphasis on the meaning of the *hōs mē*.[51]

The ancient Sceptics follow a strictly dialectic process, in which first one hypothesis is examined and subsequently its opposite. Consistently, they demonstrate that neither of the hypotheses can be adequately proven. Due to this result, dialectic examination finds itself in a crisis, which the Sceptics call *aporia*, literally 'no-passage'. The dialectic process ceases and finds no passageway to the truth. The tension observed in the *hōs mē* brings about a similar effect because a vocation – 'being married' – is also placed opposite its enactment – 'as not married'. Because of this *aporia*, the Sceptics suspend their enquiry, their famous *epochē*, suspension. It is no coincidence that, in Paul's letters, *katargēsis* fulfils an analogous role as the Sceptic *epochē*. For the Sceptics, *epochē* suspends both the affirmation and the negation of the hypothesis under examination. Likewise, Paul's *katargēsis* suspends the affirmation as well as the destruction of the worldly vocations.

At first glance, one would expect the Sceptic *epochē* to deliver a merely negative result. Dialectic examination after all finds no passage to a judgement on the original hypothesis. Nevertheless this *epochē* is everything but negative for the Sceptics because, following the image suggested by Sextus Empiricus, the body, *sōma*, of the *epochē* is followed by a very fortunate shadow, *skia*.[52] While the ancient philosophers believe peace of mind, *ataraxia*, can be achieved only by bringing the dialectic process to a final judgement, it appears, so the Sceptics argue, that the peace of mind the ancient philosophers desire is simply, as if by accident (*tuchē*), as a pure contingency or grace, granted *the very moment the dialectic quest is suspended*. Sextus compares this gift of grace with a tale about the renowned painter Apelles that circulated in ancient culture:

The Sceptic, in fact, had the same experience which is said to have befallen the painter Apelles. Once, they say, when he was painting a horse and wished to represent in the painting the horse's foam, he was so unsuccessful that he gave up the attempt and flung at the picture the sponge on which he used to wipe the paints off his brush, and the mark of the sponge produced the effect of a horse's foam. So, too, the Sceptics were in hopes of gaining quietude by means of a decision regarding the disparity of objects of sense and thought, and being unable to effect this they suspended judgement; and they found that quietude, as if by chance, followed upon their suspense, even as a shadow follows its substance.[53]

The effect of Paul's *katargēsis* and the related mode of living can be understood in an analogous fashion. These quasi-nihilistic operations of suspension are followed by a shadow, a gift of grace; this shadow is the free use. The second vocation announces that the genuine task with respect to one's worldly vocation is its enactment: the free use of one's worldly vocation implies that one is called to use this vocation while not abusing it. Hence, 'free' has nothing to do with 'easy'; rather, the strain is intensified because no worldly calling in itself offers and guarantees its good use – this can only be enacted and achieved in the actual using that avoids and resists abuse, misuse, excessive use and using up. Nevertheless, the Sceptic-Pauline *aporia* is a genuine *euporia*, an unexpected portal and passage that is mercifully granted at the very moment the first aspiration – read: the first worldly vocation – is suspended and disabled.[54] One does not lose one's vocation in the mode of 'as not', but one receives it back to use freely.

What *hōs mē* dissolves for ever is the vocation of the master in as far as the master is the figure of possession and right. The habit of the world to award possessions and rights passes; no single possession or right is the proper(ty) of the world or of the people. Paul's anthropology is, for this reason, pervaded by this insight: we possess nothing, we have nothing in our possession; not even our own existence is our true property.[55] It is precisely in the *hōs mē*-mode of living that this mode of being reveals itself. Yet, as if by grace, by suspending our attempts to possess our own existences, they are given back to us in a free use. In contrast to the way of the world and what the world thinks, the suspension of possession and right does not leave us empty-handed, but opens up our existence to a potentiality-of-being-otherwise.

This means that we are never completely familiar with or at home in the social order of the world, in which possession and right are normative. Precisely because we do not truly possess anything and are not truly masters of anything, we are cast back to a fundamental contingency, uncertainty and insecurity. Yet, by evoking the sense of an ending, this contingency becomes part and parcel of the order of the world itself. Then, all of a sudden, it is a matter of comparing the contingency of the world to the potentiality of the spirit, namely the possibility of existing in *this* world in the mode of *chrēsis*. This grace is, as Breton writes, '[f]rom Paul's point of view [...] the religious form of contingency'.[56]

CAST OUT FROM THE WORLD

The transience of the form of the world from 1 Cor. 7:31 is connected to the transience, senselessness and suffering of creation that Paul addresses in Rom. 8:20-2. For Heidegger, this transience marks the brokenness of Christian life.[57] This is not only another word for the discontinuity between the ethos of the world and the ethos of faith but also concerns the brokenness of creation itself; again, ontology and ethics, being and ethos, mirror each other. Paul alludes to this brokenness in the third meontological text fragment:

> To the present hour we are hungry and thirsty, we are poorly clothed and beaten and homeless, and we grow weary from the work of our own hands. When reviled, we bless; when persecuted, we endure; when slandered, we speak kindly. We have become like the [scum] of the world, the dregs of all things, to this very day. (Cor. 4:11–13)[58]

The scum of the world refers to people who suffer hunger and thirst, are abused, homeless, reviled and persecuted. This Pauline figure has lost nothing of its urgency and remains a figure for the present moment. In this fragment, Paul explicitly identifies himself with people who are *nothing* and who represent *nothing* in the eyes of the world. This certainly does not only concern a socio-political construction: as if people only suffer because they are rejected by society. It equally concerns what happens in the world when disasters strike, when people are born in the wrong place, when people are lost or forgotten, and so forth. It is the dark side of the contingency of the world that manifests itself in the existence of these people. Paul identifies himself with the suffering, transient, insignificant dregs of society and creation. If a preference for nothingness is to be found in Paul, it is here. When Nietzsche points to Paul's focus on those who suffer and his preference for the weak and paltry, he goes to the heart of this passage. As Agamben emphasises: '[Paul's] assimilation to what has been lost and forgotten is absolute.'[59] Yet, that this meontological passage should not be read in a nihilistic key, is immediately visible. It is not so much the destruction of the world or of these people that is at stake here as the particular *demand* that speaks from these outcasts. The suffering, the weak and the insignificant perish in history and are not recorded in one single memory or commemoration. In the history written by the victors there is no space for those who have perished. In identifying with the scum of the world, Paul answers the specific demand emanating from the lost and forgotten.

The demand that speaks from the lost or the forgotten, however, is not simply to be remembered or commemorated. Because the limited ability of our (collective) memory and our conscience does not measure up to what perishes and is lost, and because our memory and archives are all too selective in their interpretation and preservation of the past, one should understand the demand of the lost and the forgotten in a different way. Paul's identification with the dregs of society and the scum of the world offers no list of names or monuments for the fallen but rather means to carry the forgotten and the lost in and with oneself as that which needs salvation. The forgotten always remain anonymous: those who are genuinely lost and forgotten are those who have no place in the order of the world and are never mentioned or named there.[60] The second vocation and identification thus enforce detachment: one needs to disengage oneself from the first vocations and related identities, from one's privileged place in the order of the world, in order to catch sight of what falls outside the current order and what is not allowed to flourish within this order.[61]

At this point, the *hōs mē*-formulas acquire an ontological peak when the field of application of the identification with 'the scum of the world' is extended. Meontologically, this may perhaps be expressed by another *hōs mē*-formula: 'being as being-not(hing)'. The identification with what is nothing expands the attitude of 'as not' beyond the boundaries of our own relations to the world in order to enact the very transience and contingency that we share with all that is. In this way, insignificant being is included in the call constitutive of Paul's *hōs mē*: this being too becomes new, and this non-being is called to being.

Thus, along the lines set out in this chapter, it has become clear how Paul's meontology is anything but nihilistic and how the accompanying ethos or mode of living and thinking is anything but defeatist or indifferent. It rather aims to draw our attention to the two corresponding poles or axes that span the space of his proclamation, namely the outcast cast out from the present order of being, granted no place or position therein, and the revivifying spirit capable of quickening the outcast and of calling into being that which is not.

NOTES

1. Critchley, *The Faith of the Faithless*, 177ff. Meontology is derived from *to mē on*, the non-being, and *logos*.
2. See also the New Living Translation (NLT). The *agenē tou kosmou*, the lowborn or ignoble of the world, literally means 'uncreated'; see Van Kooten, 'Paul's Stoic Onto-Theology', 140.
3. The standard example of ontotheology is 'Book Lambda' from Aristotle's *Metaphysics*. See Van der Heiden, *Ontology after Ontotheology*, 1–21.
4. See Heidegger, *Phänomenologie des religiösen Lebens*, 97/67; and Badiou, *Saint Paul*, 50/47. Van Kooten's provocative title 'Paul's Stoic Onto-Theology' raises the following question: is the spirit of God and the spirit of the cosmos also identical for Paul, which indeed provides for an onto-theology? Or is there reason to discern, in Paul's letters, a meontology that is specifically deployed to demonstrate that God prefers the lower and the inferior in the order of being? The discussion of contemporary philosophers with Hegel's dialectic, which Chapter 1 touches on and which will be further discussed in Chapter 4, concerns exactly this issue.
5. This somewhat general claim on Heidegger's assessment of Plato and Aristotle will be developed in more detail with regard to Plato and the philosophical conception of time in the next chapter.
6. Marion, *Dieu sans l'être*, 132n72/256n74.
7. Agamben, *Il tempo che resta*, 92/96.
8. Van Kooten's analysis – that Paul too does not endorse a similar 'creatio ex nihilo' – seems to correspond to this; see 'Paul's Stoic Ontology', 141. His claim that Badiou suggests that Paul anticipates such a 'creatio ex nihilo' (138) is less evident, because it must first be clarified what exactly the 'not' of *ta mē onta* means: for Badiou, it does not concern creation but rather the 'Christ-event'.
9. Van der Heiden, 'The Dialectics of Paul', 180. Also see Van der Heiden, 'On What Remains', 130.
10. Agamben, *Il tempo che resta*, 87/90, 92/96.
11. Ibid., 93/97.
12. For the etymological argument, see ibid., 94–6/99–100. The *Lutherbibel* (1545) indeed renders *katargeō* as *aufheben* in the case of 1 Cor. 15:24 and Rom. 3:3.
13. Van Kooten, 'Paul's Stoic Onto-Theology', 141.
14. Schelling, *System der Weltalter*, 113. He also alludes to this sense of *mē on* in Schelling, *Philosophische Untersuchungen über das Wesen der menschlichen Freiheit*, 45n22 [= SW 373]: as long as it is understood in the sense of mere nothingness, the dictum of *creatio ex nihilo* will remain completely incomprehensible.
15. Schelling, *System der Weltalter*, 113. Translation: Joey Kok.
16. Heidegger, *Hölderlins Hymne 'Der Ister'*, 27/24.

17 Heidegger uses this contrast in *Phänomenologie des religiösen Lebens*, 121/86.
18 Deleuze, *Différence et répétition*, 343/267.
19 'For this reason non-being should rather be written [...] ?-being.' Ibid., 89/77.
20 Also see Heidegger, *Metaphysische Anfangsgründe der Logik*, 222/173; cited in Crowe, 'Heidegger on the Apostle Paul', 47.
21 Heidegger, *Phänomenologie des religiösen Lebens*, 120/85–6.
22 For those familiar with Heidegger's *Sein und Zeit*, it will come as no surprise that precisely this category of the present figure of the world and the related way of the world are precursors of *das Man*, 'the They', the anonymous power we continuously comply with.
23 Compare this to the end of § 3 of chap. 2 in which the notion of *initium* interrupts the course of the world as an eternal return of the same.
24 See also Marion, *Dieu sans l'être*, 182/127.
25 Ibid., 171–81/119–26.
26 Žižek, *The Puppet and the Dwarf*, 64–5.
27 Arendt, *Love and Saint Augustine*, 55. The idea of the announcement of something at the point of being born and for which there is not yet a clear form or order available can also be found in Derrida, *L'Écriture et la différence*, 428/370.
28 The term 'potentiality-of-being' translates Heidegger's *Seinkönnen*; by adding 'otherwise', I aim to emphasise how this potentiality concerns the potentiality of change and becoming otherwise. 'Potentiality-of-being-otherwise' is also my translation of *pouvoir-être-autre*, Meillassoux's conception of contingency in *Après la finitude*, 77/56. See Van der Heiden, *Ontology after Ontotheology*, viii–ix, 216–17, 267–70.
29 Taubes, *Die politische Theologie des Paulus*, 75/53.
30 Agamben, *Il tempo che resta*, 29/23.
31 1 Cor. 7:17, 20, 24 and 26; see Heidegger, *Phänomenologie des religiösen Lebens*, 118/85.
32 Ibid.
33 Ibid., 121/86.
34 The next two paragraphs also refer to Agamben, *Il tempo che resta*, 29–31/23–5, unless stated otherwise.
35 In a similar vein, but more strongly emphasising the 'impossibility' when considering what I call here potentiality-of-being-otherwise from an immanent point of view, Marion interprets Rom. 4:17 as follows: 'The *onta* do not dispose here of any "principle of change within themselves", of any intrinsic potentiality that would require or prepare completion. The transition befalls them from the outside.' Marion, *Dieu sans l'être*, 129/87.
36 See Van Kooten, 'Paul's Stoic Onto-Theology', 153–9 and 'Paulus als anti-filosoof en messiaans nihilist?' I agree that Taubes depicts Paul's *hōs mē* passages as nihilistic but am less convinced of Van Kooten's analysis of Agamben because the latter's reading culminates in the crucial,

non-nihilistic concept *chrēsis*; moreover, the emphasis on 'messianic nullification' (149–50) neglects that Agamben always understands this 'nullification' in terms of Paul's *katargēsis* or suspension.
37 Taubes, *Die politische Theologie des Paulus*, 74–5/53.
38 Ibid., 75/54. See also Løland, *Pauline Ugliness*, 152–3.
39 Taubes, *Die politische Theologie des Paulus*, 74/53.
40 As Taubes notes in the discussion included in Schatz and Spatzenegger, *Wovon wirden wir morgen geistig leben?*, 136. Translation taken from Muller, *Professor of Apocalypse*, 487.
41 Agamben, *Il tempo che resta*, 28/22. He attributes eschatological indifference in the first place to Max Weber; see, e.g., Weber, *Die protestantische Ethik*, 68/43.
42 In this context, Heidegger therefore speaks about a new sense granted by the 'as' of the 'as not': 'these relations to the surrounding world receive their sense not out of the formal significance they indicate; rather the reverse, the relation and the sense of lived significance are determined out of the original enactment.' Heidegger, *Phänomenologie des religiösen Lebens*, 118/84–5.
43 Agamben, *L'uso dei corpi*, 48–55/24–30.
44 This notion is of crucial importance for Agamben's oeuvre as a whole. It plays a fundamental role in *Altissima povertà* and in *L'uso dei corpi*.
45 Agamben, *Il tempo che resta*, 31–3/26–9.
46 Also see Heidegger, *Phänomenologie des religiösen Lebens*, 119/85.
47 Agamben, *Il tempo che resta*, 31/26.
48 Here Agamben refers to the *usus pauper* (ibid., 32/27), further explored in *Altissima povertà*.
49 See Van der Heiden, 'Exile, Use, and Form-of-Life' for a critical discussion of whether Agamben can truly think the possibilities of abuse, misuse and using up that inhabit every use.
50 Van Kooten, 'Paul's Stoic Onto-Theology', 154. He is moreover not the only one arguing that the alternative of Agamben remains empty or nihilistic – see, e.g., Žižek, *The Puppet and the Dwarf*, 112–13. Both authors seem unaware of the specific role *chrēsis* plays for Agamben.
51 For Agamben's relationship with Scepticism, also see van der Heiden, 'Contingency and Skepticism in Agamben's Thought'.
52 Sextus Empiricus, *Outlines of Pyrrhonism*, I.28–9.
53 Ibid.
54 Also see Van der Heiden, *Ontology after Ontotheology*, 117–26.
55 Agamben, *Il tempo che resta*, 31/26.
56 Breton, *Saint Paul*, 63/92.
57 Heidegger, *Phänomenologie des religiösen Lebens*, 120–1/85–6.
58 The expression 'scum of the world' can be found, among others, in the NIV.
59 Agamben, *Il tempo che resta*, 45/41. Badiou, *Saint Paul*, 60/56.
60 For the category of the anonymous, see Yazıcıoğlu, 'The Anonymous'.

61 In the vocabulary of Lacan's psychoanalysis, Žižek points out that this identification with the scum of the world is also a kind of *kenōsis* of our symbolic identity, that is, of the identity we have in the nexus of meaning formed by the current order of the world. Approached in this way, *kenōsis* should be understood as a form of detachment from the current order of the world and the identities it entails; see Žižek, *The Fragile Absolute*, 24–47.

4. *Time, Event and Exception*

The second line of thought to be explored in order to derive an ontology and an ethics from Paul's letters brings us to the themes of time and event. Moreover, this line allows us to address in more detail the sense of exception at stake in Paul's dialectic. The importance of time, temporality and event in the contemporary European philosophical reflections on being hardly needs to be stated. Emblematic in this respect are the titles of Heidegger's *Being and Time* and Badiou's *Being and Event*, but many more books with less iconic titles and many more authors may be added to these. Elsewhere, I have extensively examined and assessed how the critique of the ontotheological constitution of metaphysics has guided contemporary continental ontology in the direction of reflections on the event, so I will not repeat this analysis here.[1] However, in this chapter, I do want to show why, amid the many sources available from ancient culture, it is Paul, rather than, say, Plato or Aristotle, who offers the philosophical means to think event and time in such a way that these provide a genuine alternative to the ontotheological paradigm. Moreover, I argue that the alternative arising in this way significantly contributes to the other dialectic legacy of Paul pursued in this study.

For clarity's sake, let me add that this also means that I am less interested in the role that the philosophical reflection on time and event play in the conceptualisation of the end of history, which framed several approaches to Paul in the 1990s and early 2000s. In fact, it is not the end of history or a particular version of the apocalypse that guides my reading here, but rather the very sense of the historicality and temporality of existence that is experienced when the contingency and transience of the world and of human life is confronted in the present. This also means that, in this chapter, I enter into a dialogue with some of the readings of Paul with the two following questions in mind. How and in what sense do the letters of Paul provide the means to think time and event? How do they contribute to a dialectic of exception?

In our everyday use, the word 'event' can refer to anything that happens, to all kinds of incidents and occurrences in the world. Yet, 'event' can also be used for incidents with a significant impact on the world or on our lives and for occurrences that have gained particular significance for us. The philosophical use accords with this distinct sense of the event and uses the term to mean an incident that challenges the present order of the world or of our present understanding of this order since it confronts this order and this understanding with something utterly new, which subsequently transforms the order and reorients the understanding. In this sense, the concept of the event provides a particular variation on the Greek *archē*, if we understand this term in Heidegger's sense as meaning both beginning, *Anfang*, and rule, *Herrschaft*.[2] An event interrupts the status quo in existence and understanding, and it opens up new possibilities for human action. As Badiou notes, for instance, an event in this philosophical sense of the word breaks history into two, into a time before the event and a time after. As such, the event makes history and opens up a new epoch; the event in this sense is always an *exception* to the given order and to the given understanding of the world.

These general remarks guide us to the more detailed questions of this chapter: What is the event or what are the events proclaimed by Paul? How is the Pauline event as exception capable of avoiding the Scylla of monism and the Charybdis of dualism, a duality which in modernity appears in the guises of Hegel and Nietzsche (or Schmitt in the context of the question of political theology as discussed in Chapters 5 and 6), respectively? The first two sections of this chapter are devoted to the dialectic structure of exception that marks the event proclaimed by Paul. The last two sections are devoted to the specific sense of temporality of the Pauline event.

DEATH AND RESURRECTION

It goes without saying that the death and resurrection of Christ are core themes in Paul's letters. As we have seen, they are *the* stumbling block for Nietzsche, who complains that Paul completely ignores Jesus' life and instead only needs his death, to which he adds the illusion of his resurrection. For Nietzsche, this is not only exemplary of Paul's hostility to life but also reveals his profound dualism: the actual life of Jesus of Nazareth is strictly separated from that other, true life that only commences with death. Nietzsche's dispute with Christianity therefore concentrates on the Christian glorification of the pairing of 'death and resurrection.'

(a) Speculative Good Friday

Nietzsche's objections to Paul's Christianity are important to help us to understand another account of the Pauline legacy captured under the heading of 'death and resurrection'. In modern thought, the work of Hegel, the modern heir of the Stoic concept of spirit, offers such an account. The nucleus of Hegel's dialectic philosophy is the productivity of the negative. The negation of a position is not the end (of the) position – and does not result in a form of nihilism – since it itself can also be negated and in this way become the prelude to a higher, more encompassing position. Epistemologically, Hegel's model is quite attractive. Is he not right that only in the negation of our present views and experiences do we find the necessary passageway to new perspectives, to a spiritual (*geistlich*) enrichment of our understanding of reality? Yet, how exactly should we understand this productivity of negativity, this 'magical power',[3] as Hegel himself writes? Where does it come from?

Viewpoints and experiences that can be negated, are necessarily finite. Their negation shows that they have limits and conditions. If they are valid, they are so only within certain limits, up to a certain point: they are only relatively valid and not absolutely so. It is the negation that allows the limitations and conditions of our views and experiences to appear to us and actually become part of our understanding. Each time our conceptions and experiences are justifiably contradicted or negated, we become aware of their finitude. And so, every insight that first seemed to present an unconditional truth, comes to its end: it proves to be relative, conditional knowledge. This applies to *each* of our insights.

For Hegel, this is not only an epistemological issue but also an ontological one. *Everything* that seems to exist in itself and appears to be unconditional is negated as soon as its conditionality and relativity is manifested. Consequently, in this logic of negation, the concept of 'infinity' seems, at first, to express that eventually everything – all viewpoints and all beings – can be negated and revealed as finite. At the end of Hegel's essay 'Faith and Knowledge', we find a striking version of this idea that displays its Pauline sense. Infinity appears, in the first instance, 'as the abyss of nothingness in which all Being is engulfed.'[4] Echoed herein is the line from the Dutch poem 'Insomnia' by J. C. Bloem: 'And every being is created for non-being.'[5]

If infinity is indeed this abyss, it is simply the name for nihilism itself. Indeed, before Nietzsche characterises this form of nihilism as 'the death of God', Hegel writes: 'God Himself is dead.'[6] The death of God characterises the speculative 'abyss of the nothing'; this is Hegel's speculative interpretation of the death of God at the cross, whence his description of this nihilism as 'the speculative Good Friday'. Yet, for Hegel, this nihilism of the death of God is not the endpoint or the final stage, but only *the next to last* moment of development. This nihilism can be overcome, Hegel suggests, by using the Pauline paradigm of 'death and resurrection'. Death is the negation of every finite life. Yet, death itself can also die, the negation can itself be negated. For Hegel, resurrection is this death of death itself, the ultimate outcome of the productivity of negativity. From death rises an infinite spiritual life that is no longer conditional or finite. Therefore, the last sentence of 'Faith and Knowledge' says that from the extreme 'Godforsakenness' of reality, having fallen prey to nihilism and disappeared in the abyss of nothingness, 'the highest totality can and must achieve its resurrection solely from this harsh consciousness of loss, encompassing everything, and ascending in all its earnestness and out of its deepest ground to the most serene freedom of its shape.'[7]

This apotheosis of reality to the level of absolute spirit is not only programmatic for Hegel's dialectic philosophy, but it at the same time also indicates the Pauline character of his views. Yet, his is a *specific* kind of dialectic Paulinism. In the final instance, the death of God and the entire finite reality's falling prey to nothingness is understood as a moment in the development of absolute spirit. Seen from the viewpoint of absolute spirit, this development cannot take place in any other way. Every moment in this development is necessary and immanent to the self-development of spirit. This self-development has and *is* rational order. In Chapter 1 we discussed why this interpretation of Paul is, at the end of the day, contrary to the crucial divide between the spirit of the world, which possesses the capacity to create and transform only up to a certain point, and the spirit of God, which is the principle of a revivifying of what is dead that cannot be explained in terms of the last convulsions of what is dying.

The philosophical notions of 'event' and 'exception', as well as the claim that these notions are crucial to understanding the role played by the resurrection in Paul's letters, should therefore be understood as an attempt to find a passage between the Scylla of Hegel's immanent and necessary self-development of the spirit and the Charybdis of Nietzsche's nihilism. Hegel's interpretation of the spirit's self-development repeats the Pauline paradigm of Christ's death and resurrection on a speculative-philosophical level and knows to convert it to a dialectic system of philosophical thinking. For this reason, the question of the relationship of the contemporary philosophical interpretation of death and resurrection to Hegel's Pauline alternative is highly significant. Paul may be the source of inspiration for the Hegelian system; yet, as I would like to maintain, the letters voice an experience of reality that cannot be translated into this system without remainder. In this debate, the event is therefore the exception that remains when rendering Paul in a Hegelian logic.

To what extent do the notions of event and exception succeed in breaking with Hegel's dialectic, and especially with the appropriative and totalising tendencies in it?[8] This question touches on a core issue within twentieth- and twenty-first-century philosophy. Hegel's dialectic is uncommonly powerful, as this form of thinking has a mobility and flexibility through which it appears capable of even absorbing the extreme thought of nihilism as a moment of its own development. More specifically, this implies that everything that appears as different from what is experienced or thought – and, hence, points out the finitude of the content of these experiences and thoughts – can eventually, via the dialectic movement, be understood in an encompassing concept. In this sense, Hegel's spirit does encounter otherness and difference everywhere, but only so that it can be appropriated by its own movement, and, hence, difference and otherness turn out not to be absolute, but only relative to the comprehensive viewpoint and the 'highest totality' of absolute knowledge.

Derrida's *Margins of Philosophy* contains an intriguing preface that summarises, in programmatic fashion, the task facing contemporary philosophy, when confronted with Hegelian thought. Derrida notes that philosophy has always insisted on thinking the other(ness) that surpasses thinking but that, as surpassing, also elicits thought. Yet, at the same time, philosophy aims to think this other(ness) in such a way that it ultimately can appropriate it and integrate it into itself. In the logic of Hegel's dialectic, as soon as the other(ness) is thought as the other *of* thought, the dialectic movement of the *Aufhebung* is able to incorporate this other(ness) in philosophy. Yet, is it not the case, Derrida wonders, that, precisely when philosophy appropriates this other(ness), it actually misses what is genuinely other in this other(ness) and only discerns and captures what it can appropriate – missing even its missing of what is genuinely other?[9] It misses this other(ness) because in the movement of appropriation it is yet again experienced and thought of *as* what belongs to thought and hence no longer *as* other than thought. Differently put, does philosophy, in that which it thinks, not eventually only retrieve itself – its own self-portrait, gradually filled out – and retrieve of the other only what the other shares with thought itself, thus forgetting to think, in a melancholic awareness of what it can never fully appropriate or reach, the other(ness) in its very otherness?

Confronted with such questions, it is important to understand that these do not only concern the issue of the other(ness) and do not only concern the question of whether there is something that falls outside of philosophy's grasp, but also concern the *origin* of thinking, of what makes us think and of what calls thinking to life. As Waldenfels argues, philosophy does not begin as *logos* but rather as *pathos*, understood here as the other of thinking. Philosophy does not commence with the clarity of genuine understanding and sharply delineated concepts. It commences with the dazzling wonder about what it does not understand.[10] Thinking, in the first instance, *answers*, Waldenfels suggests, to a claim or appeal based on this *pathos*. As response, *logos* is not only not the first, but it also does not have – and can never gain – any hegemony over that to which it responds. For Hegel, by contrast, the development of *logos* culminates in the hegemony of the absolute spirit. In a philosophical discussion of Paul, notions such as miracle and exception therefore play a very specific role: they occasion the suspension and deactivation of Hegel's dialectic machinery, which appropriates everything in the history of the spirit of the world, and they demand attention to what is new and other, announcing itself as miracle and exception to those attuned to wonder.

Following this detour, we now return to our question: to what extent do the notions of event and exception succeed in breaking with Hegel's dialectic? To answer this question, I devote the remainder of this section to a critical description of Badiou's 'antidialectic', which is based on his interpretation of the resurrection and his particular lack of attention to the cross, which serves as a contrast to my own dialectic account which will take shape in discussion with Badiou. Subsequently, in the second section, I develop the notion of exception in order to introduce, with the help of Kierkegaard's *Repetition*, another dialectic.

(b) Antidialectic

If there is anything in the letters of Paul that deserves to be qualified as a 'miracle', transcending the immanent laws of the *kosmos*, it must be the resurrection. In 1 Cor. 15, Paul emphasises that without the resurrection both his proclamation and the faith of the members of his community in Corinth are bereft of any meaning. In 1 Cor. 15, the resurrection is explicitly understood in terms of the principle of the spirit since it is the life moved by the spirit, the transformation of the mortal, mundane and natural life into a spiritual life that is itself a vivifying force. Christ, as 'life-giving spirit', is juxtaposed with Adam, 'a living being' (Cor. 15:45): 'for as all die in Adam, so all will be made alive in Christ' (Cor. 15:22).[11]

De Vries shows that the notion of the miracle (in Dutch: *wonder*, hence etymologically closely related to the pathos of wonder – in Dutch: *verwondering* – which elicits thought) can also be found in contemporary philosophy.[12] The examples the author provides make clear that Badiou's notion of event plays a crucial role for him in understanding the miracle and that, especially in the context of Badiou's reading of Paul, the resurrection is the paradigmatic sense of the miracle he has in mind. If we follow this interpretation of resurrection as miracle, we should, however, add a comment in order not to go down the wrong track. The event of resurrection is strictly de-subjectivised in the following sense: for Badiou, it is important that Paul does not mention any miracle-doer. The frequently recalled fact that Paul omits the vicissitudes of Jesus' life, with the exception of his death, does not, according to Badiou, point to a hostility to life, as Nietzsche thinks, but rather to a specific purity in Paul's considerations. Badiou appreciates that Paul is not interested in the 'religious thaumaturgy and charlatanism' that the gospels recount.[13] Only the resurrection counts. When other types of miracles are mentioned, Badiou fears, the narration of miracle-making only aims to give credit to a miracle worker, as if the event of resurrection could be helped by proofs or other guarantees. By contrast, Paul's discourse about the resurrection is 'without proof, without miracles', and only offers the bare event of the resurrection, without additional credentials.[14]

This means that, of the term 'miracle', we retain only the following characteristics: to describe an event as a miracle implies that it is totally unforeseen and unforeseeable, thus truly falling outside the given *order* of existence and its laws. Such an event is strictly contingent and without grounds. It is thus withdrawn from the well-known metaphysical principle of sufficient reason, formulated by Leibniz, which holds that for everything that exists and everything that happens there should be sufficient grounds or reasons why it exists and why it happens. An event in Badiou's strong sense of the word is a surplus of happening, a hyperbole and a surpassing of the incidents subsumed under Leibniz's principle. Badiou's event is an exception to this principle.[15]

The term 'hyperbole' suggests that the notion of 'contingency' might not be strong enough to characterise an event. In explaining what is at stake in this hyperbole, let me first clear a possible misunderstanding regarding the miracle of resurrection. Paul attaches great importance to the material, 'empirical' resurrection of Christ. He provides witnesses to the risen Christ and also presents himself as a witness (Cor. 15:5–8). For philosophers such as Hegel and Badiou, however, the resurrection as something to which one might bear witness hardly plays any part; it rather seems an obstruction to its speculative reinterpretation. This can already be seen in Hegel. He is not interested in this death and resurrection of Christ but only in the paradigm of death and resurrection resumed on a speculative level. Similarly, Badiou repeatedly remarks that the event that Paul proclaims is a fable.[16] A *real* event, however, cannot be a pure fable. Nevertheless, the 'poet-thinker' Paul devised a formal structure that is philosophically extremely fertile, as Hegel and Badiou demonstrate.

Paul's citation of witnesses confirming the resurrection in 1 Cor. 15 has a specific role. For him, it is not so much about establishing this particular resurrection. The event is important because it is the first in a series; after Christ follow those belonging to him (Cor. 15:23). The latter makes the term 'resurrection' so suitable to conceive of the event in Badiou's sense of the word: an event is not only a contingent, exceptional incident that happens once and once alone, but is rather something from which springs the possibility of a new and real – 'immortal', as Badiou echoes Aristotle – life according to the spirit. Hence it is an event with high significance; it opens up the possibility of another mode of living to those faithful to it, a possibility which did not exist or was impossible in the order of the world without this event. For this reason, Badiou can posit that 'the Gospels, the Good News, comes down to this: we *can* vanquish death' and '[t]he apostle is then he who names this *possibility*'.[17]

For Badiou, a real event can for example be found in the slave uprising of Spartacus. This revolt reveals the idea of equality beyond the distinction between slave and master that was the norm in antiquity. To this idea one could – and can – hold true by developing a new life. The life that is subsequently lived in accordance with this idea is for Badiou an example of a new life according to the spirit. In a society where the distinction between slave and master is the norm, the emergence of this idea may be called a miracle in the sense of an event. This event brings something into play that cannot be understood from the existing order, but also does not have anything supernatural: the group of slaves is preeminently an example of a 'part that has no part', to borrow Rancière's term to which I return in Chapter 6, a group that did not have the possibility of freedom and independence in ancient culture. It is in a Pauline vein to identify with these slaves and proclaim their possibility of a resurrection to a new life.

Resurrection as the poetic name for the possibility of conquering death, not only for the figure of Christ but also for other people, thus drives Badiou's interpretation. The contingent event acts as a foundation of the distinction between death and life understood as distinction between two modes of living. Deathly life is not concerned with the event, while the resurrected life is faithful to it. It is, however, important to note that this effect of the resurrection on modes of living is founded in the specific hyperbolic mode of being of what Badiou calls 'event'. The attitudes to life that correspond with 'death' and 'life', respectively, can thus only be identified 'retroactively'. Only after the resurrection, the mode of living people adopted before (the proclamation of) the Christ-event is identified as 'flesh' and 'death'.[18]

In this hyperbolic mode of being of the resurrection, Badiou discovers an alternative to Hegel's dialectic interpretation of the Pauline coupling of 'death and resurrection'. The Hegelian *Aufhebung* of death implies that death is abolished but is thereby also assimilated into and preserved in the resurrection. Badiou resists *this* dialectic. Resurrection, he argues, is precisely *not* the dialectic consequence of death, as if death as productive negation could yet deliver a positive contribution to the resurrection and its meaning. That would fail to appreciate the quality of newness of the resurrection and convert it to automatic, rational development already implicit in the world itself: 'If the theme of resurrection becomes caught up in [Hegel's] dialectical apparatus, it must be conceded that the event as supernumerary givenness and incalculable grace is dissolved into an auto-foundational and necessarily deployed rational protocol.'[19] Hegel's dialectic fails to appreciate exactly this 'supernumerary givenness', the hyperbolic nature of the resurrection. For this reason, Badiou juxtaposes it with his own 'antidialectic of death and resurrection'. Indeed, the resurrection chronologically follows the crucifixion of Christ but does not follow *from* this crucifixion.[20] Badiou insists on this because otherwise suffering and death *contribute* to the resurrection. He resists the latter suggestion because – for his Paul – the inevitability of suffering and death does not belong to the order of resurrection and new life, but is rather 'the law of the world'.[21] Suffering and death are an integral part of the current form of the world from which the resurrection breaks. The resurrection, however, is a pure gift, a genuine new beginning interrupting this law of the world.[22]

Paul gives, so Badiou argues, life according to the spirit the name 'faith'. A specific attitude is required of the human being to relate to the Christ-event. One cannot theoretically check if the resurrection has taken place or not – the resurrection is no such event. One can only know of it by living according to the spirit that emanates from it. This can be seen from the example we gave earlier. The slave revolt of Spartacus can indeed be historically located, and we can, without participating therein, know that it did take place. The event Badiou finds in this slave revolt, namely the idea and the ideal of equality and emancipation, cannot be recognised in the same way. The very heart of this event is that it invents and discloses the possibility of another life, namely life according to the rule this ideal prescribes. The event is the inauguration of this rule and is in this sense indeed *archē* as beginning and rule in Badiou's thought, but only as an always already presupposed *archē* for the subject it makes possible. The other life it makes possible demands fidelity to this spirit of the event and demands perseverance in its ideal. Hence, such an ideal and the life that springs from it cannot be known 'objectively', but do make a subjective knowing and acting possible. 'Subjective', then, does not mean relative or individual, but rather it means that the human being becomes a subject, that is, a loyal servant and confidant – *doulos* – of this ideal. Similarly, 'knowing' points to being convinced of the event and its spirit, and 'acting' becomes a posture of loyal service to this spirit. Exercising the self in this conviction or mode of thinking as well as in this service or mode of living is the process that Badiou names 'subject'. The Greek philosophical term *hupokeimenon*, which has come to be translated over time as 'subject', means that which underlies and that which carries. The subjects, the people who live according to the spirit of the event, are the bearers who carry out the spirit of the event and deliver it into the world, making it true and real in the world by transforming the world in light of the event.

In this explanation, Pauline faith does not concern the holding-to-be-true of what is not true, as Nietzsche argued. Faith should much rather be understood in the same register Foucault finds among the ancient Cynics. The Badiouan-Pauline subject perseveres in another mode of living with a view to transforming the world. While Nietzsche *opposes* the slave Paul to the creative artist, Badiou understands the slave Paul as the one who is faithful to an ideal and committed to creating another world. In this light, Badiou recalibrates the terms 'truth' and 'truth procedure', which appear on average more than once per page in his relatively small book on Paul. The truth of an event is not concerned with the question of whether the event took place or not. It is rather concerned with the spirit of an event, which has not yet fully taken place or completed itself. An event initiates and opens up the possibility of a life according to the spirit. This life is not aimed at the shaping of the self – so it is no art if we understand this term to mean how we should work on our little egos as a work of art – but rather at making *true* and *real* this ideal in the world in which we live. 'Truth' and 'truth procedure' refer to the process of this truthmaking, with which the life of the subject is raised up from its own factual existence and becomes part of a more comprehensive uprising against the present order of the world; the subject becomes part of a process in which he or she works together with numerous other subjects to create another world.

(c) Scandal of the Cross

The above considerations give rise to two reflections. First, for Badiou, the resurrection is a beginning that has not yet reached its completion. Rather, it is a merely a beginning that needs subjects and their fidelity in order to become true and be made real. Therefore, Žižek argues the following about Badiou's spirit of the event: 'Spirit is a *virtual* being in the sense that its status is that of a subjective presupposition: it exists only insofar as subjects *act as if it exists*.'[23] Although this seems to deny the real nature of the event, it strikingly reveals how precarious the event's mode of being is; it is a genuine potentiality-of-being-otherwise of the world in which the event takes place. The present in which the subjects live is therefore the time of the truth procedure in which the event should be completed and its potentiality actualised. Yet, one might wonder whether this event is not made too precarious and too much dependent on the subject's work. Does Badiou not forget to relate the event to the spirit of God and its life-endowing and existence-granting character?[24]

Despite his awareness that the event still has to become true and be fulfilled in the world and although the end of the present order of this world is positioned in the horizon of the new world the subjects are working on, Badiou has no eye for Paul's discourse on the Second Coming. What hampers him from speaking about the Parousia seems to be the idea of the Last Judgment with which it is closely connected for Badiou. He refuses to read such a last judgment in Paul's letters, as the subjects would only be 'inspired' to live their lives in this way at risk of this judgment. If Paul were to found faith and love on this judgment and, consequently, on the punishment and demise of the infidels, the affirmative nature of Paul's faith would be nullified; faith and love would be based on a negativity – for instance, the demise of the unfaithful – of hope.[25] Therefore, Badiou interprets hope differently, namely as principle of perseverance in light of the transformed world that beckons.

The ground that Badiou thus offers for his refusal to think through the importance of the Parousia remains, however, too Nietzschean. His account seems to uncritically follow the gist of Nietzsche's insistence on resentment in Christianity when the philosopher with the hammer refers to Aquinas's description of how, in the afterlife, the faithful revel in the sight of the punishment of the infidels: '"Beati in regno coelesti", he says as meekly as a lamb, "videbunt poenas damnatorum, *ut beatitudo illis magis complaceat*" [The blessed in the heavenly kingdom will see the torment of the damned *so that they may even more thoroughly enjoy their blessedness*].'[26] It is therefore left as a task to think the Second Coming as another event proclaimed by Paul with significant implications for a philosophical sense of the history and the time of the event.

Second, it should come as no surprise that Badiou is not interested in the passages from 1 Cor. 7:17–31 and the life in the mode of *hōs mē* recommended there. For him, this mode has little to do with the new life that is made possible by the resurrection, and it is certainly not militant enough for him. Characteristically, he singles out another citation from 1 Cor. 7, which is concerned with indifference in a different way: 'Circumcision is nothing, and uncircumcision is nothing' (Cor. 7:19).[27] The difference between circumcised and uncircumcised is part of the nexus of meaning that is significant in Paul's surrounding world because circumcision is the mark of being Jewish, and being uncircumcised is the mark of the heathen. These are, however, characteristics and differences that are only of importance in the present order of the world. It is the task of the subject to reconsider, in light of the event to which it is faithful, the meaning of everything it encounters in the surrounding world. Paul reckons that the practice of circumcision as a whole is indifferent to the resurrection. It is precisely this issue, Badiou argues, that forms the core of Paul's dispute with the 'Jewish-Christian faction' in Antioch, which led to a convention in Jerusalem, as described in Acts 14–15. Should believers be circumcised or not? The problem of the faction with which Paul is at odds is that '[i]ts conception of the subject is dialectical.'[28] Because of this, those who adhere to it believe that circumcision is relevant because those believing the resurrection come from Judaism. Hence, for Badiou, the dialectic origin of the 'Christ-event' is the true point of dispute here: the Jewish-Christian faction affirms this dialectic origin, whereas Badiou's Paul rejects it and claims that the customs in the world leave the faithful subject totally indifferent.

Yet, the Pauline subject, whether of Jewish or heathen descent, has to ensure that such indifferent tokens do not stand in the way of the new life according to the spirit. This means, as Badiou writes, that the subject is a Two. On the one hand, the subject is faithful to the event that is at odds with the existing order of the world. On the other hand, it is itself, as human being, part of this order and etched with its customs, tokens and nexus of meaning. In this context, Badiou cites Paul: '[W]e have this treasure in earthen vessels' (2 Cor. 4:7), and explains that this treasure is nothing but the event with its precarious status of being.[29] Its fulfilment depends on subjects, and these subjects themselves are etched with the mundane, carrying the marks of the present order of the world and its customs, worries and nexus of meaning. It is at this precise moment that negation comes into play again; yet, this negation does not precede the event and is not constitutive of the resurrection – as in Hegel's dialectic – but it follows (from) the event. The present order of the world has to be negated by the subject in as far as it threatens to impede its loyal work. Therefore, Badiou once more concludes: 'Paul [...] is not a dialectician.'[30]

However, with this antidialectic Paul, Badiou falls prey to dualism. After all, is it not extremely fitting with a (crypto-)Marcionite dualism to say that first comes the affirmation of the spirit, and only in its wake does there emerge a negation derived from this affirmation that, for example, rejects circumcision in light of the affirmation of the resurrection? In this way there is no longer a link between the first order of the world and its renewal in light of the event. The only difference with ancient forms of dualism is that the event is not eternal but rather contingent and historical, even though Badiou does characterise the life stemming from it as immortal.[31] Due to this perspective, a number of important issues in Paul's letters simply elude Badiou. He has, for instance, no regard for the much more complex relationship of Paul to Judaism and Israel, and the pneumatic hermeneutics of Paul is simply erased. I will return to this in Chapters 5 and 6. Here, I want to focus on another significant gap in an antidialectic approach to Paul.

Due to the strong resistance to Hegel's dialectic, the concept of death becomes the mere opposite of true life in Badiou's Paul. Death, law and flesh directly oppose life, grace and spirit. This strict opposition renders Badiou incapable of acknowledging another meaning of death in Paul. Christ is not discussed in terms of resurrection alone but in terms of death and resurrection. Christ's crucifixion plays a crucial part in Paul's rhetoric, which is suppressed by Badiou, as has already been noted by, for instance, Boyarin, Welborn and Žižek.[32]

Apart from the philosophical question whether Badiou's antidialectic does not threaten to degenerate into dualism, there is this other important issue regarding the crucifixion of Christ. The fact that Christ's death was a death on the cross gave Paul's letters an unprecedented rhetorical impact. In Hellenistic culture, the cross was the social symbol of absolute scandal. Even if countless crucifixions took place in the Roman Empire, these mostly sealed the fate of slaves. In the culture of free citizens, this shame and disgrace was to be concealed completely. In this context, consider the following telling citation from Cicero: 'The very word *cross* should be far removed, not only from the person of a Roman citizen, but from his thoughts, his eyes and his ears. [...] The mere mention of such a thing is shameful to a Roman citizen and a free man.'[33] In connection to these words, one cannot help but think of the Roman formula *damnatio memoriae*, that which is to be removed from memory, which inspires Bradley's notion of 'unbearable life'.[34] The image of the cross is the image of what is not allowed to be seen or remembered; it is the image of what, in the world of the Roman citizens, is prohibited to *be*. *It is the pure image of the outcast*, that is, of that which is to be cast out from the world and from every memory. Hence, Paul can identify himself with the scum of the world, because Christ has first become the very figure of the outcast.

Thus, Paul's specific mention of Christ's death on the cross shows that Christ indeed represents the ultimate scandal.[35] In Paul's letters, death thus does not only represent the reverse of a life according to the spirit. In Hellenistic culture, death on the cross is so repulsive that the idea that someone who has died such a death could rule is scandalous and unprecedented. Death in the sense of the death of Christ thus represents the absolute exception that Christ is to the life lived in Paul's surrounding social world. For Paul, this death symbolises everything that the Roman world wants to exclude from it. With his emphasis on the affirmative and positive sense of the resurrection, an antidialectic reading simply neglects this dimension of humiliation and emptying out, the ultimate *kenōsis*, as mentioned in Philippians:

> Let the same mind be in you that was in Christ Jesus, who [...] emptied himself [from: *kenoō*], taking the form of a slave, being born in human likeness. And being found in human form, he humbled himself and became obedient to the point of death – even death on a cross. (Phil. 2:5–8)

Formulated differently, the antidialectic Paul only knows to interpret the figure of the slave, *doulos*, in terms of a readiness to help a higher ideal – and who would ever object to such a servitude? – but is incapable of incorporating the disgrace and humiliation that accompanies this figure in ancient culture. To be, subsequently, the slave of someone who was crucified is simply unthinkable in civilised ancient society. Thus, the antidialectic Paul misses a central key in Paul's letters that reaches a climax in Phil. 2:7, where Christ embraces this scandal of cross and its (self-)humiliation.

The question is how we should interpret the self-humiliation Paul encourages among the members of the community in Philippi. With Nietzsche and Foucault, one might fear that these passages offer proof of a specific 'hostility to life' characteristic of Christianity and of a Christian asceticism, which would propagate the complete death of the self. At this point, however, another interpretation is more useful. Above, I quoted Žižek's remarkable description of God as 'the name for the purely negative gesture [...] of giving up what matters most to us'.[36] For him, this detachment from what is of utmost importance – and, ultimately, what is the most important thing in life but the perseverance in one's own existence and taking care of one's own existence? – corresponds to the following sense of historical reality. The death of Christ is not the death of the God who is presented as 'a transcendental caretaker who guarantees the happy outcome of our acts, the guarantee of historical teleology'. This death rather 'refuses any "deeper meaning" that obfuscates the brutal reality of historical catastrophes.'[37] The deeper meaning refused here is in the first place the one that arises *as a matter of rational course* in Hegelian dialectic. Instead of this dialectic negativity, another significance of the *kenōsis* of Christ arises here: it is not the *negation* of 'the brutal reality of historical catastrophes' or of what Agamben calls the 'ontological squandering', but rather the *identification* therewith.[38] This identification is not concerned with the sheer affirmation of a brutal reality but rather with the *disclosure* of the very crisis and bankruptcy of the existing order of reality in the form of this identification. Disclosing the bankruptcy of the existing order is nothing other than voicing and making audible the *demand* for justice and deliverance that can no longer come from the mouth of what has perished, because it has lost its voice, but that is voiced in the proclamation of Christ's death on the cross.

Consequently, if we truly interpret Badiou's concept of the event in terms of the Pauline paradigm of the resurrection of Christ, it cannot be described in Badiouan terms alone, namely as nothing but affirmation. Only in the crucifixion does the divine preference for non-beings really become manifest. Badiou's *exclusive* identification of non-being with the event of the resurrection makes a hyper-being out of non-being; and this is a flagrant distortion of Paul's meontology. It is, however, only in a situation in which outcasts exist that their lamentations are gathered and voice a demand. Only because Paul considers death and Christ's resurrection *together* – and, for example, in 1 Corinthians emphasises death – it emerges that, for him, God prefers the outcast, the remnant that is not allocated any proper place in and by the world because it is prohibited to exist and condemned to non-existence in this order of the world. Grace is partial and prefers the outcasts and honours the demand emanating from their lamenting voice of misery. Crucifixion and resurrection belong together, not because death is 'productive' – for instance, as negation in a Hegelian dialectic – but rather because the *demand* of the lost and the outcast finds its voice in Christ's death to which the revivifying spirit of God answers.

DIALECTIC OF EXCEPTION

How to integrate the Pauline event in a framework that is not antidialectic? In order to do so, let us begin with the following fragment: 'So too at the present time there is a remnant, chosen by grace' (Rom. 11:5). Here we have a case of a gracious election, *eklogē*, that prefers and chooses a remnant, *leimma*. Undeniably, there is *preference* here. Paul may in many regards be a thinker of universalism, the sense of partiality must be integrated in the concept of the event – and one way to do so is by emphasising that the event is a *gift*, which is necessarily partial because it singles out a receiver. We can trace this even in Badiou's own examples. The uprising of Spartacus occurs at a particular time, in a particular world. Only there, and nowhere else, is history split into a before and an after. The principle of the spirit worked there and then and makes a new life possible for those who lived in its aftermath. There and then, for the first time, the effective identification with and choice for the demand that rang out from the lamentations of the slaves became possible. Because Badiou is only interested in the possibility of the new life that presents itself in the *wake* of the event, he addresses the event as having-already-happened, not in terms of what still awaits to happen or what is happening in the present; in this way, the actual and contingent *giving* of the event simply disappears from sight – the event is for him only what has always already been given, a gift or treasure already received. Yet, precisely the *contingency* and *partiality* of the gift of the event is necessary to ensure that the alternative to Hegelian dialectic is not sought in an antidialectic, but in a genuine dialectic of exception.

If it is correct that it was Schmitt who put the notion of 'exception' on the politico-philosophical agenda, this agenda was inherited from Kierkegaard. For when introducing this notion, Schmitt refers to Kierkegaard's *Repetition*, and particularly to the concluding letter in which the exception is introduced as dialectic concept.[39] An exception implies a general rule, norm or law; it implies a dimension of the universal to which it is an exception. As exception, it erodes the universality of the rule. In this regard, the relation between the universal and the exception is never a dualist one: they refer and are related to each other; the exception cannot stand alone without reference to a rule, norm or law.[40]

It seems to me that the importance of Kierkegaard's understanding of the exception has implications that far transgress Schmitt's peculiar reinterpretation – or: misinterpretation – of it and that returning to Kierkegaard's *Repetition* is necessary to capture in a more profound sense what a Pauline dialectic of exception exactly entails.

Kierkegaard describes the relation between exception and rule as a 'dialectic struggle'. For him, too, the concepts of 'dialectic' and 'universality' refer to Hegel and the Hegelians of his time. In his own description of the dialectic struggle between the exception and the universal, Kierkegaard attempts to turn Hegel's dialectic on its head. With Hegel, the dialectic struggle between the exception and the universal eventually leads to the *assimilation* of the exception by the universal. This means: an exception shows that a viewpoint that considers itself universal is still in a certain respect only particular since it does not include the exception, but the negation that results from this confrontation between exception and viewpoint is for Hegel always the prelude to an *Aufhebung*, in which the contradiction between the exception and the universal is appropriated in a new enriched universal viewpoint. By contrast, Kierkegaard argues that the struggle between the universal and the exception is rather a test, trial or ordeal of the exception to see if it is able to continue to exist as exception, to see if it is a genuine exception. This struggle is therefore a spiritual exercise or test for the exception itself as well as for the universal. During this exercise, it becomes clear whether the exception positing itself as such is justified or not. Kierkegaard describes this struggle as follows:

> On the one side stands the exception, on the other the universal, and the [dialectic] struggle itself is a strange conflict between the rage and impatience of the universal over the disturbance the exception causes and its infatuated partiality for the exception, for after all is said and done, just as heaven rejoices more over a sinner who repents than over ninety-nine righteous, so does the universal rejoice over an exception. On the other side battles the insubordination and defiance of the exception, his weakness and infirmity. The whole thing is a wrestling match in which the universal breaks with the exception, wrestles with him in conflict, and strengthens him through this wrestling [...] [T]he universal is polemical toward the exception, and it will not betray its partiality before the exception forces it, as it were, to acknowledge it.[41]

Intriguingly, the universal is described here to be *in two minds* about the exception. It is profoundly ambiguous in its conflict with the exception. To fully understand Kierkegaard's implicit discussion with Hegel, this being in two minds is crucial, that is, the universal's hesitation and wavering between two different *pathē*, two different attunements to the exception.

The first attunement of the universal is anger and impatience because the exception resists appropriation in a higher moment of the universal. This is the pathos of Hegel's dialectic in which thinking, when it is confronted by that which is other than itself, still seeks to integrate this other(ness) in a higher, enriched moment of itself. The second attunement of the universal, however, is one of a 'partiality' for the exception. As opposed to the attempt to appropriate and integrate the exception into the law of universality, this pathos shows an elective dimension that prefers and chooses the exception as exception and rejects the transformation of the exception into a merely particular case of an encompassing universality. It is this second attunement that shows that the universal itself suspects that the exception that cannot be appropriated without remainder, that is, that the very significance of a true exception is to defy appropriation indefinitely, to be inappropriable. By allowing for a hesitation between these two attunements, Kierkegaard announces a duplication of the exception in a false exception that can be appropriated and a true exception that cannot be appropriated.

Due to this double pathos, the universal wants to annul the exception but at the same time has a passionate, elective preference for it. In this way, the passage from Rom. 11:5 with which I opened this section, returns in Kierkegaard's description of the dialectic struggle and the second pathos of the universal: a remnant, an exception, is preferred and elected by the universal.

The universal, however, does not stay in two minds. The dialectic struggle between the exception and the universal is a struggle to decide which attunement will gain the upper hand. If the exception does not appear powerful enough and does not know how to maintain itself, the first pathos will gain the upper hand and annul the exception. In this case, the struggle turns out to be the mediating movement of appropriation: the exception is but an expression of the universal that allows the universal to return to itself, enriched by this addition. There is, however, also another possibility. The exception that is capable of persisting in its exceptionality will eventually force the other pathos of the universal to gain the upper hand, so that the universal will truly and openly manifest its preference for the exception. In this case, the struggle is nothing less than *an immediate contact* between universal and exception: the universal does not discover itself expressed in the exception, but rather encounters and touches the exception itself and values this exception as the exception it is.

In Hegel's dialectic, an antithesis is annulled in a higher understanding, but the mediating dynamic of the spirit of the world itself is never annulled. Ultimately, thinking, when confronted with something that it does not yet know, always appears powerful and flexible enough to appropriate this other and, in this way, still manages to find an entrance to a universality that also includes that which merely appeared to be an exception. Kierkegaard's alternative interpretation of the dialectic struggle between the exception and the universal, however, reveals that *katargēsis* might have another meaning than annulment or *Aufhebung*. Through the perseverance of the exception, dialectic thinking that strives to appropriate what is different, repeatedly comes across a resistance it cannot overcome. Here we thus find ourselves in a situation similar to that of the Sceptics as described in the previous chapter. In the dialectic process, the Sceptics repeatedly come across an *aporia*. The process of coming to a judgement finds no way through. Therefore, they feel necessitated to suspend and deactivate the dialectic inquiry. This deactivation returns in Kierkegaard's description of the dialectic struggle: the first pathos of the universal striving for the annulment of the exception is itself annulled, suspended and deactivated when the exception knows to persevere in its exceptionality.[42] The exception paralyses the dialectic process guided by the first pathos. Where the Sceptics refer to a peace of mind, *ataraxia*, that follows the *epochē* like a shadow, Kierkegaard's interpretation of the dialectic struggle between the universal and the exception suggests that the *epochē* of the attempt to appropriate clears the way for the second pathos of the universal. The passionate partiality of the universal for the exception can now truly and unambiguously manifest itself.

One could wonder whether Badiou's objection does not in fact gain in momentum here, namely that suffering plays a *productive* role here. For Kierkegaard, the dialectic struggle with the universal indeed causes the exception to suffer. It is, however, no passive suffering and no struggle that the exception merely undergoes in order to be taken up in a higher form of the universal. Rather, the struggle is a trial and an ordeal of both the exception and the universal. To borrow an image from Plato's *Gorgias*, the exception is tested like gold; the universal's attempt to appropriate is the very touchstone – *basanos* – to prove whether a genuine exception is encountered here.[43] Here, the universal does not appropriate the exception, but witnesses – in the double sense of the word – that the exception is truly exceptional. Kierkegaard's model of the dialectic of exception is thus of crucial importance to understand how the universal's attempt to appropriate reaches its limits in its struggle with the exception, allowing its real and deepest, but hidden preference for and recognition of the exception to become manifest.

Translating Kierkegaard's description of the dialectic struggle and the double attunement of the universal into the basic terms that guide this study, we see that in its first attunement, the universal represents the spirit of the world or the present order of the world that nevertheless reaches its limit in those forms of not-being, *to mē on*, that turn out not to be simply nothing. The attempt to appropriate them runs the risk of not recognising the crisis of which they are the symptoms. Opposed to the first pathos of the universal, the preference for, or the affirmation of, what is not and what is totally rejected – of which Christ's death on the cross is the Pauline paradigm and most pure figure – manifests itself in the event of the resurrection *of the exception*. The universal in its first mind represents philosophical thinking following the paradigm of Hegelian dialectic. In this model, the struggle between universal and exception is a mediation that allows the universal to appropriate the exception as its individual manifestation. Yet, this attempt of the *logos* is not only motivated by a particular *pathos* or attunement, but its appropriating tendencies also find a limit in the other pathos of partiality, preference and 'election', to use the theologically charged term. This second pathos is the symbol of *contingency* in Paul's letters. Preference and partiality are themselves contingent on the progress of the dialectic battle and disappear in case the exception is incapable of maintaining its status as exception and is appropriated after all. Yet, the pathos of preference also includes the recognition of the *possibility* that not everything may be taken up in the spirit of the world and its necessary development. The exception is contingent because the result of the dialectic struggle is not given in advance and is not characterised by any rational necessity. The exception may be able to maintain its exceptionality but it may also turn out to not be a genuine exception. The dialectic battle is the stage of this either/or, with no determined outcome. In this battle, the universal hides its preference for the exception, even though the battle is much more a test and an ordeal that aims to purify the exception as exception than it is a rational and necessary process of appropriation. The attunement to the exception by the pathos of preference does not aim for a mediation between universal and exception but rather concerns an immediate contact and communication of universal and exception, which the universal does not appropriate, but cherishes and witnesses.[44]

PAROUSIA AND POTENTIALITY-OF-BEING-OTHERWISE

The question of the event proclaimed by Paul cannot be settled by an interrogation of the resurrection alone, as noted above. The phenomenon of death has to be taken into account to capture Paul's dialectic. Yet, there is more to be said on this issue. Another perspective on the Pauline event is opened up by the analysis of the Parousia. This other perspective will not only deepen our sense of the exception, but will also offer us a better sense of the specific temporality at stake in the event as well as the dialectic struggle inherent in it. In particular, it will offer us a better understanding of the contingency of the event and the extent to which Paul is engaged in the experience of this very contingency. I explore this perspective in dialogue with Heidegger's reading of Paul.

Let me begin by briefly introducing Heidegger's reading of Paul and show why the stakes of this reading resonate strongly with those of this study. Heidegger's approach to the apostle's letters is preceded by a long methodological introduction, which essentially covers the first half of the series. Actually, if his students had not complained about the level of abstraction of these methodological considerations, they would probably have been even more extensive. Upon their complaint, Heidegger abruptly interrupts the flow of his course and starts interpreting Paul's letters, but not before snapping at his students: 'under the assumption that you will misunderstand the entire study from beginning to end'.[45] Despite Heidegger's apparent worry, the available part of the methodological reflections provides sufficient material to help us understand why he turns to the apostle's letters in the first place.

The point of departure for Heidegger is the pervasive philosophical tendency to understand time and history from the primacy of an atemporal or omnitemporal permanence and presence: the temporal version of ontotheology.[46] The order of the *kosmos*, in which all temporal, historical and finite beings have their proper place, is ultimately anchored in a form of being – be it Aristotle's God or Plato's realm of the ideas – that is permanent and stable, that is, marked by eternal presence. This eternal presence or *ousia* is thus the atemporal measure and norm for the philosophical conception of time and history.[47] This conception is not only Plato's and Aristotle's, but also, albeit in a different way, Hegel's and that of other modern philosophers. The question for Heidegger, however, is whether the temporality of human existence cannot be experienced and elucidated *out of itself*, without reference to an external yardstick. In this regard, Paul's letters are of crucial importance because they offer the articulation of an experience of time that *does not* have recourse to an external norm and they do so specifically in the explication and proclamation of the Parousia. Hence, Paul's letters offer anything but a Platonism for the masses. In the frame I am putting forward here, the interpretation of the Parousia contributes to another account of the Pauline event that also, but now along the lines of the questions of time and history, breaks with the ontotheological constitution of metaphysics.

Heidegger's methodological considerations substantially contribute to this latter point.[48] Philosophical theories of time and history are, each in its own way, characterised by 'theoretical tendencies-to-secure'. Hence the philosophical quest for an atemporal norm and measure has a particular significance and is guided by a particular tendency, namely to find a secure hold that offers a grip on, and in, the everchanging contingency which humans experience in time and history. Platonism – but Heidegger could just as well have mentioned Aristotle, as he does in *Being and Time* – offers the paradigm for this peculiar tendency. The time and the movement of the sensuous world as well as the uncertainty and the disquietude experienced in a human existence marked by transience and contingency is thus thought as anchored in the permanence of the intelligible realm. Despite the temporality of human existence, the human capacity to think is capable of attuning to this eternal realm that provides humans the possibility to transcend the contingency of life and focus on what is stable and permanent. The Platonic model thus secures time and history in the supratemporal. Even though Heidegger does not discuss Hegel, one could, *mutatis mutandis*, make a similar claim about the sense of time and history following from his dialectic: history is the self-development of spirit, and each historical movement or moment is thus only a moment of this encompassing history, which itself is characterised by rational necessity and therewith loses the uncertainty and disquiet that characterises the human experience of life and its temporality.

By this anchoring, however, the actual disquietude of human life and the experience of uncertainty, insecurity and contingency that mark it, remain unexamined. This is problematic because it hides from view the particular *human motivation* to develop philosophical theories that offer certainty and security amid the contingent vicissitudes of human history and life is itself neither understood nor accounted for.[49] Philosophy's theoretical perspective is *not* a given, but is a human *creation* motivated by and founded in human experience and existence. Since humans experience their existence as uncertain and disquieting, human existence is captivated by the distress to secure itself and by a care to find a hold for itself. On the one hand, the 'theoretical tendencies-to-secure' motivating philosophy are an expression of this human concern. On the other hand, however, by attempting to secure what is uncertain and insecure in an eternal, permanent and stable reality, philosophy actually hides the contingency and disquiet of human existence from our view: rather than interpreting this experience from itself, it interprets it in light of what is created to overcome and tranquilise this experience.[50] Whether it concerns Plato or Hegel, their theories cover over the experience of disquietude and contingency by constructing a rational order; thus, they fail to address directly 'that which, in the historical, genuinely disturbs us'.[51]

In an interview about his novel *4321*, Paul Auster recounts how, at the age of fourteen, he watches a bolt of lightning kill a boy before his eyes. During a walk in the forest, they got caught in heavy weather, and Auster recalls:

> Someone said we should get to a clearing, and we had to crawl, single file, under a barbed wire fence. As the boy immediately in front of me was going under, lightning struck the fence [...] I've always been haunted by what happened, the utter randomness of it.[52]

In another interview, he adds to this scene: 'Suddenly I understood: *anything can happen, at any moment, to anyone.*'[53] This is the understanding of our transitory existence that the experience of contingency elicits in us: 'anything can happen, at any moment, to anyone.'

Human existence is thus marked by a disquieting potentiality-of-being-otherwise. The question is how one can experience and understand this mode of being. Even if we agree on a theoretical level with Auster's verdict that 'anything can happen, at any moment, to anyone', we still very seldomly live in accordance with it. Quite the contrary. In almost everything we do, we anticipate that everything or most things to go as expected and, hence, the unexpected withdraws from our anticipation, hitting us in the face when it does turn up. In this sense, the experience Auster so concisely foregrounds in these interviews is usually absent from our everyday dealings with – *Umgang*, *chrēsis* – things. Yet, as absent, this experience is simultaneously motivationally present, as is evident from the tendencies with which we keep on trying to get a grip on the world, clinging to the dream of eliminating the exception of contingency in higher systems, theories, technologies and concepts. This leads us to the question: how to face up to this contingency and bring it into view?

Regarding this question, Paul points the way because he incites the members of his community to face up to the disquietude and contingency of Christian life. In fact, the capacity to face up to this disquietude and experience is the very touchstone that decides whether one is an exception or not to an order of the world that seeks to secure itself and that only affirms itself. Paul's letters thus do not posit the event as an axiom, but rather the event is the very name for the disquietude and contingency of Christian life. Paul calls on readers to adopt a new attitude to life so that their existence can be experienced in light of such an event, that is, in light of its contingency and its disquietude. In Paul's letters, the phenomena of human concern for existence and its disquiet are thus not shrouded in 'tendencies-to-secure'; rather, these tendencies are resisted by exercising a particular mode of living of which *hōs mē* and *chrēsis* are the keywords, so that contingency can actually be experienced and understood. Hence, the pre-philosophical motivation that remains hidden in the philosophical theories about history, are disclosed in Paul's letters, albeit under the specific heading of a Christian experience of this contingency.

(a) Rupture in Existence

1 Thessalonians includes the experience of human temporal existence elicited by the Parousia. Yet, this letter first describes another Pauline event, namely the rupture in human existence commonly referred to as 'conversion'. In the letter, Paul describes this particular rupture with the verb *genesthai*, which means 'to come into being', 'to come into a new state of being' or simply 'becoming'. Heidegger renders this verb as *Gewordensein*, which is translated in English as 'having-become'. This latter translation is somewhat unfortunate as it erases Heidegger's attempt to emphasise that *genesthai* concerns a particular *mode of being* of the Thessalonians and not simply a new state they have come into. Their existence is indeed marked by a fundamental change, namely their acceptance of Paul's proclamation, by which they have come into a genuinely new mode of being.[54] Yet, this rupture is not an incident that once happened and subsequently belongs to the distant past for the Thessalonians; it is in this sense not a new *state* of their existence. While indeed the event of conversion in a certain sense has happened, it at the same time has not yet finished happening. *Genesthai* rather *is* their present mode of being, as Heidegger insists: 'Having-become [*Gewordensein*] is not, in life [just] any incident you like. Rather, it is incessantly co-experienced, and indeed such that their Being [*Sein*] now is their having-become [*Gewordensein*]. Their having-become is their Being now.'[55]

This Heideggerian emphasis on the specific status of the Thessalonians' coming into a new mode of being can be integrated in the dialectic of exception I am putting forward. That the Thessalonians *are* this rupture in their existence means that they *are* the exception to the mode of being, thinking and living prescribed by the present order of the world. The verb 'to be' is italicised in the previous sentence to emphasise that this rupture places them in a continuous dialectic struggle. To be an exception is not a state but only exists in the enactment of one's existence as exception, that is, it exists only in the struggle with a world that wants them to return to its order. The cross and its scandal symbolise the rupture with the mode of living that Paul calls 'the world'. In the eyes of the world, a mode of life that commits to the scandal of the cross deserves to be emphatically rejected and discarded. The scandal of the cross expresses of the deepest disquietude and concern of having to live in the mode of *genesthai* in such a world. The rupture in Paul's existence as well as in that of the Thessalonians is therefore experienced as the brokenness of existence, of an existence that has been fundamentally disrupted – and to be able to endure and hold out this brokenness is the touchstone of this exceptional existence. In the experience and Pauline explication of the Parousia, this touchstone is fully elaborated. It is in this sense that, for the Thessalonians, the event of their coming into a new mode of being can only be understood in relation to the Parousia, which further clarifies the dialectic struggle in which they are engaged.

(b) Experiencing Time

The Parousia is a second ingredient of the Pauline event in 1 Thessalonians and all comes down to the question of how the believers await and experience the Second Coming, as Heidegger emphasises: 'The awaiting of the *Parousia* of the Lord is decisive [...] the experience of the *Parousia*.'[56] In this experience, all the basic characteristics of the Pauline life experience come together in the following succinct and enigmatic way:

> The experience is an absolute distress [...] which belongs to the life of the Christian himself. The acceptance is an entering-oneself-into-anguish. This distress is a fundamental characteristic, it is an absolute concern in the horizon of the *Parousia*.[57]

By accepting Paul's proclamation, the Thessalonians have not entered a blissful life of happiness, but have placed themselves in a dialectic battle: their lives have become a continuous test and ordeal; whether they can endure this test is the very anguish and distress of their existence. Hence, by accepting, they have placed themselves in a mode of living that knows no security.[58] The Parousia and its particular temporal structure allow Paul to elucidate this. Let me elucidate in two steps what my dialectic of exception adopts from – and how it relates to – Heidegger's approach to the Parousia as the exemplification of event and contingency.

First, the Second Coming is of the order of possibility, of what can-be, and not of the order of actuality, of what already is. Paul raises this possibility in a striking way. If we speak about a future event, nothing seems more natural than asking when exactly it will take place. Characteristic for an upcoming event, after all, seems to be that it will be present and take place at a certain moment in time; in this sense, the future of an event seems to be a mere modification of the present. And so, one wonders: When does it take place? How long does it take until Christ returns? But precisely these questions are misleading according to Paul:

> Now concerning the times and the seasons, brothers and sisters, you do not need to have anything written to you. For you yourselves know very well that the day of the Lord will come like a thief in the night. (1 Thess. 5:1–2)

This is a remarkable response. Paul does not indicate a particular point in time for the Second Coming, but he also does not say that he does not know when this point in time is. The question about knowledge of the exact point in time is apparently irrelevant. Or, more precisely, those who are seduced by the question of when the Parousia will take place are false exceptions who cannot pass the test of the Parousia.

Paul does mention another form of knowledge, though: 'you yourselves know very well.' This knowledge concerns the self-knowledge of the Thessalonians about their conversion. If they know the uncertainty in which this change in their existence placed them, they understand what it means to await the Second Coming as something that comes 'like a thief in the night'. Awaiting the Parousia is not about waiting for the passage of a particular interval of time until this event takes place at some point in the future; awaiting or expecting is rather about the present, that is, about expecting, here and now, the unexpected, being prepared, here and now, for that for which one cannot prepare. The image of the 'thief in the night' thus expresses the profound uncertainty and insecurity, experienced here and now, in the present. Consequently, the possibility of the Parousia, that it can happen, should not be experienced as a future possibility – it may happen tomorrow or next week – but should be experienced as a *present* possibility: it may happen now, in this very moment. Rather than imposing an image of the future as a modification of the present, the imminent possibility of the Parousia changes our sense of the present. The present is not simply what is here and now actual, but the present should rather be experienced as that which is pregnant of the unheard-of possibility of a complete reversal of all that is and which can be born in this very moment. The present is not only the *now* in which all kinds of incidents actually occur, but it is also the very *moment* when the Second Coming *can* take place. The now is not the now of actuality, but rather the moment filled with the possibility of rupture, the potentiality-of-being-otherwise, of the exception. The Thessalonians ought to live in such a way that their enactment of life is delineated by the realisation that the Second Coming is possible at any moment.

Second, the Second Coming is not so much concerned with an actual transformation of reality, in the form of an apocalypse or otherwise; the Parousia rather concerns the very experience of *the potentiality-of-being-otherwise* of everything that is. For Breton, grace is the religious form of contingency for Paul. For Heidegger, the Pauline experience of contingency is pre-eminently that of the Second Coming. 'Anything can happen, at any moment, with anyone.' The anguish facing Paul – Auster and the apostle – has everything to do with the inherent difficulty of expecting the Second Coming in this way, to live (with) the Parousia in every moment. One is habitually inclined to understand oneself in terms of one's worldly callings, but therewith one misunderstands precisely the potentiality-of-being-otherwise that characterises our existence and that marks its very rupture. Thus, the expectation of the Parousia connects to explications of the *hōs mē*-passages as discussed in the previous chapter. What else does this attitude to life require than to enact everything one is and does in the present order of the world – married, delighted, bereaved – in such a way that one does not identify with it because one experiences it in light of its potentiality-of-being-otherwise? Every identification distorts and covers over the potentiality-of-being-otherwise that gives itself to understand when the Pauline event is the horizon of one's existence. Thus, we may summarise, conversion is truly the whole turning around of the whole soul in which one leaves behind the attitude that understands and affirms the order of the world as a given and instead embraces an attitude receptive to the world's potentiality-of-being-otherwise – other than it is and other than one thinks it is.

BETWEEN PAST AND FUTURE

The event of death and resurrection and the event of the Parousia, respectively, are complementary in Paul's letters. Therefore, it might make sense, in line with Agamben's suggestion, to account for the

Pauline event by combining them: 'Paul decomposes the messianic event into two times: resurrection and *parousia*, the second coming of Jesus at the end of time.'[59] Death and resurrection mark the first temporal dimension of the Pauline event: it has already happened. This character is repeated and retrieved in the rupture the believers experience in their own existence, that is, their *genesthai*, their coming into a new mode of being. Without this 'already' of the event, there is no real anchoring of Paul's proclamation, and a mode of living in accordance therewith would not be underpinned by anything in the existence of the believers. At the same time, this already should not be mistaken for a mere point in the past. Should the Pauline event be purely and solely 'already', and a mere incident in the past, it would be complete(d): *it has completely happened*. The Parousia therefore emphasises the other dimension. The Second Coming has *not yet* happened, but it is *imminent* and it is given as a possibility can happen at every moment, that can happen here and now. Including the Parousia in our understanding of the Pauline event allows us to say that it has *already* begun but is *not yet* fulfilled.

Yet, as Arendt emphasises long before Agamben, exactly this double structure of the time of the event – *already* and *not yet* – implies that the time of the present is the gap between past and future in which humans live their lives in an incessant dialectic battle: 'a gap in time which "his" constant fighting, "his" making a stand against past and future, keeps in existence'.[60] This time is returned to the believers as the time in which their existence is enacted in accordance with the event. This present time of the event is the time of the exception. It is the time in which the dialectic struggle takes place and the humans are tested whether they truly are the exception, whether they are capable of maintaining an attitude that discerns in the world its potentiality-of-being-otherwise. In this sense, this time is the time that humans are gracefully given to adopt and enact the new mode of living enabled by the event. The resurrection has disclosed the potentiality-of-being-otherwise of the world, has shown that an exception is possible: the present figure of this world is not permanent and need not have the final word. Without this rupture of the resurrection, this potentiality-of-being-otherwise would not be part of any horizon of understanding. In this way, the resurrection represents the principle of spirit, the principle of transformation in its activity. On the other hand, the resurrection is not the name for the completion of this transformation; it offers the believers a transformation in their mode of being that grants them the possibility to live differently, to prove themselves to be exceptions to the way of the world and to be receptive to the world as being other than it is and than one thinks it is. The Parousia represents the principle of the spirit in its imminence and potentiality.

The event, extended between *already* and *not yet*, thus returns the capacity to live and to act *here and now*, in the present – the objective time created in the beginning, *in principio*, is revivified and transformed in the time of the *initium*, of human initiative and the enactment of human existence in a dialectic struggle with the order of the world. Where they were first caught up in the time of the world and its mode of living, now this time and order are suspended and a qualitatively different time is opened up. It is the time in which the new life happens. More precisely, since it has already begun but is not yet completed, and since this completion is not a certainty but rather a demand and test, it might be better to say: *now it may be happening*. The resurrection has granted the *dunamis* for the new creation to be, and for the believers this means that they can now life by this *dunamis*. The time that remains is the time in which humans prove or disprove themselves to be exceptions. It is the only time humans *have* to live well according to the possibilities granted – as Kierkegaard already noted: 'Spiritually speaking, everything is possible.'[61] This marks the urgency and the disquiet of the time that remains for humans: *now* is the time to act, to use as not abusing, because now it is happening or it will never happen. The time that remains humans is the time of the touchstone to test whether they live up to the potentiality-of-being-otherwise, to the exception.

NOTES

1 The concept of the event is also of the utmost importance beyond the discussion on Saint Paul in contemporary thought; see, e.g., Raffoul, *Thinking the Event*; Van der Heiden, *Ontology after Ontotheology*. For a whole range of references to the concept of the event in contemporary phenomenology and continental philosophy, see the introduction of Filiz, 'Event and Subjectivity'.
2 Heidegger, *Wegmarken*, 247/189: '*Archē* means, at one and the same time, beginning [*Anfang*] and control [*Herrschaft*].'
3 Hegel, *Phänomenologie des Geistes*, 30/19.
4 Hegel, 'Glauben und Wissen', 431/190.
5 'En elk zijn is tot niet-zijn geschapen'. Translation: Joey Kok.
6 Nietzsche, *Die fröhliche Wissenschaft*, 159/119–20 [= Book III, § 125]. Hegel, 'Glauben und Wissen', 431/190.
7 Ibid., 431–2/191.
8 See Chapter 1 for the characteristics of appropriation, totalisation and mediation. The character of mediation is also challenged, but is, it seems to me, not genuinely overcome in the thought of authors such as Derrida; it is explicitly addressed, however, by Kierkegaard in his account of the exception.

9 Derrida, *Marges de la philosophie*, I–II/x–xii.
10 Waldenfels, *Platon*, 9–15.
11 The opposition between Christ and Adam is thus, in accordance with the Stoic tendencies in 1 Cor. 15, that between *pneuma* and *psuchē*.
12 De Vries, *Een kleine filosofie van het wonder*.
13 Badiou, *Saint Paul*, 35/32.
14 Ibid., 56/53.
15 For an extensive account of the relation of the principle of sufficient reason and the concept of the event in present-day thought, see also Van der Heiden, *Ontology after Ontotheology*.
16 See, e.g., Badiou, *Saint Paul*, 5/4, 62/58, 116/108.
17 Ibid., 47–8/45.
18 Ibid., 77/68.
19 Ibid., 69/65.
20 Similarly, Badiou notes that Paul's conversion in no way follows from his previous life: it is 'a thunderbolt, a caesura, and not a dialectical reversal.' Ibid., 18/17.
21 Ibid., 71/66.
22 According to Badiou, Paul consequently also does not glorify suffering: there is indeed mention of the cross and the crucifixion, but not of the Via Dolorosa in Paul's letters, as this does not contribute anything to the new beginning introduced by the resurrection; see ibid., 71–2/66–7.
23 Žižek, 'The Necessity of a Dead Bird', 180.
24 See also Barclay, 'Paul and the Philosophers', 181.
25 See Badiou, *Saint Paul*, 99–100/93–4.
26 Nietzsche, *Zur Genealogie der Moral*, 298/29 [= First Essay, § 15].
27 Badiou, *Saint Paul*, 24/23.
28 Ibid., 23–4/22–3.
29 Ibid., 56–7/53–4.
30 Ibid., 118/110. This is confirmed in Badiou, 'From Logic to Anthropology', 46–7.
31 This dichotomy of world and event is not occasional but rather an integral part of Badiou's systematic work; see *L'Être et l'événement*.
32 For Žižek, the dialectic role of death – the necessity of the crucifixion for the resurrection – is crucial; see *The Ticklish Subject*, 169. See also Løland, *The Reception of Paul the Apostle in the Works of Slavoj Žižek*, 41–51; Boyarin, 'Paul among the Antiphilosophers', 113; and Welborn, 'The Culture of Crucifixion'.
33 Cicero, *Pro Rabirio Perduellionis Reo* 16; see Cicero, *Orations*, 466–9. Cited in Welborn, 'The Culture of Crucifixion', 135. See also Løland, *Pauline Ugliness*, 77.
34 Bradley, *Unbearable Life*, 4–5.
35 See also Barclay, 'Paul and the Philosophers', 182–3, who emphasises that leaving out this point constitutes a profound weakness in Badiou's reading of Paul.

36 Žižek, *On Belief*, 150. For a comparable analysis of detachment, see Žižek, *The Fragile Absolute*, 140.
37 Žižek, 'The Necessity of a Dead Bird', 179–80.
38 Agamben, *Il tempo che resta*, 43/40.
39 Schmitt, *Politische Theologie*, 21/15; Kierkegaard, *Repetition*, 226–8. Schmitt's reference to Kierkegaard is extensively cited and commented on in Agamben, *Homo Sacer*, 19–35/15–29.
40 Agamben, *Homo Sacer*, 21–2/17–18.
41 Kierkegaard, *Repetition*, 226–7.
42 Agamben argues in his discussion of Schmitt that the relation between exception and rule should be understood as suspension; see *Homo Sacer*, 22/18.
43 Plato, *Gorgias* 486d. See also Foucault, *Le Gouvernement de soi et des autres*, 340–1/366–7.
44 In the terminology used in 1 Cor. 14, the chapter on speaking in tongues, Paul distinguishes between *pneuma* and *nous*. The former term describes the part of the human where the immediate contact with the divine can take place; the latter term, which we could render as 'mind', describes that which can be understood interpreted and shared with others; see Van der Heiden, 'Interpreters of the Divine', 97. This same distinction basically structures Kierkegaard's *Fear and Trembling*, which also refers to the speaking in tongues and which has been written in the same period as *Repetition*.
45 Heidegger, *Phänomenologie des religiösen Lebens*, 65/45.
46 For a more critical account of Heidegger's way of reading Paul, see Boulnois, *Saint Paul et la philosophie*, chap. 1.
47 See also Heidegger, *Sein und Zeit*, § 6, esp. 34–5/22–3.
48 For what follows on the first part of this lecture series, see Heidegger, *Phänomenologie des religiösen Lebens*, 39–55/27–37, esp. 45–51/31–7.
49 From this Heideggerian point of view, the Badiouan way out of Hegel's dialectic by positing an event as axiom suffers from a similar philosophical forgetfulness and blindness: rather than elucidating the fundamental uncertainty attached to each and every socio-political ideal, Badiou fantasises his way out of it by positing the event as axiom thus fleeing for or at least assuaging the genuine experience of disquiet with which the affirmation of each event goes hand in hand.
50 Heidegger, *Phänomenologie des religiösen Lebens*, 78/54.
51 Ibid., 45/31.
52 Laity, 'Paul Auster: "I'm going to speak out as often as I can, otherwise I can't live with myself."'
53 De Veen, '"Het is veel spannender om met imaginaire personages te leven."' Translation: Joey Kok; my italics.
54 Heidegger, *Phänomenologie des religiösen Lebens*, 93–4/65–6.
55 Ibid., 94/66.
56 Ibid., 97/67.

57 Ibid., 97–8/67.
58 'There is no security for Christian life; the constant insecurity is also characteristic for what is fundamentally significant in factical life. The uncertainty is not coincidental; rather it is necessary.' Ibid., 105/73.
59 Agamben, *Il tempo che resta*, 69/69.
60 Arendt, *Between Past and Future*, 11.
61 Kierkegaard, *Fear and Trembling*, 44; at 46, he cites Matth. 19:26: 'for God, all things are possible.'

5. Law, Promise and Grace

The question of another legacy of Paul is often addressed in terms of its socio-political ramifications. In the previous chapters, I have shown that one cannot limit this legacy to these ramifications: a present-day philosophical portrait of Paul should begin with painting the ontological and ethical features of these letters. Yet, this obviously does not mean that the socio-political dimension of this legacy can be left aside. In this and the next chapter, I argue that this legacy concerns in the first place how the notions of outcast, spirit and exception affect our understanding of law and community. This chapter examines what the Pauline dialectic of exception means for Paul's account of the law. The next chapter continues this examination, focusing on community.

In the cultural, modern reception of Paul's letters, there is probably no issue as important as that concerning *nomos* or 'law'. The modern, especially Protestant interest in Romans, from Luther to Barth, concerns exactly Paul's suspension of the law. For a philosophical interpretation, *nomos* is also a key focus since it directly concerns Paul's statements about law, faith and grace, which are the conceptual resources of a new politico-philosophical language at the heart of the question of political theology.

Paul's use of the term *nomos* raises several questions, not least with respect to which law he actually means. Does he refer to the Jewish law, the law of the cosmos, or Roman law, that is, does the law concern the ethical, the cosmological, or the political or constitutional law? Taubes suggests that '[i]t is all of these in one', thus making the concept even more complex.[1] Moreover, Paul's letters reveal a strong *antinomianism*, a resistance to or even rejection of the law. In several instances, he connects the law with the figures of flesh and death, thus pitting the law against gospel, spirit, life, covenant and grace. The law often belongs to those dimensions of the world that are passing away. Thus, this antinomianism seems connected to a specific *eschatology*, which consists in preparing a mode of thinking, being, and living in accordance with this passing away of the laws – cosmological, ethical and political – that regulate the present order of the world. This raises several complicated questions: Is Paul pleading for the law to be abolished? What are the implications of this antinomianism when Paul is read in a socio-political register? Can he be pleading for a socio-political order without law?

Yet, at the same time, Paul does not seem to be consistent in his antinomianism. His hesitation can be seen when he uses the key verb *katargeō*, to suspend or to deactivate, in relation to the law. What does this suspension of the law exactly mean when Paul also writes: 'Do we then overthrow the law by this faith? By no means! On the contrary, we uphold the law' (Rom. 3:31). Moreover, in relation to the often-discussed passage in 2 Thess. 2 on the *katechon* – that is, the deferral of the arrival of the last things and the withholding of their presence – the term *anomia* seems to refer to a lawlessness explicitly rejected by the apostle.[2] Adding to this confusion, he also does not strictly distinguish between law and faith. Besides the 'law of works' (*nomos tōn ergōn*), which he problematises, he also speaks of 'the law of faith' (*nomos pisteōs*; Rom. 3:27) and embraces it. Moreover, he writes of himself that he is 'under Christ's law' (*ennomos christou*; 1 Cor. 9:21) and, hence, bound to this law.

This leads to the following questions. Which specific domain does Paul suspend in his thought about the law, and which domain is opened up when the law is suspended? How does he revalue the law? That such a transvaluation comprises faith and grace is clear enough, but how the relation between law, faith and grace should subsequently be understood is less evident. Nevertheless, the flexibility with which Paul uses *nomos* suggests that it very well might be a dialectic term taken up in a pneumatic hermeneutics moving from the natural law of works to the spiritual law of faith or Christ.

STATE OF EXCEPTION

In the present-day debate, beginning with Taubes, the question of the political theology of Paul is usually staged as a discussion with Schmitt. Let me therefore begin by clarifying and identifying a number of relevant notions and arguments in Schmitt's political theology. A number of the concepts introduced in the previous chapters find a politico-legal sense when understood a Schmittian vein. In the first chapter of *Political Theology*, Schmitt turns to the notion of the exception in order to flesh out '[t]he political potential of Kierkegaard'.[3] In fact, the notion of exception appears in the famous first sentence of the first chapter: 'Sovereign is the one who decides on the exception.'[4] Schmitt writes that the title of sovereign is applicable to the one who has the power to proclaim the state of exception, thereby suspending the legal order that is valid in normal circumstances in a society.[5] Declaring the state of exception is thus nothing less than 'the suspension of the entire existing order'.[6] Hence, in Schmitt, the terms 'exception', 'order', 'law' and 'suspension' obtain a distinctly political meaning.

Let me briefly explicate the political significance of Schmitt's distinction between normal and exceptional. Every society 'demands a normal, everyday frame of life' to which a norm can be applied. For this norm to function, a 'homogeneous medium' is required. Hence, the functioning of a legal order presupposes a particular societal homogeneity. Consequently, only a society that is not incoherent, that is not reigned over by differences that threaten this homogeneity, knows an 'effective normal situation' where norms and laws can truly be applied.[7] Situations such as, for instance, the threat of terrorist attacks may obstruct the adequate application of the law; when they do, the law has to be adjusted in such situations. These situations form a 'state of emergency': society loses the coherence and homogeneity needed for the proper functioning of the legal order.[8]

Schmitt's theory of the sovereign is often explained in decisionist terms: the sovereign decides on the state of exception without having to defend themselves before a tribunal. That a decision has to be made is obvious; yet, this decision is itself a response to an emergency situation in which society risks losing its homogeneity. The sovereign's response is in the first place the acknowledgement or affirmation that society finds itself in a particular distress – *Not* – or emergency and that, therefore, the state of exception needs to be declared.

Differently put, Schmitt's idea of the state of exception cannot merely be understood in terms of a metaphysics of the will, as if the emergency itself were the sovereign's making. Prior to the sovereign judgement, there is something that induces a decision: the proper functioning of the legal order is under threat. The sovereign needs to judge the extent of this violation. Hence, prior to this judgement, a differential element is found, a heterogeneity in society that *could* threaten its homogeneity. However, differential elements always exist in a society. There are always differences between groups in a society that often lead to political discord under normal circumstances. Yet, this implies that the possibility of an emergency situation is always real: certain socio-political differences can always manifest themselves politically. If this happens, and the purely differential manifests itself as a potential violation of the required homogeneity of society, the sovereign can intervene with a decision. Following Schmitt's lead, one may phrase this as follows: there is an ongoing dialectic struggle between the homogeneity of society and its differential elements; if this struggle escalates, it is the sovereign who settles the dispute and chooses one of the two options: either the differential elements do not threaten the legal order, or they do. A sovereign's decision is thus the political *proclamation* or *declaration* that the differential element confronting the political community is indeed an exception to the homogeneity required in a society.

For Schmitt, the state of exception is not a permanent state. It is rather a period of transition during which a *new* homogeneity of the political community is founded, making a new constitution possible. Consequently, the state of exception is the sphere of the pre-legal and the pre-constitutional. Hence, it is not simply a sphere *outside* the law; it is rather a sphere of a power that *precedes* the constitution; it is the space of configuring and constituting the constitution. Hence, the following distinction applies. The power exercised by the state based on the law is called *constituted power*, as this power is justified by the state's constitution. Conversely, the power that is exercised during the state of exception is called *constitutive power*, as it is not justified by any existing constitution but constitutes a constitution and requires no justification in the normal situation that results after the state of exception. The aim of constitutive power is to transform the political community. During the state of exception, a new political community is created with a new identity and homogeneity.

What does the sovereign need to do to establish a new homogeneity? To respond to this question, Schmitt introduces the important and well-known distinction between friend and enemy.[9] This distinction converts the differential elements at play in every homogenous situation into a simple *opposition*: for each of the differential elements, a decision is made whether it belongs to the category of 'friends', and thus contributes to the new homogeneity, or to the category of 'enemies', and thus should at all costs be banned to make a new homogeneity possible. The very introduction of such oppositions is the political act par excellence and establishes a new people with a new homogeneity.[10] Needless to say, such a theory by a scholar in the employ of the German Nazi regime is deeply unsettling.

In order to show how these considerations are relevant for the question of Paul's conception of the law and that of the true legacy of Kierkegaard's exception, let me conclude this section with two remarks. First, although we have explained a number of Schmitt's notions, we did not yet explain what he means by political theology. In a nutshell, this term states that central ideas from political philosophy – such as sovereign, law, people, but also the state of exception, and the friend–enemy distinction – have theological roots. The political sovereign is, for instance, understood as an analogy of God, who sovereignly rules over His creation. As God is able to intervene with miracles in His creation, the sovereign can suspend the existing legal order by declaring the state of exception.[11] Yet, this theological heritage is in many respects a Pauline one. Second, following Taubes, one may argue that the Paul implicitly present in Schmitt's writing is actually a Marcionite Paul, and the friend–enemy distinction is the socio-political translation of Marcionite dualism, obscuring the *dialectic* character of Paul's political theology.

PAUL'S DIALECTIC POLITICAL THEOLOGY

Let us begin our discussion on the nature of Paul's political theology in terms of the debate between Taubes and Schmitt. According to the former, the political dimension of Paul's legacy is eminently revealed in Romans. The opening verses of this letter disclose a profound dispute with the Roman Empire when Christ is described as resurrected from death and invested with power through God (Rom. 1:1–7). To our modern ear, this might sound like a standard Christian message, but Paul is probably writing this around 57 CE to the Christian community in Rome, the seat of the Roman emperor. If this date is correct, Taubes suggests, Paul writes this shortly after the death of the emperor Claudius in 54. The Roman Senate interpreted the latter's death as an ascension: Claudius was elevated to the Roman gods. In this period, Paul writes to the community in Rome that not Claudius but rather Jesus Christ was elevated: 'The Epistle to the Romans is a political theology, a *political* declaration of war on the Caesar.'[12]

More precisely, it is declaration of war on the law. Paul's contemporary culture, whether Jewish, Greek or Roman, was marked by an 'apotheosis of nomos'.[13] Each group understood the law in its own way; yet, each bestowed a divine status upon it: the law ruled. When Paul opposes the law, he opposes its all-encompassing apotheosis and indeed attempts, as Nietzsche suggests, to substitute it by another value. This opposition can be heard in the proclamation of the death of Christ: the Messiah has been nailed to the cross by the law. Christ's crucifixion is not embraced as an exaltation of death and suffering but rather as the most fundamental protestation against the authority that has this death on its conscience: *nomos* or law. Pauline theology is in this way true political dynamite.

Yet, how does this relate to Schmitt's political theology? While Schmitt borrows important principles for his political theory from Paul, in his interpretation of them he relies on the Marcionite tradition.[14] In light of German history, it is telling that it is specifically the anti-Semitic tradition of Marcion that resounds in Schmitt's work. Two crucial concepts from Schmitt's political thought can be reinterpreted when taking into account this difference between a Marcionite and a genuinely Pauline tradition: (1) the distinction between friend and enemy that determines the shape of a political conflict, and (2) the role of the sovereign in the state of exception.

(1) Without conflicts there is no true politics and a constitutive conflict divides a community into two groups: friends and enemies. For Schmitt, as discussed before, the latter distinction between friend and enemy concerns the heart of the political. Yet one should be aware that this distinction is a politico-theological one with Pauline roots.[15] At this point, Taubes has captured the stakes very well. Schmitt has understood that the political task facing Paul is the same as the one facing the sovereign, namely 'the *establishment and the legitimation of a new people of God*'.[16] The old, first people of God, Israel, founded by Moses and his laws, has apparently run into such a crisis that it can no longer be the people of God. To draw a distinction, Paul addresses this first people of God indeed as enemies: 'As regards the gospel they are enemies of God' (Rom. 11:28). The conflict underlying the distinction between friend and enemy concerns the proclamation of Christ, and in this conflict, Israel is addressed as the enemy because it does not accept this proclamation. According to Schmitt's political logic, Paul creates a group of enemies to be able to establish a new people with a new homogeneity. However, by *absolutising* the value of the distinction between friend and enemy, Schmitt adopts a political variation of Marcion's dualism, including the anti-Semitism contained therein.

Yet, exactly at this point, Schmitt proves to be a bad reader and discerns a dualism where there actually is a dialectic. The precise argumentation in Rom. 11 is crucial. In this chapter, Paul first indicates that the disbelief and unwillingness to accept the proclamation of Jesus Christ, as he finds it among a part of Israel, have a precedent in the history of this people. In other words, this refusal does not oppose a group of 'friends' with Israel and its history but rather repeats and resumes this history in a different way. Paul points to passages from the books of the prophets who complain that Israel does not follow God's path. For this reason, he interprets this history as follows: 'What then? Israel failed to obtain what it was seeking. The elect obtained it, but the rest were hardened' (Rom. 11:7). In a similar reading – repeating and resuming Israel's history and sacred texts – Paul proves himself to be no Marcionite aiming to destroy this history or these sacred texts. He does not place Israel in a rigid friend-enemy opposition but rather describes a *dialectic*: 'So I ask, have they stumbled so as to fall? By no means! But through their stumbling salvation has come to the Gentiles, so as to make Israel jealous' (Rom. 11:11). Paul continues his argument by suggesting that he is the apostle of the nations (*ethnēn Apostolos*). Yet, he does not preach salvation to the nations alone to make the divine message accessible solely to them, but also to make his own people jealous and thereby inspire them to still convert (Rom. 11:13–14). According to Paul, it is a divine 'mystery' that the hardening and impiety of a 'part of Israel' is only temporary, that is, 'until the full number of Gentiles has come in' (Rom. 11:25). Thereafter, 'all Israel will be saved; as it is written' (Rom. 11:26).

Hence, the conflict between friend and enemy is but a moment in a larger dialectic development that culminates in all Israel being re-assimilated into the people of God that is yet to be founded. (The relation between 'all Israel' and the establishment of the people that Paul sketches in Rom. 11 will be examined in the next chapter.) Rom. 11 can thus be read to contain a sharp dialectic critique of Schmitt's definition of the political in terms of the opposition between friend and enemy as well as of his claim that this conflict establishes the new people. Conflict is but a moment in a larger development of the people of God that Moses founded: in the yet-to-be-founded new people of God, Israel maintains its share. Paul's political project does not exclude Israel, but rather aims at a *transfiguration* of Israel. Not the dualistic principle of conflict and opposition, but the dialectic principle of the spirit plays a key role in Paul's political theology, both hermeneutically and politically.

The terminology used in Rom. 11:15–16 is highly illuminating in this regard. In the first verse, the rejection of Israel is mirrored in 'the reconciliation of the world'. The first part of this verse suggests a genuine dualism: the Greek word used for reconciliation, *katallagē*, is also the word that expresses the exchange of money (e.g. in an exchange office): Israel is exchanged for the world. Hence, the first half of this verse could be read in a perfectly Schmittian vein. Yet, the verse continues stating that 'their acceptance be but life from dead': the dualism of rejection and reconciliation, the exchange of Israel for the world, is *supplemented* by the acceptance of Israel, which is nothing less than the work of the spirit of God, which grants life to the dead. Hence, not the logic of exchange, *katallagē*, but rather that of life from dead, *zōē ek nekrōn*, is at stake here, as Rom. 11:15–16 emphasises: Christ is the firstfruits, *aparchē*, of the logic of *zōē ek nekrōn* that pervades all, both Israel and the world.[17]

Moreover, this transformation of the people of God is concluded not in a new, homogeneous community *on which a legal order can be built*, as Schmitt's political theology suggests. This transformation rather implies a fundamental change of the role of the law itself. The law is also subject to the principle of the spirit. God's people is no longer the community determined by a legal order or by blood relations. The latter are characteristics of the people Moses founded. The alternative foundation is the new covenant.[18] This transition from law to covenant forms the background of Paul's aforementioned antinomianism. An alternative has to be found to the law because the law stands for the old people of God and obstructs the renewal of the people and of the relation of God to the people. To better understand this transition, we turn to a second pair of concepts from Schmitt's political theology: exception and sovereign.

(2) Schmitt's account of the sovereign and the state of exception can also, in part, be traced in Paul's letters.[19] Yet, also with respect to these notions, Schmitt is Marcionite. To understand this, let us first address in more detail the problem of constitutive power: even if this power eventually founds a new legal order, the power and violence used for this constituting cannot be justified in this new legal order. Hence, the new order is based on an unjustified and unjustifiable power and violence inscribed in the foundation of its constitution, but that, being unjustified, should be excluded from this new order.

To capture this problem, Žižek understands this constitutive moment as a trauma that makes the new order possible only in as far as it is excluded from and forgotten by it. Yet, because this trauma is constitutive for the new order, it continues to haunt it like 'a permanent spectral presence, an undead ghost'.[20] According to Žižek, this means that this constitutive power is the 'perverse core' of the new political and legal order. He thinks that this structure can also be traced in Christianity. The examples he points out are the betrayal of Jesus by Judas and the Fall caused by Adam. Such incidents, Judas's betrayal and Adam's Fall, constitute the necessary condition for salvation and, hence, are necessary ingredients in the history of salvation.[21] In Žižek's conception of Paul's Christianity, these exceptions thus become a perverse core, and it is only based on this core that a new pneumatic order is possible in the first place.

In itself, this is an interesting reading. Yet, in line with my argumentation at the end of Chapter 1, it seems to me that Žižek does not frame the issue of exception in genuinely Pauline terms. One of the conditions for such a reading is that a new order truly arises and that it does so based on a temporary state of exception as period of transition. In Paul's rhetoric, however, it seems more reasonable to suppose, as my discussion of Rom. 3, 4 and 7 aims to show, that no new legal order emerges from Paul's state of exception. In fact, in the domain opened up by the suspension of the legal order, sovereign arbitrariness does *not* reign. For Paul, the exception has a completely different relationship with justice and justification than the Slovenian philosopher seems to think.

The notions of exception and suspension of the law will make or break Paul's argument, it seems to me. Everything depends on whether the exception is possible. This applies in particular to the problem of the law. Do we see the world in light of the apotheosis of the law, or do we consider an exception to be possible? In Schmitt, this exception is decided on and declared by the sovereign. Schmitt suggests that this sovereign is a theological notion, based on a God who can intervene in the natural order with miracles. However, for Paul, a miracle – if that is the most suitable term – is not in the first place the deed of a miracle worker who strengthens their credibility with a show of force, as discussed in the previous chapter. The true 'miracle' is the identification with the disgraceful and the powerless, as mentioned in 1 Corinthians and as sealed by the figure of the cross. Paul's God is thus rather concerned with the merciful selection and resurrection of the rejected and lost ones than with powerful displays of miracle-making.

Rom. 4 is the crucial chapter in which Paul discloses his points of view concerning the suspension of the law and the specific determination of the pre-legal sphere that exceeds and constitutes the law. In this chapter, Paul's conflict with Moses concerning the people of God comes to the fore and Paul's pneumatic hermeneutics can be seen in action: he reinterprets Israel's past in such a way that the basic characteristics of this people are transformed. In this way, Rom. 4 bears witness to yet another difference with Schmitt. For the latter, the suspension of the law and the proclamation of the state of exception is, in fact, a leap into the void and thus a leap into the space of sovereign arbitrariness and display of power. It seems the pre-legal is truly a blank page on which another, new dividing line can randomly be drawn that splits the page and so redistributes the population into friends and enemies. Paul, however, sketches a far more complicated picture. He differentiates between the covenant of God with his people and the Law of Moses in which this covenant further takes shape. These two *do not coincide* because the covenant is *prior* to the law. The suspension of the law then does not open up an empty space or blank page in Paul's political theology, but rather the primordial space of the covenant.

One could ask whether this does not imply a variation of Schmitt's sovereign arbitrariness hidden in God's preference for Israel: why this people and not another? This is a legitimate and important question to which we return in the next chapter because it concerns community. In the logic of Rom. 4, however, the isolation of the people of Israel from the other nations has a specific rhetorical function. Paul does not oppose law and circumcision to sovereign arbitrariness, but to *another kind of exception*, namely one that interprets Israel's past in another way disconnecting it from the (necessity of) law. If Moses represents the law, Abraham represents the original covenant, which comes into view when law and circumcision are suspended. Abraham appears prior to Moses in Jewish history. Paul's suspension of the law could thus be read as moving back in time, to a time *before* the law, to the law's prehistory. Compared to Moses, Abraham has the oldest testimonials: 'the law, which came four hundred thirty years later, does not annul a covenant previously ratified by God, so as to nullify the promise' (Gal. 3:17). This citation mentions a promise. Exactly this term, the promise, describes the form of the covenant before the law.[22] Although the law in some way supplements and seems to substitute for the promise, it cannot nullify the promise because the latter is the primordial form of the covenant between God and his people. Hence, the suspension of the law does not open up the space of constitutive violence, but rather that of God's primordial promise to and preference for the people of Israel.[23] This relation between exception and preference was already present in the description of Kierkegaard's account of the dialectical battle offered in the previous chapter.

Rom. 4 explains the implications hereof. Because the promise is more original than the law, there is a latitude between both countenances of the covenant. This latitude is the space that opens up the possibility of a pneumatic interpretation of the history of Israel and, more particularly, of the covenant. Abraham is not called based on his actions – Paul refers here to the law of works and thus the law of Moses – but based on his faith and trust (Rom. 4:2–5). Paul poses the rhetorical question: Was Abraham, at the time that *pistis*, faith and trust, were attributed to him, circumcised or uncircumcised? Was he under the law or without the law? He was not circumcised yet, is his immediate answer. Circumcision was 'a seal [and sign] of the righteousness that he had by faith while he was still uncircumcised' (Rom. 4:11). So, when arguing that the covenant begins with a promise that is not grounded in arbitrariness but in *pistis*, in the reliability and the trust of both parties to this covenant, Paul can also complete the transformation of God's people into another type of community:

> The purpose was to make him the ancestor of all who believe without being circumcised and who thus have righteousness reckoned to them, and likewise the ancestor of the circumcised who are not only circumcised but who also follow the example of the faith that our ancestor Abraham had before he was circumcised. (Rom. 4:11–12)

Not only those who are under the law, and thus circumcised, are part of the people of God but also those who are uncircumcised and share in the faith and trust of Abraham. Moreover, the circumcised are also part of the covenant, which not only means they uphold the law but also that they belong to God's people in as far as they share in God's and Abraham's *pistis* – faith in the sense of trust and trustworthiness – and promise.

The way in which Paul's pneumatic logic works can perhaps best be seen in Rom. 4:14: 'If it is the adherents of the law who are to be the heirs, faith is null and the promise is void [again: *katargeō*, to suspend].' Paul is not concerned with annulling the 'first' covenant but rather with re-illuminating the specific nature of the covenant of God in contrast with the interpretation that identifies this covenant with one of its historical countenances, namely the law: the *identification* of law and covenant suspends the original form and countenance of the covenant, which is faith and promise. The law may supplement but not substitute this original countenance.

Unlike what Schmitt thinks, the space opened up by the suspension of the law is not that of sovereign constitutive violence. Rather, where the law of works does not prevail, righteousness or justice *apart from the law* do (Rom. 3:21). This righteousness, *dikaiosunē*, is the sovereign beginning of the covenant and implies that the ethos expressed by *pistis* is obediently following instructions but rather consists in the exercise of justice, trusting the reliability of righteousness. The law may supplement this justice, that is, be inspired by it, but can never substitute it. Paul's focus on the stratification of the first covenant – first faith and promise, and subsequently the sealing of this heritage in the law – shows that this 'righteousness apart from the law' – or 'outlaw justice' as Jennings somewhat provocatively calls it – does not institute another principle but the one sealed and assumed by the law.[24] Thus, Paul does not speak about the negation or destruction of the law, but about fulfilling the law (Rom. 13:10), and he describes Christ as the end of the law (Rom. 10:4). Agamben points exactly to this: 'Justice without law is not the negation of the law, but the realization and fulfilment, the *plērōma*, of the law.'[25] The law finds its source and its completion in this justice.

This last sentence, which articulates the precise sense of Paul's antinomianism, might initially seem more difficult to understand than it actually is. Do we, after all, not trust that the legal order of a society is in some way an expression of justice? This is a politico-theological idea. When speaking of 'an expression', two things are implied: first, that justice precedes and inspires the legal order; second, that the legal order does not coincide with justice and could for this reason also lead to unjust consequences. Jennings suggests that one might recognise here Derrida's conception of the relation between justice and the law as developed in *Force de loi*, which is more Pauline than Derrida might be willing to acknowledge.[26] However, for Derrida, the law is *necessarily* unjust. This, it seems to me, is *not* a Pauline statement. For Paul, even though the law does not coincide with justice, it sets out as promising (the good) life; it is only because of the crisis of the law – as discussed in Rom. 7, to which we turn in the next section – that the suspension of the law becomes necessary. This, however, is a historical necessity and not a structural one.

Nevertheless, this still implies that the *fullness* of the law is never to be found in the legal order itself but has to be sought in the trust or faith in the righteousness that underpins it as well as in the faithfulness to it. Moreover, we say more, perhaps without realising it, when we claim that the legal order does not coincide with righteousness. We trust that at those moments when the legal order leads to injustice, there are people who understand that and who themselves, in their power of discernment, may embody righteousness – ancient Greek has the more eloquent term *empsuchos*, which could perhaps be translated with 'ensouled' or 'inspired' – and suspend the legal order not to enforce their own violence or will, but to recall the law to its origin. It is for good reasons that, in such cases, reference is made to the spirit of the law, that is, the sense of justice and righteousness the law should embody and express.[27] The surplus of justice over law is no variation on Schmitt's arbitrariness but is nothing other than the Pauline grace, *charis*, through which humans are not at the sole mercy of forces of law and sovereign constitutive violence. Righteousness is the sphere before the law from which the law originates: without the primordial trust in, faithfulness to and reliability of righteousness, law truly is abyssal and the expression of nothing but an arbitrary constitutive violence.

DUALISM OF LAW AND GRACE?

In the context of the political theology of Paul, the question of dualism versus dialectic does not only concern Schmitt but also concerns the relation between law and grace. What exactly is the specific role and sense of grace, *charis*, as the Pauline alternative to the law, as so clearly expressed in Romans: 'you are not under law but under grace' (Rom 6:14)? This question guides me in this and the next section.

Badiou quickly identifies grace in terms of his conception of the Pauline event: 'The pure event is reducible to this: Jesus died on the cross and resurrected. This event is "grace" (*kharis*).'[28] The event liberates the subject from the law: *not* under the law, *but* under grace. This 'not ..., but ...'-construction is Badiou's point of departure for his interpretation of Paul's conception of the law, and, for him, it forms a binary opposition between law and grace, which represent two heterogeneous principles: 'For Paul, the Christ-event is heterogenous to the law.'[29] By this account of grace, Badiou tends to embrace a dualistic Paul, which does have problematic implications for his appreciation of the role of the Jewish identity in Paul.[30] Moreover, in this way, Badiou tends to miss the complex and peculiar logic Paul develops when speaking about the law, as discussed in the previous section.

Yet, such a dualistic account of *nomos* and *charis* is not sufficient. In order to get a better understanding of the Pauline 'state of exception', two other elements need to be highlighted in relation to Paul's notion of grace: (1) the relation between grace and contingency, and (2) the specific failure of the law.

(1) Grace cannot be anticipated, calculated or deduced in any way. Grace is indeed 'incalculable grace'.[31] This incalculability should be understood in contrast to a specific form of philosophical rationality.[32] The term 'grace' stands for that which goes beyond the order of the foreseeable and the anticipatable. Grace can in no way be deduced from the situation or the present order of the world in which it presents itself. Among others, Badiou has a keen sense of this incalculability. According to him, Paul preaches the 'exceptional "but" of grace', and grace is 'a pure gift' and 'without cause'.[33] Hence, there is no ground or reason to be found in the present order of the world that explains grace. For this reason, grace is, from the perspective of the contemporary world, as much a miracle as it is unthinkable.

With the latter descriptions, we get to the heart of the form of rationality that gets no grip on grace, which goes back to Leibniz's *principle of sufficient reason*. This principle holds that everything that is or happens has a sufficient reason or ground to be or to happen. We can account for everything that is or happens, according to this principle, and eventually we can even pronounce upon what can and cannot be or happen. This principle then enables us to completely rely on our knowledge of reality and to build on the expectations we deduce from our knowledge. When we lift the word 'grace' from Paul's vocabulary, we do so to indicate that, for Paul, the event transcends this philosophical rationality of sufficient reason. This event can in no way be deduced from what we know or could know. The event introduces something entirely unexpected in light of the principle of reason and forms a genuine exception to it. Thought that strives to provide sufficient grounds and reasons for everything will come up against and collapse in the face of a reality characterised by grace. To capture this, several authors, such as Breton and Badiou, have characterised grace as a form of contingency.[34] Breton delicately notes that Pauline grace is 'a gratuitousness that excludes any justificatory recourse to a "principle of reason," be it external or internal. From Paul's point of view, grace is the religious form of contingency.'[35]

Grace thus gives contingency its own place in Paul's thought, and it cannot be included in a comprehensive dialectic system. Yet, in line with what I have argued in the previous chapters, it also does not need to lead to a variation of an anti-dialectic crypto-dualism. In a Pauline political theology, contingency does not concern the arbitrariness of a sovereign will, as Schmitt suggests, but is rather encountered under the heading of grace. The dialectic of exception, as described in Chapter 4, appears as a dialectic of grace as soon as we see that grace is the groundless preference for the exception to laws and regularities. Grace is another name for the Pauline exception.

(2) Moreover, in relation to the law an exception in the form of grace is necessary for Paul. In this context, we turn, as promised to Rom. 7.[36] The law forbids all kinds of things and thus makes us aware of what is sinful (Rom. 7:7), but because the law forbids things, it arouses desires and 'sinful passions' in us (Rom. 7:5). Or as Paul specifies:

> But sin, seizing an opportunity in the commandment, produced in me all kinds of covetousness. Apart from the law sin lies dead. I was once alive apart from the law, but when the commandment came, sin revived and I died, and the very commandment that promised life proved to be death to me. For sin, seizing an opportunity in the commandment, deceived me and through it killed me. (Rom. 7:8–11)

The law introduces the possibility of sin, even providing sin its power and ability, so Paul writes. Because the law sets boundaries, crossing this boundary does not only become possible but also alluring. Paul uses the contrast between life and death here as a contrast between two modes of living, between a dead life and a true life. Law promises genuine life. Life without the law, in which there was no mention of sin, was apparently not much more than a dead life. Nevertheless the law does not succeed in its intention. Instead of awakening us to a new life, it awakens sin in us. Despite the fact that the law is 'holy', and 'the commandment is holy and just and good' (Rom. 7:12) – and it cannot be otherwise, according to Paul, because it is the expression of the first covenant – the law does not lead to life. Sin uses the law to entice us to break the law. Instead of us coming to life, sin comes to life in us; thus, the law leads to death. This brings Paul to the following troubling conclusion: 'the very commandment that promised life proved to be death to me.' The promise of a new life, which Paul perceives in the covenant between God and Abraham, ultimately does not come to flourish in the law of Moses, built upon the promise, but is actually in danger because the law, albeit aimed at life, through its complex relationship with sin actually leads to death. The law is the work of the spirit – it is, after all, sign and seal of the promise – but it becomes its opposite because we are 'of the flesh', 'sold into slavery under sin' (Rom. 7:14). Hence, we see that the original intent and significance of the law has turned into a crisis, which is here addressed under the heading of 'sin'.

Sin is often linked to a specific understanding of the will and of acts of freedom. The issue of the human will only arise once it is taken seriously that we, despite our insight into what is good, still prefer to do evil, in order to deliberately break the law. This idea was foreign to Socrates: for him, the correct understanding of the issue was also sufficient reason and incentive to lead a just life. This point of view is perhaps not so strange when we consider that in ancient culture, the understanding of the true always involves a change of our mode of living. In principle, there is no leeway between mode of living and mode of thinking for the philosopher. Every deviation from the true life is a sign of an incorrect understanding. Also with Paul it seems incorrect to imagine that the problem of sin should simply be understood from human free will, which sins despite real understanding. Paul famously writes:

> I do not understand my own actions. For I do not do what I want, but I do the very thing I hate. Now if I do what I do not want, I agree that the law is good. But in fact it is no longer I that do it, but sin that dwells within me. For I know that nothing good dwells within me, that is, in my flesh. I can will what is right, but I cannot do it. For I do not do the good I want, but the evil I do not want is what I do. Now if I do what I do not want, it is no longer I that do it, but sin that dwells within me. So I find it to be a law that when I want to do what is good, evil lies close at hand. (Rom. 7:15–21)

Paul notes that he acts contrary to what he understands and to what he wants. His understanding *and* his will both agree with the law. Yet, sin, which works in him as a power stronger than both his understanding and will, does the opposite. Will, then, is not an active ability that leads to sin; we find here rather the idea of a subconscious or unintentional active sin in us.

Badiou's summary of this problematic is insightful and helpful: '*Sin is the life of desire as autonomy, as automatism.*'[37] Autonomy does not mean *our* autonomy – after all, we appear incapable of imposing the law on ourselves – but the automatism of sin. Sin imposes its own law on us, and we find this lawfulness in ourselves as a heteronomy – as the law of another – and, consequently, as an automatism. Violating the law of God is not intentional. By contrast, as Paul writes: 'I delight in the law of God in my inmost self' (Rom. 7:22). Hence, sin does not happen wilfully, but automatically. Thus, sin concerns an obstruction or caesura between thinking and acting that prevents our understanding from being expressed in our actions. Paul indeed understands what is just, but he lacks the power to make his actions be guided by this understanding. Death as an attitude to life is nothing but this caesura or obstruction, as Badiou argues: '[K]nowledge and will, on the one hand, agency and action, on the other, are entirely disconnected.'[38] He continues: 'Basically, sin is not so much a fault as living thought's inability to prescribe action.' Sin is the name for a deep powerlessness and inability in us.

Wasserman shows that the incapacity to influence action with thought is a theme more common in antiquity.[39] The *pathos-logos* nexus, which we discussed before, is helpful here. Paul describes a situation in which reason does not rule over passions, but where the passions themselves rule. Wasserman parallels Paul's self-analysis in Rom. 7:23 – where he writes that with his mind he agrees with the law, but in him sin is stronger than this mind – with Medea's self-analysis in Euripides' eponymous tragedy. Medea expresses the struggle between reason and anger in comparable terms: 'And I know to what bad things I go, but louder than all thought doth cry Anger, which maketh man's worst misery.'[40] Such similarities are indeed striking. However, they should not make us lose track of the uniqueness of Paul's self-analysis. Despite the parallel between Medea and Paul, the latter argues that this is not only his own singular situation but rather that of everyone. The caesura between *logos* and *pathos* has become universal.

The outlines of the crisis in which Paul – or, rather, Paul's God – feels compelled to proclaim a state of exception and to suspend the law, now become clear. The law, which is supposed to lead to life, apparently leads to death. The law, which is supposed to draw a distinction between those who uphold it and those who do not, apparently draws a distinction between no one and everyone, because no one observes the law (Rom. 3:10–20). In this way, the machinery of the law is deadlocked. In this situation, a state of exception is proclaimed to deactivate this mechanism of law and sin and to annul the distinction between everyone and no one it generates. The terms 'grace' and 'justification' obtain their full meaning at this point. Justification is the reuniting of thoughts and actions, of mode of thinking and mode of living, by removing the obstruction of sin.[41] In whichever way one conceives of it – Lutheran or otherwise – the point of Pauline justification is that the power of justice and righteousness is given (back) to humans in the ability to express thought in action, and this is the very work of grace. Resurrection or living according to the spirit means that sin no longer 'dwells within me' (Rom. 7:17) but that 'it is Christ who lives in me' (Gal. 2:20).

Paul often describes the latter condition as another law, the law of Christ. While the letter of the law nests between thought and action like a wall separating them, the law of Christ reunites them again, thus reviving and quickening the human. This living law is not chiselled on stone tablets (2 Cor. 3:7); rather, the members of the communities to which Paul writes are themselves a 'letter of Christ, prepared by us, written not with ink but with the Spirit of the living God, not on tablets of stone but on tablets of human hearts' (2 Cor. 3:3). The image used here and its accompanying logic mirror that of Socrates as described in his conversation with Phaedrus in Plato's eponymous dialogue.[42] According to Socrates, normal writing, in ink, is vulnerable to all kinds of dangers, which result in it not leading to true understanding but rather to deceptions. Paul traces and radicalises a comparable problem in his description of the law and its works. Writing, for Socrates, could lead to knowledge, but rather leads to misunderstandings, deceptions and distortions; similarly, the law, for Paul, could and should lead to the good life but has instead led to sin. Socrates opposes normal writing to writing in the soul: writing in the soul is an image for understanding and can for this reason not be deceptive or distortive. Likewise, Paul describes the law of the spirit as the law written in the heart that does not remain external to us or our abilities.

Ancient culture developed the term *nomos empsuchos* for this. I have used it before to describe those who embody the law or, even better, en-soul the law, as the Greek term suggests, and are inspired by justification. *Nomos empsuchos* is the living, inspired law that opposes the written law. Unlike the dead law that is only written in letters, this living law is lived by us. The term is used in the first place for the sovereign who embodies and justifies the law, who is the saviour of the people, and who therefore belongs with the gods. It is not surprising that this title is also used for Christ, but it can in fact also be used as the name for those who have risen with Christ, as Paul explains, and in whose soul justification is written according to the principle of the spirit.

KATARGĒSIS AND CHARIS

Let us continue the discussion of the relation between law and grace by reflecting upon the notion of *katargēsis* in more detail. To this end, let us begin by returning to some of the conclusions of the first section. In his struggle with Moses, Paul certainly positions the law of works against those of faith and the promise, but he also argues that in the history of the people of God, prescription and promise intrinsically belong together. The law, including circumcision, is a sign and seal of the promise: the legal prescription refers back to the promise as its origin. In sum, Paul discerns the promise in the prescription, which transcends the prescriptive character of the law and for this reason leads us to the pre-legal sphere from which the law stems, characterised by justice, promise and faith. Consequently, without righteousness as the basic characteristic of that sphere, the law is ultimately powerless. However, the focus on the law and its demands tends to conceal this primordial sphere from our view and to replace it. In this way, the law threatens to cut its ties with the primordial sphere of the promise by presenting itself as foundation: the law of works positions itself as grounds for justice; the law autonomises itself from its pre-legal sphere, thus causing its own crisis. To this problem, Paul protests: 'the law [...] does not annul [or: deactivate, *katargeō*] a covenant' (Gal. 3:17).

Let us focus on this *katargēsis*. The law cannot deactivate the covenant. The covenant remains active, even if the law presents itself as having become independent from it. In Chapter 3, we saw that *katargeō* is opposed to the Greek *energeō* and Aristotle's *energeia*, actuality or being-at-work, which contains the Greek *ergon*, work. For Aristotle *dunamis*, possibility or potentiality, finds its *telos*, aim or completion, in this *energeia*. For Paul, however, the completion of *dunamis* no longer lies in a specific human work or activity, but is completely due to grace. Thwarting the Aristotelean order, the apostle writes: 'but he said to me: "My grace is sufficient for you, for power [*dunamis*] is made perfect [*teleitai*; related to *telos*] in weakness [*astheneia*]"' (2 Cor. 12:9).[43] The perfection of the *dunamis* of *charis* is not the completed work (*ergon*) of the law but is rather found in an inability or weakness, *astheneia*. This sounds as a strange, alien form of perfection. In which sense can weakness be the perfection of a particular power or potentiality?

Agamben's remarkable reflections on potentiality – not only in his study on Paul but spread over many of his works – might be helpful here.[44] For him, the phrase 'I can', as in 'I can do X' or 'I can be Y', necessarily implies 'I can also not do X' or 'I can also not be Y'. This is the very nature of potentiality. When the law reigns, the question of whether I can complete the works of the law is not a potentiality in this sense because the law *prescribes* these works: I am under the obligation to them. Whether one is of the Kantian persuasion *Du kannst denn du sollst*, 'You can because you have to', or rather of the Sartrian-Derridean persuasion *Tu dois donc tu ne peux pas*, 'You have to therefore you cannot', in both cases the emphasis is on the obligation. This means that with respect to the law, we cannot not obey. This might be Agamben's interpretation of the Sartrian-Derridean *Tu dois donc tu ne peux pas*: because the law obliges us to a work, we are no longer in a position of potentiality, not only because we might now be able to keep this law, but because the obligation robs us of the potentiality, which includes both 'I can complete this work' and 'I can also not complete this work'. In this context, Paul suggests that grace returns *dunamis* to us which is completed in weakness. *Astheneia* here has a double sense: by being aware of one's incapacity to uphold to law, one cultivates an openness or leeway where grace can appear; more importantly, however, with respect to the law where the completion of the work is the only option, grace truly returns *dunamis* to us, granting the possibility *not* to complete the work.[45]

By specifying the law as the law *of works*, a space of play opens up in Paul's vocabulary to reserve the term 'law' for a larger category in which a distinction can be drawn between the law of works (*nomos tōn ergōn*) and the law of faith (*nomos pisteōs*). That is not an ornamental gesture in Paul's rhetoric, as Agamben observes, because 'the law [of works] has become entirely unobservable, and, as such, only functions as a universal principle of imputation'.[46] One can interpret the nature of this imputation as one likes, but it is in fact nothing other than the expression of the Pauline basic given that the original power or the original ability of the law cannot reach completion. Moreover, if righteousness is the genuine concern and ground for the original ability of the law, we encounter here the very aporia of the law: the law eventually offers no passageway to complete justice in or by works. Hence, as in Rom. 7, the law is an obstruction.

Yet, in the pre-legal sphere – and now it is important to emphasise that this is the sphere preceding the law *of works* – no opposition between *pistis* and *nomos* exists. In this sphere, faith – understood as trust and trustworthiness – and law belong together, as one can easily see when one considers the fundamental role played by the promise in this sphere. The one who promises is (or is not) trustworthy, *pistos*. Hence, the phenomenon of the promise necessarily includes *pistis*. Moreover, every promise brings with it an obligation to keep the promise, that is, a *nomos*. In this sense, *pistis* and *nomos* are always connected rather than opposed in the phenomenon of the promise.[47]

In *The Sacrament of Language*, devoted to the oath, Agamben points out that the promise is a basic characteristic of human language.[48] The relationship between word and deed – a variation of the relationship between thinking and acting – is understood in terms of vow and commitment: the one who speaks implicitly pledges and commits to act in accordance with what they say. *Either* this promise is kept faithfully, in which case one's speaking is a *blessing*. In the truthful promise and by showing oneself to be trustworthy, our ability to keep our promise is fulfilled. *Or* the speaker does not – or cannot – keep their word. In that case, language and thought become *curse* and *sin*.[49]

In this context, the specific status of the law of works can be accounted for. It is the law that has become independent and isolated from the pre-legal sphere of the promise. Yet, if the link to the promise is severed, the law also loses the connection between word and deed because this connection resides in the (truthful) promise. Thus, the independent legal sphere is handed over to the curse of language, separating word and deed since it has lost every connection to the source that can connect them: the ability to promise truthfully and to keep one's promise faithfully. On its own, the law becomes an external norm that has lost its relation to the promissory dimension which it was supposed to supplement, not substitute.[50]

This analysis offers a crucial ingredient for any understanding of Paul's antinomianism. Sin, or the crisis of the law of works, is for Paul the name for the caesura between word and deed or thinking and acting, so disturbingly described in Rom. 7. This caesura, following Rom. 4, is the consequence of the isolation and the becoming independent of the law: it loses its ground, the promise connecting word and deed, and hands us over to the *incapacity* to be truthful. This reveals what Badiou's analysis is lacking. For him, there is nothing more to the law than the automated, independent law that obstructs our actions. Yet, for Paul, the law has its original resource in the original ability to promise and to be truthful and faithful to this promise; the law's *crisis* consists in being isolated from this resource.

Consequently, Paul's antinomianism is not a rejection of the law as such, but rather of the claim that the law can function independently. Differently put, the law and its prescriptions can only express justice if they are upheld in the correct *enactment*, namely one that is not guided by the letter but by the spirit of the law and that only follows the letter because and in so far as it expresses the spirit of the law. We may perhaps describe this attitude with another *hōs mē*-formula: one follows the letter of the law *as not* following it. Following the letter of the law for the sake of this letter is betraying and incapacitating its original resource. Following the letter of the law for the sake of the spirit of the law expressed therein, however, enacts the law by trusting the promise of justice that grounds it: only then one *uses* the law as not *abusing* it.

One of the discussions regarding the notion of *pistis* concerns Paul's expression *pistis Christou*: should it be translated as the trustworthiness or trust *of* Christ Himself or the trust *in* Christ.[51] In a Lutheran interpretation, which specifically concerns itself with the question of whether people truly have faith in Christ, the latter meaning dominates. However, in the context of an understanding of *pistis* and *nomos* as suggested above, the former meaning gains in significance. If the independent and isolated *nomos* represents our inability to be trustworthy and truthful, then the trust and trustworthiness of Christ offers an alternative for Paul. When the apostle emphatically posits that the law of works cannot abolish the original promise, he also means that this original promise has to be kept and fulfilled *differently*. The old fulfilment in the law has led to a crisis. Therefore, faith and law have to be united differently. The possibility of such a different unity is termed 'grace'. The provenance of this grace resembles the Sceptic and Kierkegaardian approach of dialectic discussed before: confronted with an aporia, one should not try to overcome it, but one should rather abandon the chosen course. Paul's *katargēsis* of the law brings with it, unexpectedly, the shadow of grace – the exception to maintaining the law – that raises the prospect of a different fulfilment of the promise. With a view to the relationship between *pistis* and *nomos*, it is not so strange that the *pistis* of Christ forms the grace that re-establishes a connection between *pistis* and *nomos* in the law of faith.

In this way, the law is *not* opposed to grace. Rather, grace is the exceptional element that is needed to overcome the opposition of faith and law of works. A dialectic relation between faith, law and grace thus arises. Because *nomos* originally supplements the promise, one finds positive comments about the law in Paul's letters: as a whole, the covenant comprises prescriptions *and* promise. According to Paul, the promise of justice and of a flourishing life – the number of descendants promised to Abraham – lies at the heart of the covenant, and for this reason he can speak about a law of faith as the result of the graceful reconnection of law and faith. When Paul writes: 'Do we then overthrow the law by this faith? By no means! On the contrary, we uphold the law' (Rom. 3:31), it does not contradict his analysis of *katargēsis* but actually confirms the status of the law and its origin. Because promise and faith form the heart of the law, Paul does not abolish the law, but the law can be pneumatically reinterpreted as the law of faith. Similarly, to emphasise this once more, 'righteousness apart from law' (Rom. 3:21) should not be understood as a negation of the law – 'outlaw' – but as the original righteousness that inspires and fulfils the law.[52] For Paul, the tension between promise and commandments is for this reason not a tension between two opposite or mutually exclusive principles. Promise and prescription belong together as much as trust and obligation. If I entrust myself to something or someone, I also fulfil the obligations that show my loyalty. If I promise someone that I will do something, I am also thereby obliged to deliver what I promised. That is the natural connection between promise and obligation. The obligations of the law appear not to be redeemable when they are separated from this original trust and justice.

In the case of the covenant between God and His people, this natural connection between promise and obligation means that trust is expected from both parties. For the people, this reciprocity means that they have to observe the law. When one of the parties cannot fulfil its obligations, however – which is the case in the crisis that Paul perceives in God's people – the other party can ward off this crisis by giving more than might be expected in a reciprocal relationship. This 'more' is expressed in the excessive faithfulness of God that Paul evokes under the label of 'grace' (*charis*). In Rom. 11:15–16, we encountered an analogous difference between *katallagē*, expressing economic reciprocity, and the transgression of reciprocity expressed by *zōē ek nekrōn*, life from death. Grace similarly quickens and revivifies a relation of which the reciprocity is in a crisis. The inability of the people creates a space between law and faith in which grace may manifest itself. Let us emphasise 'may': grace is not necessary; there is no reason why the party who did not meet their obligation should be met by the other party with excessive faithfulness. Therefore, grace is rather marked by contingency and unfounded preference. Thus, grace is the dialectic response to the caesura that emerged between *nomos* and *pistis* through the crisis of the covenant.

All of this, however, does not mean that there is no longer space for the notion of good and just works or that the antinomianism of Paul would be a licence to do whatever we please. In reference to 2 Cor. 9:8 – 'God is able to provide you with every blessing in abundance, so that by always having enough of everything [*autarkeia*], you may share abundantly in every good work' – Agamben affirms the connection of grace to abundance and excess. God gives in grace the sovereign (*autarkeia*, rendered as 'enough of everything') ability to do an abundance of good deeds beyond the obligations of the law. The human capacity to act is freed through grace to be used (*chrēsis*) again; to use *as not abusing*. Along the line of this interpretation, this sovereign ability is connected to the life of the spirit and Paul's understanding of love that fulfils the law.[53] The space of grace cannot be put in writing, as in the Mosaic Law: the fixing of obligations in letters chiselled into stone tables cannot do justice to this grace that exceeds all set obligations.

This interplay between *katargēsis, charis* and *chrēsis* shows how grace, in the wake of the suspension of the law, gives humans (back) the ability to abundantly use righteousness and to reunite word and deed or mode of thinking and mode of living by *pistis* – *pistis* in its double sense of the human capacity to be true to their word and of the divine being true to the promise to gracefully grant this capacity. This release of righteousness to be used *is* the good cause, *is* grace itself. Grace thus comes equipped with a mode of the living of the Pauline community. With this, we are at the threshold of the next chapter. What is this Pauline community that cannot be institutionalised because its form can only be lived and 'not chiseled on stone tablets' (2 Cor. 3:3)?

NOTES

1 Taubes, *Die politische Theologie des Paulus*, 37/24.
2 Many authors interested in the question of the *eschaton* and the end of history – one of the themes permeating the turn to Paul in the 1990s – are (also) concerned with the politico-theological problem of the *katechon*, the restraining force. The question then is how to understand Paul's reference to this restraining or withholding force in 2 Thess. 2, delaying the Parousia. It seems to me that *katechon* is a rather marginal and somewhat peculiar topic in Paul's letters, even though it had an important politico-theological reception as De Wilde, 'Politics between Times', shows. This reception places this theme in light of an apocalyptic, nihilistic reading, one which I aim to avoid.

The discussion between Taubes and Schmitt on the *katechon*, displaying their different sense and appreciation of the *eschaton*, clearly displays how the question of the *katechon* concerns the apocalypse. Schmitt's conservative attitude guides him to want to maintain the state. He supports the idea of a restraining force not so much to delay the coming of the Lord, but especially to prevent and delay the arrival of the 'human of lawlessness', who will create utter chaos. The former, by contrast, is willing to accept this chaos because it will bring the arrival of the Lord closer, that is, the full transformation of the world (Taubes, *Die politische Theologie des Paulus*, 139/103). Here, the temporal relation to the *eschaton* is fully understood in terms of a future present of the Parousia which is preceded by another future present, namely the presence and arrival of *ho antrōpos tēs anomias*

(2 Thess. 2:3), the human of lawlessness. The difference between the Schmittian and Taubesian relation to this future depends on their different investment in the present socio-political order; see also Muller, *Professor of Apocalypse*, 503.

Yet, the connection between *katechon* and apocalypse is not a necessary one, as Heidegger shows. Although Heidegger's treatment is only very marginal, he interprets *katechon* in line with his account of temporality shaped by his interpretation of the Parousia. The imminent arrival of *ho antrōpos tēs anomias* intensifies the distress and concern of Christian life in the present (Heidegger, *Phänomenologie des religiösen Lebens*, 107–8/75–6, 156/110–11). Hence, for Heidegger, the reference to the *katechon* does not add anything substantially new. (Consequently, I am not convinced by Coyne's bold claim in *Heidegger's Confessions*, 40–9, that 'the mystery of the *katechon* lies at the very heart of Heidegger's commentary'.)

3   Taubes, *Die politische Theologie des Paulus*, 96/69.
4   Schmitt, *Politische Theologie*, 13/xliv. Translation slightly adapted.
5   Ibid., 19/13.
6   Ibid., 18/12.
7   Ibid., 19/13.
8   In what follows, I use 'state of exception' rather than the more common 'state of emergency', in order to stress the link to the concept of the exception.
9   Schmitt, *Der Begriff des Politischen*, 26–45/25–45.
10 Terpstra, 'The Management of Distinctions', 254–8.
11 Schmitt, *Politische Theologie*, 43/36.
12 Taubes, *Die politische Theologie des Paulus*, 27/16.
13 Ibid., 36/23.
14 Ibid., 72/51.
15 Schmitt, *Der Begriff des Politischen*, 64/65.
16 Taubes, *Die politische Theologie des Paulus*, 42/28. See also Welborn, 'Jacob Taubes', 71.
17 See also 1 Cor. 15:23 for the identification of Christ's resurrection with *aparchē*, the firstfruits.
18 Taubes, *Die politische Theologie des Paulus*, 42/28.
19 Also see Agamben, *Homo Sacer*, 48–56/41–8.
20 Žižek, *The Fragile Absolute*, 59, 85–90.
21 Žižek, *The Puppet and the Dwarf*, 14–18.
22 Agamben, *Il tempo che resta*, 113/115.
23 See also ibid., 111/114.
24 Jennings, *Outlaw Justice*.
25 Agamben, *Il tempo che resta*, 101/107.
26 Jennings, *Outlaw Justice*, 69.
27 It is possible to further extend this analysis by applying the law to 'normal circumstances'. Applying the law is never self-evident or automatic. The

application requires (or is) interpretation: judges decide whether and how a law applies to a specific case or not. As Derrida notes in *Force de loi*, confronted with a case, judges have to decide if it indeed falls under a certain law or if it constitutes an exception. Is this latitude of the judge the space of a decision guided by a sense of justice or a mere arbitrary one?

28 Badiou, *Saint Paul*, 67/63.
29 Ibid., 60/57. When Agamben, in his reflection on the contrast between law and promise, writes that Paul does not oppose 'two heterogeneous principles' and 'exclud[e] works in favor of faith', (Agamben, *Il tempo che resta*, 112/119), he does not only aim to correct Luther but also Badiou.
30 By insisting on this contrast of law and grace, which returns also in the opposition between law and faith and law and promise, Badiou adopts a fundamentally different attitude with regards to the Jewish identity than Paul and Taubes do. For a critical reading regarding Badiou's (and Žižek's) relation to both Judaism and Islam, see Topolski, 'The Islamophobic Inheritance of the Resurrected Paul'.
31 Badiou, *Saint Paul*, 69/65.
32 See several considerations in Van der Heiden, *Ontology after Ontotheology*.
33 Badiou, *Saint Paul*, 77/73, 81/77.
34 Badiou speaks of 'radical contingency'; ibid., 81/77. He emphatically connects event, grace and exception; ibid., 67/63.
35 Breton, *Saint Paul*, 63/92.
36 See, e.g., Badiou, *Saint Paul*, 83–9/79–85. On this point, he is indebted to Lacan, *Le Séminaire, Livre VII*, 101; see De Kesel, *Eros and Ethics*, 163ff.
37 Badiou, *Saint Paul*, 83/79.
38 Ibid., 87/83.
39 Wasserman, 'Paul among the Ancient Philosophers', and Wasserman, *The Death of the Soul in Romans 7*. Also see Stowers, 'Paul as a Hero of Subjectivity', 170–2. Arendt, *Between Past and Future*, 159, also points to this similarity.
40 Euripides, *Medea*, 57 [= 1078–80; see Euripides, *Cyclops, Alcestis, Medea*, 382–3]. See also Wasserman, 'Paul among the Ancient Philosophers', 72. In Arendt, *Between Past and Future*, 295n14, the first part of this citation reads as: 'and I know which evils I am about to commit, but *thumos* is stronger than my deliberations.'
41 Badiou, *Saint Paul*, 87–8/83–4.
42 Plato, *Phaedrus* 267a.
43 See Agamben, *Il tempo che resta*, 91–4/95–9.
44 See, e.g., the corresponding essays in Agamben, *Potentialities*, as well as the reflections in chap. 3 of part I of his *Homo Sacer*.
45 See also Van der Heiden, 'Interpreters of the Divine'.
46 Agamben, *Il tempo che resta*, 101–2/108, which refers to Rom. 3 where the law as universal imputation is discussed.
47 Ibid., 106–7/113–14.
48 Agamben, *Il sacramento del linguaggio*, 74–81/54–9.

49 This double role of language is reminiscent of Heidegger's analysis of language in *Being and Time*, § 44. On the one hand, a statement – *Aussage* – is capable of letting a particular being be seen as it has been discovered. This possibility is, in Agamben's terminology, the very blessing of language. This blessing depends on the intrinsic relation between language and discoveredness, *Entdecktheit*. On the other hand, however, a statement can also be treated as a being itself, used by people *separated* from its capacity to show something in its discoveredness. This is the curse of language, in Agamben's terminology. See also the next footnote.

50 Agamben speaks of the two unrelated principles, *nomos*'s 'normative and the promissive elements', which are opposed in *nomos* itself, which makes it a dialectic notion marked by the opposition between these two principles; because of this, for Paul, *nomos* is subject to either its promissive blessing or its normative curse; see *Il tempo che resta*, 91/95.

51 See, e.g., Morgan, 'Narratives of *Pistis* in Paul and Deutero-Paul', 165–6; Morgan, *Roman Faith and Christian Faith*; Gignac, 'Agamben's Paul', 168; Petersen, 'Paul's Use of *Pistis/Pisteuein* as Epitome of Axial Age Religion', 241–2; Žižek, *The Puppet and the Dwarf*, 102; Agamben, *Il tempo che resta*, 107–8/114–15.

52 Ibid., 101/107.

53 Ibid., 102/108.

6. Community, Exception and Outcast

The Pauline political issue par excellence is the establishment of a new people of God. Hence, the question of community goes at the heart of it. With an eye to Rom. 13, it is often suggested that Paul wants to leave the authority of the Roman Empire largely untouched. As, for instance, Wright summarises: 'Most have assumed that Romans 13 means that Paul was politically quiescent.'[1] Yet, his continued identification with groups that count for nothing in the existing socio-political order of the world grants these letters political and revolutionary potential. How should we understand this identification, and what kind of community is established by it?[2]

A basic idea of our modern legal system, as expressed by Article 7 of the Universal Declaration of Human Rights, is that 'All are equal before the law'. Yet, who exactly is, and who determines who is, this 'all' or 'everyone'? Who shares in this community of equals before the law? A Pauline approach to community departs from the viewpoint that the 'all' is not all and that, despite any pretence of the socio-political order to represent and do justice to 'all', there are those excluded from this 'all'. They are exception and outcast. In this sense, the Pauline approach to community is the socio-political analogue of the ontological issue we addressed in Chapter 3 concerning the *kosmos* and the non-beings that are symptomatic of the crisis of this *kosmos*.

Schmitt's genealogy of the legal order provides a rather disturbing answer to the above questions. Equality before the law reflects the homogeneity of the political community. This homogeneity, however, is based on a preceding, constitutive separation of friends and enemies. The community of equals before the law is that of 'friends'. Consequently, in the equality before the law, a preceding dispute is inscribed and no equality is granted to the enemies of the state; rather, they are identified as the outcast and scum of this political community and are banned from it. They form the all's perverse core, hidden from view. If we stick to the notion of an order in which *everyone* is equal before the law, these enemies can only appear in the paradoxical guise of 'the enemy of all'.[3] This 'all', then, exists only by the grace of the outcasts not counted among the community of equals.

Hence, in the context of Schmitt's thought, the stakes of a Pauline approach to the question of community are affirmed. It is only possible to speak of an 'all' of the political community – whether it be in the grandiloquent, cosmopolitan form of 'humankind' or 'the open society' or in the parochial form of one's own nation, culture, tribe or people – on the basis of a specific remnant excluded from this 'all'. Rather than the state of exception in a Schmittian sense, it is this group of outcasts that captures the primary, political significance of the notion of exception. Agamben suggests as much: 'We shall give the name *relation of exception* to the extreme form of relation by which something is included solely through its exclusion.'[4] Enigmatic as this might sound, it is exactly this relation that applies to the Schmittian 'enemy of all': based on their exclusion from this 'all', the enemies are paradoxically 'included' by this 'all'. Rancière's expression proposed in *Disagreement*, namely *une part des sans-part*, that is, a part consisting of those who have no part or share in the 'all' of society and its distributions, offers one way of describing this political meaning of the exception, and I discuss this expression in the third section.

In this constellation, the demand for another kind of community arises, namely one for which the exclusion of a part that has no share in the all is *not* constitutive. This politico-philosophical issue as such and its many tangible, present-day examples clearly exceed the boundaries of this study. Yet, the philosophical relevance of the question of the Pauline community is found in this issue. If the exception that is banned from the whole forms the core problem for thinking another kind of community, then how to conceive of a community that includes this exception differently?

Moreover, in the preceding chapters, we have seen how Paul engages with the question of the identity of those belonging to the communities he addresses and the implications of their being called. In 1 Corinthians, the community in Corinth is identified as the outcast of the world. In 1 Thessalonians, Paul repeatedly addresses the members of the community in Thessaloniki in terms of their having come into a new mode of being. Their calling, *klēsis*, radically changed their mode of living and thinking. Together, they form the *ekklēsia*, the community or assembly of those summoned to this new mode of being.[5] Hence, this community comprises members with knowledge of their change. They are mindful of this change in how they live, act and think. One of the questions that need to be addressed in this chapter is how the community of outcasts as the part without part relates to this Pauline community of those who are called. These two senses of community are related but not simply identical.

Finally, there are different and conflicting approaches to the Pauline community available in the literature. The controversy concerning the exact nature of the Pauline community guides us in this chapter. Interestingly, this controversy mirrors the tension between the all and the exception just mentioned. It is expressed in the following alternative. Is Paul the thinker of a *universal* community in which everyone shares, or can share, equally? This proposal connects several, different proponents, ranging from Paul's universalism elaborated in *The New Perspective on Paul* by Dunn, to considerations about the Pauline heritage for Western thought concerning ideas about the individual, as a study by Siedentop argues,[6] and to the sense of equality and emancipation developed in French political thought. Or is Paul rather the thinker of an intensified sense of *particularity* and exception? Authors who pay particular attention to the Jewish background of Paul, such as Taubes and Boyarin, seem to support this proposal, but also the specific ethnic dimension of Paul's proclamation contains elements of this proposal. To clarify this controversy and find my own way among the different accounts of the Pauline community, I engage with the different positions concerning Paul's universalism and particularism and, in dialogue with several authors, I propose which balance between them is required by a Pauline dialectic of exception.

ALL ISRAEL

Let me begin by continuing a line of inquiry developed in the previous chapter. The political impact of Paul's letters ensues from the crisis of the old people of God, founded by Moses and his law. The impossibility of meeting the requirements of the Mosaic Law brings God's people into a state of exception that requires the suspension of this law. In this state of exception, the true political question is that of the establishment of a new community that is no longer the people of the law but rather the people of the promise. In contrast to Schmitt's antagonism of friend and enemy as the vehicle for the sovereign to establish a new homogeneous community, I argued that Paul does not simply and only position Israel as 'enemy of the gospel', but rather understands Israel from within a dialectic, pneumatic logic. How exactly does Paul do that in terms of community?

Taubes's analyses, for whom the word *pan* or *pas*, the whole and all, is a keyword in Paul's letters, provide a first, important orientation. 1 Corinthians, as he suggests, is a 'whole fugue around the word *pas*'.[7] Yet, the whole expressed by *pas* or *pan* is not simply the totality of all nations or of a universal community of each and everyone. The essential focus is rather *pas Israēl*: 'And so all Israel will be saved' (Rom. 11:26). This verse is the conclusion of the dialectic reasoning unfolded in Rom. 11. Israel at first rejected the gospel, and so Paul became the apostle of the nations, but in order to make Israel jealous. Paul's universalism – his going to other nations and including everyone in his proclamation – is therefore not the final destination or eventual aim of his proclamation. Emphasising this, Taubes argues that, for Paul, the universal or cosmopolitan community that comprises all nations is but a moment in a logic that goes one step further. The Scylla and Charybdis through which Paul attempts to navigate when it comes to the establishment of community, are here represented by the names of Hegel and Schmitt. Against Schmitt, Taubes argues that the nation Paul founds is not 'all nations' minus its enemies, and against a certain Hegel, he argues that 'all nations' does not simply mean universalism. The genuine completion is found in Rom. 11:26; the true goal is the salvation of all Israel as already described by the prophet Isaiah (Isa. 59:20).

This dialectic that absorbs the universal moment – 'all nations' – in a dialectic of salvation of Israel confirms that God's preference for Israel is not simply an arbitrary point of departure ultimately suspended in a universalism of the proclamation of the gospel to all people but is rather the permanent guiding principle of the dialectic of salvation: 'So it's a universalism, but one that signifies the selection of Israel. Only that Israel is now being transfigured, and then in the end it says *pas* Israel.'[8] Paul's universalism cannot be understood when it is no longer viewed through the lens of God's inexplicable preference for a singular people. These claims by Taubes are indeed supported by the imagery used in Rom. 11:17–24 of the branches and the tree: Israel is called the natural branch of the cultivated olive tree, while the Romans are branches of wild olive trees grafted on a cultivated one. This difference between wild and cultivated olive trees – *agrielaios* versus *kallielaios* (Rom. 11:24) – remains intact and is not suspended as if it were indifferent. Israel is and remains a natural, *kata phusin*, branch of the cultivated olive tree and the Romans are grafted 'contrary to nature', *para phusin*, onto the cultivated olive tree.

At this point, it is intriguing to see that while Schmitt attempts to provide Kierkegaard's notion of exception with a politico-philosophical translation, Taubes understands much better what Kierkegaard actually meant by the dialectic struggle between the universal and the exception. If the exception knows to maintain its position in the battle with the universal, this universal will confirm the status of the exception and even prefer and elect the exception *as exception*. The exception changes in the dialectic struggle, as Paul knows better than anyone: 'Only that Israel is now being transfigured, and then in the end it says *pas* Israel.' Yet, this change is not towards a Hegelian universalism but rather towards an increase and a clear manifestation of preference.

The importance of election is illustrated in the context of Rom. 9–11 by the example of the two brothers Esau and Jacob. While the oldest brother, Esau, is rejected by God and even hated in the womb, the other is accepted and loved by God (Rom. 9:13). As Taubes comments rather wryly: 'In other words, things aren't happening according to enlightened philanthropy.'[9] There is no mention here of a charity to – or equality of – all, but rather of an inimitable, divine preference. If universalism is hinted at in Rom. 9–11, it should be brought together with the undeniable partiality for a particular people. The universal moment, all nations, is not the dismissal of the particular people, but is involved in the transformation of and the dialectic struggle with a particular people.

Let us try to integrate Taubes's staging of the tension between the motifs of universality and particularity in Paul's basic political issue in the dialectic of exception I propose here. To confront this tension, consider the following two viewpoints that Paul brings to the fore. On the one hand, he points out that the difference between being- and not-being-circumcised – the mark of differentiation of the particular people, of Israel – is irrelevant and indifferent in light of his proclamation. On the other hand, he points out that God nevertheless sets apart a particular people from the nations and chooses them above the other ones – thus distinguishing Israel from the nations. How can these two views both be true?

To answer this question, it is necessary to bring Paul's pneumatic logic into play. With this logic, Paul first introduces a difference *in Israel itself*: 'not all Israelites truly belong to Israel' (Rom. 9:6). There is a distinction between those who were born from Israel 'in the flesh' and those who belong to Israel according to the promise or 'in the spirit'. This second, pneumatic order of the promise, however, is not identical to a simple universal extension of the promise to everyone, to all nations. The concept of 'spirit' first and foremost describes a transfiguration *of Israel*, a dialectic battle concerning this people, as depicted in Rom. 9–11. Paul commences in Rom. 9 with the election that leads to a difference *in* Israel – Israel according to the flesh and Israel according to the spirit – and consequently to a transfiguration of Israel. As soon as the principle of the spirit is introduced, the elected particular community no longer coincides with itself. This difference in the identity of this people creates the space for 'only a remnant' of Israel, about which Paul writes that it will be saved (Rom. 9:27). Furthermore, the possibility of the calling of other nations only arises when Israel no longer coincides with itself. That is why Paul *simultaneously* speaks about this small remnant *and* the calling of the nations.[10]

Only now, after the pneumatic vocation of Israel, the calling can also go out to the nations, and Paul can say that there is no distinction between Jew and Greek (Rom. 10:12). Effacing the distinction between Jew and Greek is thus dialectically grounded in the difference the principle of the spirit first makes in Israel. The fundamental question is therefore how this effacement will transform the particular people that is now divided *in itself*. The universalisation of the calling and the equalisation of Jews and Greeks is not the final part of Paul's plea in Rom. 9–11. The completion of the dialectic of salvation can be found in the aforementioned verse about the salvation of 'all Israel' (Rom. 11:26). We can draw the following two conclusions from this.

First, in light of Rom. 9, the equalisation of Jews and Greeks is of a rather specific nature. It is not the simple erasure of the distinction between Jew and Greek, if we think the result of this erasure to be: Jew = Greek. Rather, the equality concerns the following. As there is a distinction between flesh and spirit in Israel, there is also a distinction between flesh and spirit among the Greeks. The distinction between flesh and spirit does not erase the division between Jews and Greeks in the universalism of the form Jew = Greek, but rather indicates that this distinction *divides* both Jews and Greeks in themselves. The distinction between flesh and spirit transfigures the identity of Israel. There is no longer one Israel but two: of the flesh and of the covenant or the spirit. In turn, the equalisation between Jews and Greeks does not *unite* them but places them, in Rom. 10, under the same principle of the spirit. As Israel, thanks to the pneumatic transformation, no longer coincides with itself, so the Greek no longer coincides with itself. What the particular identities of Jew and Greek share is that they are divided in themselves through the caesura between flesh and spirit. This division and differentiation are the genuine sense of universality and is an integral part of a Pauline legacy that aims to describe the politico-theological consequences of a Pauline dialectic of exception.

Second, the distinction between Israel and the nations maintains the asymmetry introduced in Rom. 10. The calling and the salvation of the nations firstly presume that the people of God is no longer the people of God. This non-coinciding of Israel with itself finds expression in Paul's description of the part of Israel that hardens itself and does not believe. This unbelief and this lost remnant inspire Paul in his work as apostle of the nations: the other nations need to be reeled in to make this part of Israel envious, so that all Israel can be saved. Hence, the Pauline rhetorical strategy demonstrates that the universalisation of the gospel is not about the absorption or appropriation of every people but is rather led by the pathos of preference, along the lines we explored in Kierkegaard's account of exception and the distinction between flesh and spirit. One should perhaps say that the distinction of flesh and spirit only makes sense in relation to the exception and the dialectic battle with the exception. Interestingly, this applies both to Israel and to the members of the community in Thessaloniki, as discussed in Chapter 4. Whether members of these particular communities are an exception is only determined in the dialectic battle that serves as a test and an ordeal to distinguish between the false exception according to the flesh and the true exception according to the spirit. Therefore, as these examples confirm once again, flesh does not concern the body but rather concerns the way in which humans *enact* their being elected as a nation or their being called from the nations. Whether *pneuma* has quickened them or not shows itself in their capacity to use as not abusing their existence, their calling and everything and everyone else they encounter in their lives.

Let us briefly return to Taubes. Much of Taubes's argumentation is fruitful for a Pauline dialectic of exception. Yet, this does not apply to his account of the *eschaton*, that is, the time of the completion of this transfiguration of the people of God. This completion ultimately shapes Taubes's reading of Romans: not the resurrection but the *eschaton*, when God is all in all (Cor. 15:28), and 'all Israel' is realised. In Chapter 3, I identified and criticised a similar functioning of the *eschaton* in Taubes's account. His interpretation of life in the mode of 'as not' follows his emphasis on the *eschaton* as well as his claim that Paul propagates an eschatological indifference. The question is whether the emphasis on the eschatological moment of Rom. 11:26 does not result in a similar indifference to the time of the now – the time of the now is, after all, the time of the constituting of this community. How to save this sense of time and this resistance against indifference in an approach to the Pauline community? In order to move closer to an answer to that question, let us continue our interrogation of the motifs of universalism and particularism in the Pauline community.

NEITHER JEW NOR GREEK

Considering the subtitle of his book about Paul, *The Foundation of Universalism*, it will not come as a surprise that no theme is as important for Badiou as that of universalism. I already noted that the terms 'truth' and 'truth process' appear on average more than once per page in his *Saint Paul*. The same applies to the terms 'universal' and 'universalism'. For Badiou, Paul is an intellectual figure crucial to the history of the West, because he is 'one of the very first theoreticians of the universal' and so a 'founder' of the way of thinking about universalism that has become part and parcel of our culture over time.[11] Let us consider how this emphasis on universalism in Badiou's interpretation plays out.

In Paul, the universal is opposed to the particular laws that rule a world or society. In particular this means that the Pauline event is not to be traced back to the existing order of the world and cannot be explained in any ways as deriving from its particular laws. As a consequence, the 'Christ-event', as Badiou terms it, can in no single way be fitted into the identity politics of our social world: the event establishes something that cannot be traced back to a particular identity but is rather 'detached from [...] the particular laws of a world or society'.[12] Similarly, for Badiou, the Christian subject is in no way characterised by the particular identity of the social group in which he or she grew up; rather, the Pauline subject is characterised by a 'consciousness-of-truth' that has a universal character. Everyone can equally participate therein and no particular background – whether it concerns social identities, roles, communities, morals and customs – is privileged. For any mode of living that belongs only to a specific people, a specific individual, or a specific culture – that is, a mode of living that only, or in a privileged sense, accrues to this particular people, this individual or this culture, and cannot be lived in the same way by other peoples, individuals, cultures or eras – fails to meet the demand of such an event. The event not only separates the subjective ethos from this or that particular attitude to life but also from every particularity. In this sense, the event establishes a possible mode of human existence that is truly absolute, that is, set apart from every particular and relative mode of human existence that came before it. Consequently, only a universal attitude to life, that can be taken up by *everyone* in a given situation, can adequately correspond with an event. More precisely: this universal is no consequence but rather a defining characteristic of an event. An incident only merits the name of event if everyone can equally become a subject thereof, regardless of their individual background, and if no one is privileged by their particular circumstances. For Badiou, the universal community is thus not simply the community of all, but rather the community of which everyone *can* equally become a member, provided that they are prepared to become a subject, a servant of the event.

How can this theory of universalism be traced in the letters of the apostle? The above considerations imply that cultural identities, which normally are considered highly important in our social world, are no longer important in light of the event. Paul's letters offer a number of crucial indications supporting this view. For instance, the distinction between the pure and impure, which is a defining characteristic of the particular laws in the Jewish culture, has become obsolete due to the 'Christ-event': 'Everything is indeed clean' (Rom. 14:20): the particular food regulations, which are characteristic of cultural identities, do not matter. The apostle also writes that the distinction between Jew and Greek is no longer relevant (Rom. 2:10), the distinction between man and woman has been erased (Cor. 7:4, 10), and the distinction between slave and master has lost its significance (Gal. 3:28). These are powerful and strongly politically laden statements in a socio-cultural world in which these differences are constitutive.

Despite his disregard concerning these differences, Paul nevertheless appears to tolerate the existing differences, as for instance in Rom. 14 in which he implores his readers not to offend those who do observe the prescriptions of the particular law and do value the difference between clean and unclean food. Offending them, as Paul notes, would not contribute to his proclamation. Hence, Paul emphasises here that, even though ultimately, for him, nothing is unclean (Rom. 10:14), and everything is allowed as long as it is done from faith (Rom. 10:23), tolerance is an attitude one has to adopt because of the weakness of others. The true divide then lies with faith: weak faith can lead to clinging to differences; those whose faith is not strong enough do not (yet) see the indifference and insignificance of existing differences in the area of customs, rites and cultural identities, and as long as they still 'have doubts [they] are condemned if they eat, because they do not act from faith; for whatever does not proceed from faith is sin' (Rom. 14:23). Everything, then, depends on the *enactment* of one's actions: in a modality of faith or not. *This enactment is the only difference that truly matters* and is a sign of the continuous dialectic battle.

A similar attitude is evident in 1 Corinthians when the apostle writes that he is a Jew for the Jews, and that for those who are 'outside the law' – read: the non-Jews – he is as one outside the law (Cor. 9:19–22). Once more, Paul displays tolerance for differences. He is prepared not to offend the people with whom he interacts. However, that he himself is able to be under as well as outside of the law ultimately implies that for him these differences are indifferent *for faith itself*. Each one of the particular distinctions are irrelevant and should be made to serve the proclamation and be examined through the eyes of faith. Even though his tolerance may at first appear as a particular form of pragmatics – not offending people makes social interaction so much easier – it is rather to be understood in terms of the proclamation: in this way, one does not create unnecessary obstructions for the message to go out to all in equal fashion.

Badiou interprets these elements to mean that Paul suspends all meaningful differences in the world and *'leave[s] them be'* so that they do not hinder the proclamation. Hence, no differences remain. Yet, Badiou can only say this because he is deeply invested in the idea that the universality of the Pauline event introduces one fundamental and encompassing distinction: everything that we encounter in the world should be approached be deciding on the question of whether it belongs to the event or not. This distinction is intrinsic to the particular sense of the universality of the Pauline event: this universality is not automatically accrued to everything in reality or to everyone but rather must be assumed through a particular mode of living. The event requires believers to take it upon themselves and prove to be able to leave their differences behind, such as their particular identity as man or woman, master or slave, or Jew or Greek, since these are irrelevant for the tireless fidelity to the event. In this sense, this universality is, on the one hand, a pure *gift*, like the resurrection is pure grace, as Badiou emphasises, but on the other hand it is assigned as a *task*.[13]

The impact of the 'Christ-event' on the life of the members of the Pauline communities could therefore be seen as a bifurcation point. With the event, a fork emerges, and we suddenly find ourselves before a choice to either live according to our particular identity (as Jew or Greek, as master or slave, as man or woman) or according to the universal mode of living provided by the event, transcending every particular identity. Because one cannot get rid of one's particular identity(ies) but also always lives in a specific situation with such identities, this choice continues to encroach, and those who want to be subject of an event will have to persevere in the way of the spirit. For the subject, the event is thus a gift that is assigned as a continuous, strenuous task. The subject is a Two: 'It is of the essence of the Christian subject to be divided, through its fidelity to the Christ-event, into two paths that affect every subject in thought.'[14] Flesh and spirit prove to go hand in hand in the subject and lend it its own attitude, struggle and vulnerability. The task the Pauline event assigns thus also involves the idea that the subject, who as a historically and situated living being is characterised by the existing order, has to continue suspending this order. The subject is the place where the caesura with tradition and particular identities needs to brought about and where one needs to be engaged in the battle with the flesh over and over again. *The partitioning or the division that is constitutive for the Pauline subject thus indicates that the subject is that which no longer coincides with its socio-cultural identity.*

We have already seen how both this ethos and this non-identity of the believers is expressed in the Pauline formula of *hōs mē*, 'as not'. Badiou, however, rather embraces another one, which also expresses a tension: 'since you are not under law but under grace' (Rom. 6:14). In the previous chapter, it could already be seen that grace in this formula is, for Badiou, no third term between law and faith but rather stands in opposition to the law. He affirms the 'not ..., but ...'-formula, because Paul uses it to express the aforementioned division in the subject: 'no longer purely Greek or Jewish but called to a new life'. Yet, like the *hōs mē*-formula, this 'not ..., but ...'-formula does take an advance on a dialectic relationship between flesh and spirit that merges into a synthesis of new identity. The 'not ..., but ...' links a negative and a positive moment; the 'not' suspends the way of the flesh, so that space can be made for the 'but', the way of the spirit. Badiou identifies the subject with this formulation: 'the subject of the new epoch is a "not ... but".'[15] And that is the '*form that underpins the universal*':

> For the 'not' is the potential dissolution of closed particularities (whose name is 'law'), while the 'but' indicates the task, the faithful labor, in which the subjects of the process opened up by the event (whose name is 'grace') are the coworkers.[16]

Because the subject is the 'not ..., but ...' and continues to distance itself from its particular identity, in this way cooperating with other subjects in the process opened by grace, it becomes clear that 'the subject is no condition but a becoming'. In conclusion, it could be said that, for Badiou, the Pauline *adiaphora*, the particular practices that are proclaimed to be indifferent, are stalled in a certain area of tension: on the one hand, they are not relevant and can be tolerated, while on the other they should be rejected – in the form of 'not ..., but ...' – if they threaten to pull the subject back to its particular origin.[17]

In this regard, Badiou's argument comes close to that of Engberg-Pedersen, who points out that Paul allows Jews and Greeks to uphold their old practices as long as they do not endanger the focus on and faithfulness to the Pauline event – or the focus and the faithfulness of other members of the Pauline community.[18] Yet, at the same time, Engberg-Pedersen argues against Badiou that, through his unilateral emphasis on Paul's universalism, Badiou underestimates the ethnic and particularistic tendencies in Paul's letters.[19] He sees these ethnic and particularistic tendencies coming to the fore *precisely where Paul is concerned with founding a new community*, distinct from the Jewish and the Greek communities. The members should indeed abandon something basic belonging their old community in order to be able to participate in the new one. Every attempt to establish a new community after all assumes that this community knows how to distinguish itself from preceding or other communities. By emphasising universalism, Badiou forgets to include the sense of separation and particularism in Paul.

To assess this criticism of Engberg-Pederson and its specific philosophical relevance, it should firstly be noted that, for Badiou, the universal community coincides with the development of a new Pauline-Christian discourse. This discourse distinguishes itself from Jewish and Greek discourse.[20] In this sense, Badiou does acknowledge that the universal community is not simply the community of all. It is distinct from other communities. Yet, there is a claimed universality. As noted above, the predicate 'universal' concerns the *possibility* of becoming a subject: it is grace that this possibility is granted equally to all. In this sense, Badiou would definitely object to the characterisation of this community as an ethnic one. Nevertheless, this universalism can only exist as a particular form of *partiality*. A comment by Žižek clarifies this:

> [I]t is, rather, the difference Christians/non-Christians itself, which, as a difference, is universal, that is, which cuts across the entire social body, splitting, dividing from within every substantial ethnic or other identity. Greeks are cut into Christians and non-Christians, as are Jews.[21]

The last sentence of Žižek's citation confirms not so much an ethnicity in Badiou's version of the Pauline community, but rather a definite partiality of the Pauline subject when he continues that '*universal truth is accessible only from a partial, engaged subjective position*'. The community of subjects is a partial community that sees everything in light of the fundamental difference between flesh and spirit. It may be that in this reading, Paul's communities are open to all, and it may also be so that the members of these communities – called 'Paul's incrowd attitude' by Engberg-Pedersen – are truly equal among themselves, but this equality indeed only extends to the members, to those who belong to this community, who partake in the constitution of this community.

If we consider the constitution of this community itself, Žižek's interpretation in fact uncovers a particularly Schmittian dimension to Badiou's approach to Paul. There is apparently an absolute, and universal binary opposition – Christian versus non-Christian – that pervades the whole differential field of this socio-political community. This opposition rearranges and reorders this differential field according to the difference of friends of the gospel versus its enemies. The state of exception, founded by the event, thus fully conforms to the Schmittian structure of the friend–enemy dichotomy. If one looks at Badiou's version of the Pauline community in this way, it is far less surprising that these members are equal among themselves: is this equality truly different from the homogeneity sought by Schmitt's sovereign? Put differently, the equality of Jew and Greek, man and woman, and master and slave is only surprising against the background of, and in relation to, a world order in which these differences reign. It is far less surprising if members of the Pauline community are nothing but militants fighting side by side *against* a common enemy and *for* what they consider the one and only good cause.

With these last comments, I do not want to claim that Badiou's *Saint Paul* can be reduced to this Schmittian structure. His emphasis on universalism clearly brings to light important features of Paul's proclamation. Yet, it does seem to me that also here, a dualistic tendency tends to overtake Badiou's analysis. His considerations of the subject as Two are symptomatic in this regard, especially when compared to the descriptions offered in the previous section. Rather than a pneumatic difference in – or non-coinciding with – oneself, which has a point of contact in one's particular identity,[22] Badiou turns the faithful subject into a Janus face, that is, into a human with two identities: the old particular one that continuously needs to be warded off and the new, universal one that lacks all rootedness and individuality since it is totally absorbed in the service to a new good cause or ideal. Exactly for this reason, Badiou's attention to Paul's universalism tends to obscure the importance of particularism and of separation in Paul's proclamation.

A PART WITHOUT PART

Before addressing the importance of the notion of separation and its relation to universality, let me pause briefly on a notion mentioned before, namely that of *une part des sans-part*, a part of those who have no part or share, coined by Rancière.[23] Paul is not referred to in Rancière's text. Nevertheless, the idea of a part without part perfectly expresses what might be at stake in a focus on separation or exception: the Pauline community is in the first place the community of rejects or outcasts, of those who have no share in the socio-political order.[24]

We may even say that it offers a politico-philosophical translation of concepts introduced in Chapters 3 and 4, especially of the distinction between, on the one hand, the notion of the world expressed by the *tou kosmou*-formulas in 1 Corinthians, such as 'the present form of this world' (Cor. 7:31) and, on the other hand, the notions of outcast, scum and non-beings (Cor. 1:28), that is, of that which is nothing and has no value in the present form of the world. This distinction helps us to see what is at stake for Rancière and how his account of the part without part relates to the discussions on Paul.

The politico-philosophical translation of this Pauline distinction can be traced in Rancière's distinction between *la police* and *la politique*. *La police* is translated as 'the police'. Yet, in a broader sense, the term refers to the body of officials responsible for order. This body stands in full service of the existing order. It is therefore 'essentially, the law'.[25] For every part, every group and every party of society, this body guards and protects its proper place, that is, the place this part is awarded in the existing political and legal order. However, with respect to the configuration of the society guarded by the police, a surplus exists that eludes this body of surveillance. In its supervision, this body *only observes* that which was given a place in the order and awarded visibility in this way. This body does not see what remains invisible, what did not receive a voice in the order to speak up and what does not have the capacity to position itself as part of this society. When saying that a part exists that did not receive a voice, we mean that by clinging to the existing order, this body maintains a decisive distinction between voices. The order determines which voices are heard and understood as saying something meaningful and which voices produce mere – or, rather, are reduced to – noise.[26]

According to Rancière, the term *la politique* or politics applies to that political activity that breaks with the existing order to such an extent that we no longer remain deaf to what the voices of the part that has no part have to say. Politics – although this statement is no longer Rancière's – thus concerns a pneumatic transformation of our capacity to understand: we no longer hear these voices as mere murmurs but hear in these murmurs the cries of voices that demand to be – and also can be – heard, just like the other voices. This conception of politics implies that true political activity *makes the basic contingency of the existing socio-political order visible*: it shows that the existing order can also be different. Moreover, this contingency is intrinsically bound to that which is not, the 'non-beings' of the part that has no part in the existing order. Precisely because this part exists, because the whole of the order was not able to equally give each part its share, an imperative emanates from the part that received no share, namely: Dismantle this order! A political activity deserves to be called 'political' only if it answers to this claim of those who are rejected and neglected.

Rancière understands this claim not in terms of the pneumatic transformation I just mentioned, but rather as a claim to equality. For him, equality is the ideal to which any politics worthy of the name strives. Whether the Pauline community finds its ultimate goal in this equality remains to be seen. For now, let us note that this claim places and criticises the present order of the world, which leaves one part unheard, in light of 'the equality between any speaking being with any other speaking being'.[27] For Rancière, politics has everything to do with a form of equality, but this equality is not exactly the same as the equality of Badiou's subjects that fight side by side to remain faithful to an event and make it true in the world. The community of equals Rancière imagines is not the community of subjects à la Badiou. It is not the community based on the difference between subjects and non-subjects, which is Badiou's variation of Schmitt's friend–enemy dichotomy. Rancière rather allots equality a constitutive role: this community is based on 'the equality of any speaking being with any other speaking being'. Therefore, this community interrupts every community based on the distinction between voices that are heard and not heard. Remarkably, the latter is unthinkable in Badiou's conceptual framework: the voices of the non-subjects – the 'non-Christians', as Žižek writes – produce for the friends of Badiou's gospel nothing but noise that is not heard and cannot even be understood in the discourse founded by the event. With this emphasis on the demand associated with equality and the interruption that Rancière's community implies, with every community based on a distinction between voices, I want to turn to the question of separation for an account of the Pauline *ekklēsia*.

Before doing so, let me address one last point with regard to the part with no part, namely its relation to the universal. In order to characterise the type of universalism that follows from Badiou's understanding of the event, it is often suggested, following Badiou himself, that the event be called a 'universal singularity'.[28] The French *singularité*, or 'singularity', refers to the uniqueness of the exception that is an event. The adjective 'universal' adds that the uniqueness of this exception is to be found precisely in the universality of the call that goes out to everyone to be faithful to this event. In Badiou, this universality can only result in a community of subjects cooperating for a good cause.

The term 'universal singularity', however, appears to be more applicable to Rancière's notion of the part that has no part. Žižek strikingly interprets this concept as follows: '[T]he excluded, those with no fixed place with the social edifice, presented themselves as representatives, the stand-ins, for the Whole of Society, for the true Universality.'[29] What he calls 'the Whole of Society' is nothing but the existing order that presents itself as total and all-encompassing. With regard to this Whole, the outcasts, who have no part in it, are the 'minimal difference' of this order with a truly encompassing universality.[30] Žižek speaks of a *minimal* difference, because this part that has no part is invisible and anonymous: that and how the encompassing order differs from the universality cannot be addressed in this order itself; yet, albeit invisible, this part is not nothing. A true political act is one that dismantles the order at precisely this point, revealing this minimal difference, thereby depriving and detaching this order of the illusion of its own comprehensiveness: the outcasts *present* this order in its 'modality of non-All'; these outcasts form the 'real' of this order that this order cannot symbolise or understand.[31] If we want to speak of an event in this context, the event is the moment in which this 'real' affects the given socio-political order and in which the murmur of the outcasts is transformed in a genuine voice, a voice of misery, that calls and that demands.[32] The part without part is thereby quite a specific exception. It is the *supplement* and *representative* of the universal because, in a negative sense, it shows that the order is not truly universal and because, in a positive sense, it demands equality – 'the equality of whichever speaking being with whichever other speaking being'. The question, however, is whether the Pauline concern for community can be based on the presupposition of equality as the goal politics should reach for, or whether a higher principle is at stake.

SET APART

The notion of *aphōrismenos*, 'set apart' or 'separation', appears in Paul's self-description with which Romans opens: 'Paul, a servant of Jesus Christ, called to be an apostle, set apart for the gospel of God' (Rom. 1:1), as well as in Galatians: 'who had set me apart before I was born and called me through his grace' (Gal. 1:15).[33] This notion of separation also marks Paul's sense of community and the universality that goes hand in hand with it.

This latter claim immediately raises an obvious question. How can universalism, which follows from the unification and equalisation of particular groups, be connected to separation and exception, which ultimately and emphatically distinguish particular groups or individuals and set them apart from the rest? This question becomes even more baffling when one traces the word *aphōrismenos* and derived terms in

Paul's letters. The universal tendency seems to be operative in these letters when Paul blames fellow apostle Peter for clinging to the setting apart from Gentiles (Gal. 2:12).[34] However, elsewhere Paul notes that the believers need to set themselves apart from the non-believers (2 Cor. 6:17), emphasising a more 'ethnic' and particularistic tendency.[35] So what exactly is at stake in this separation for a dialectic of exception? Let us answer this question in dialogue with Agamben, whose emphasis on separation offers a crucial addition to our sense of the Pauline community.[36]

For Paul, the Greek term *aphōrismenos* has yet another significance since it is the translation of the Hebrew term 'Pharisee'.[37] The (Jewish) law introduces a caesura between Israel and the nations, between circumcised and uncircumcised. 'Pharisee', however, points to a seclusion *within* the people of God. As loyal and meticulous observers of the law, the Pharisees, to which Paul also belonged before his radical turn, were set apart from the ordinary people who did not honour the same meticulous observance of the law. The term *aphōrismenos* thus refers to a seclusion that is introduced by and for the law, but *within* the people of God, between the scrupulous observers of the law and the more liberal or loose ones – or better: between the scrupulous elite and the common people who were unable to observe in their everyday lives the complex arrangement of religious laws and prescriptions. In the gospels, Jesus objects to this scrupulous observance exactly for this reason: maintaining the law had become something for the elite, and it had become impossible for the common people to uphold the religious law. Jesus' reduction of the law to loving God above all and one's neighbour as oneself is an attempt at giving back the law to the common people. The elite observation of the law thus marks the crisis of the law for the common people.

While the pharisaic relation to the law is turned upside down in Paul's letters, he maintains a sense of separation, which should be taken into account if we are to understand what happens when the proclamation goes out to the nations. By it, Israel and the nations are not simply equalised. Rather, Paul *adds* a distinction, setting apart spirit and flesh.

At this point, I want to take recourse to an element of Agamben's reading which is both subtle and indispensable for portraying Paul's dialectic of exception. The flesh–spirit distinction does not simply erase the division instituted by the law in order to introduce a new distinction, as Badiou's dualistic account seems to imply. Rather, this distinction *transforms* this division by dividing it: the division of spirit and flesh does not sublate the division between Israel and the nations in a universal humanity but suspends this division *by dividing it once more*.[38] To explain this, Agamben refers to the 'division of Apelles'.

The story goes that, one day, the painter Apelles went to visit his colleague Protogenes, who unfortunately was not at home. In order to let Protogenes know that he wanted to visit him, Apelles then painted a very fine line on a white cloth. When returning home, Protogenes immediately recognised the subtlety of Apelles and used another colour to paint an even finer line over the one Apelles painted, cutting Apelles' line not perpendicularly in two but rather longitudinally. When Apelles once more visited Protogenes' house, he demonstrated his unparalleled artistry by painting a third line that could not get any finer and that once more split Protogenes' already very fine line lengthways. To understand what the dichotomy of flesh–spirit does, one needs to keep in mind this image: the Pauline proclamation divides the line itself that distinguishes the Jews and the nations lengthways in two. The second vocation, as discussed in Chapter 3, is not simply a new vocation but rather re-vokes the earlier vocations; similarly, the division constitutive for the Pauline community is no new division or dichotomy but rather the division that divides existing divisions.

This division ensures that 'not all Israelites truly belong to Israel' (Rom. 9:6): there are Jews according to the flesh and there are Jews according to the spirit – and the same happens with the gentiles. The division into flesh and spirit does not just divide Israel into two separate groups, but also the gentiles. More precisely, it is not a matter of groups – as if now four groups would remain – but the same fine line dividing the dividing line, concerns each and every individual: for each individual, particular and legal distinctions and even individual identities are no longer sufficient to determine who we are and who we can be. The division shows that there are Jews who are not Jews – Jews who are set apart from their being-Jew – and that there are non-Jews who are not non-Jews – non-Jews who are set apart from their being-non-Jew.[39] Even this formulation is not quite adequate because one may still understand the pneumatic as introducing a new identity. In a Pauline dialectic of exception, however, marked by a preference for the exception, for that which is excluded from one's identity, the pneumatic concerns this non-coincidence of someone or some group with itself. The pneumatic introduces a difference within one's identity, a surplus by which one is freed from the straitjacket of one's identity so that this identity is given back to be used freely.

In terms of Rom. 9:27, where Paul cites Isaiah who speaks about a small part or a small remnant, the division of flesh and spirit discloses that 'the comprehensive division of the peoples through the law' now leaves a remainder: where previously the division between Jews and non-Jews comprised humankind in its entirety, there are now remnants in both groups and in everyone that fall outside of any comprehensive division.

The subtlety of this approach can be further illustrated by applying it to a passage Badiou reads in terms of a dualism between law and grace to underline the universality of Paul's proclamation:

> To those under the law I became as one under the law [...] so that I might win those under the law. To those outside the law I became as one outside the law (though I am not free from God's law but am under Christ's law) so that I might win those outside the law. (Cor. 9:20–1)

According to Badiou, this passage shows that the distinction between 'under the law' and 'without law' leaves Paul unmoved: for those under the law, he is under the law, and for those without law, he is without law. For this reason, so he argues, this passage reveals Paul's universalism as being at odds with the division of the law. Yet, Paul's rhetorical strategy seems more subtle here because he inserts a sentence: 'though I am not free from God's law but am under Christ's law'.[40] This insertion implies that Paul resumes and recovers the term 'law' rather than abandoning it. When Paul writes that he has become 'as one under the law' and 'as one outside the law', this 'as' – *hōs* – means 'as if'. Paul does not associate with Jews and non-Jews with the indifference of someone who appears just to be as comfortably under the law as outside the law. The mystery of Paul's relation to the law is expressed in the peculiar phrase in the middle and the double negative he uses there: not *anomos*, not outside the law. According to the logical law of the excluded third – and the distinction that the Mosaic law makes employs this logical law: either circumcised or uncircumcised – there are only two options. One is either under the law or outside the law. There is no third option. However, the Pauline, pneumatic division of this comprehensive distinction between 'under the law' and 'outside the law' does not conform to this logical law and introduces a third term: 'not outside the law', a negation of a negation, a dialectic movement through which the negation of the negation does not return to the original position – in this case that of the Mosaic law – but rather lets the law appear in another, transfigured form. When this third term is acknowledged, 'not outside the law' is not identical to 'under the law', but rather signifies a remnant beyond the distinction between 'under the law' and 'outside the law'. Paul's phrase 'not free from law' then does not point to the *indifference* of the difference between 'under the law' and 'outside the law', but rather *points out that this distinction is not all-encompassing*. The law of Christ is this remainder: 'not free from law'.

In the context in which Paul uses it, 'not free from law' means the following. When he poses as someone who is outside the law and presents himself as representative of the uncircumcised, he cannot be identified as uncircumcised because he carries this sign in his flesh. Rather, Paul enacts his being 'outside the law' in a specific way. When he presents and behaves as non-Jew, outside the law, he does so as being 'not free from the law', which means as non-non-Jew.[41] Here, Paul's 'as not', *hōs mē*, returns. When he is outside the law, he is a non-Jew, but he enacts being non-Jew as not being non-Jew, that is, as non-non-Jew. When he is under Mosaic law, he is equally Jew and not Jew. Agamben describes this non-coincidence of the non-Jewry with itself (and of the Jewry with itself) that reveals itself in the attitude of 'as not' in terms of the remnant that indicates that a nation does not coincide with itself: '[The non-non-Jews] are something like a remnant between every people and itself, between every identity and itself.'[42]

The new law, then, does not propagate, *pace* Badiou, an indifferent tolerance towards the differences of the law but rather shows that every part of the whole – the part of the Jews, of the Greeks, of the peoples – in itself harbours a remnant that does not conform to the given order instated by the law. Reprising his own analysis of the vocation as the revocation of every existing worldly vocation and linking it with his analysis of 'as not', Agamben writes that the second vocation 'sets apart' every vocation from itself: 'Jew *as non*-Jew, Greek *as non*-Greek.'[43] There is no universal point of view to be found in Paul – 'no universal person, no Christian can be found in the depths of the Jew or the Greek, neither as principle, nor as goal'[44] – but only the sustained labour of the suspension of identities set up and maintained by the law, the existing order, and the body that guards this order. These very remnants form the link for a transformation of every part, and with that of the whole; they make it possible to live according to the spirit. In Rancière's argument, true political activity reveals a similar remainder and gives this remainder a voice.

Hence, one could read the remnant as the Pauline version of Rancière's part without part: for both, the political is concerned with this remnant. However, it is crucial to be aware of one essential difference. Rancière's part without part is the part that is in need of *salvation*. It needs to be granted a voice, or its voice needs to be heard so that it can begin to demand and take its own place in a socio-political environment. In this sense, Rancière's conception of politics remains indebted to the structure of abandonment and the ban that marks the state of exception. In fact, the part without part is basically another variation of bare or unbearable life in need of salvation. These forms of bare life, as Agamben suggests, are produced in and by the Schmittian logic of the exception – or, in Rancière's logic, they are maintained by the police. *The Pauline remnant, however, is not 'the object of salvation', but rather the 'instrument' that makes salvation possible*: 'So that, in the time of the now [*en tō nun kairō*] a remnant is produced, chosen by grace' (Rom. 11:5).[45] Consequently, the Pauline remnant is an exception in the Pauline and not the Schmittian sense of the word. The last citation also shows how this remnant is connected to the notion of time as the time granted to humans to use their own voice to speak and to use their own body to act. Rancière's part without part is characterised as a part that utters noises that are not understood in a society as voices that address. Therefore, politics concerns the capacity to perceive in these noises the political demand – *esigenza* – to be heard as voices. Paul's remnant, however, is the product of grace and of the pneumatic transformation: the remnant is that part of and in us that is granted the capacity to speak, to act, and to understand beyond the boundaries of our alleged socio-political identities – whether they are awarded a part in a society or not. That is, it is that part of us that is granted the capacity to find and use our own voice. Once people have the capacity to use their own voice to speak and to use their own bodies to act, they are no longer the object of salvation and are twisted free from any 'soteriological machine'.[46] In this logic, not the goal of *equality* determines the demand, but the pneumatic *difference* by which someone finds one's voice. Unlike the part without part that makes demands based on the presupposition that equality should be aimed at, the remnant is the very difference from any order in which the pneumatic call to life and the power of revivification resides. The Pauline objection to order is not the lack of equality; this lack is at best a symptom of a deeper problem, namely its lack of pneumatic life.

Let me compare this account of the remnant with Taubes's reading of Rom. 9–11, in which the dynamics of the Pauline remnant and the universalisation of the proclamation *does* constitute part of Paul's 'peculiar kind of soteriological machine'. For Taubes's Paul, this 'machine' finds its culmination in the salvation of 'all Israel' when God will be 'all in all'. In this culmination, the remnant no longer plays a part and is suspended in a Pauline conception of the fullness of time. Agamben distances himself from Taubes's eschatological perspective. He is not interested in the eventual perspective of the *eschaton*, and I tend to side with him on this issue.

The true value of Paul's thought lies elsewhere: 'But in the time of now, *the only real time*, there is nothing other than the remnant.'[47]

In Taubes's version of Paul, the idea of the *eschaton* runs the risk of falling prey to Nietzsche's claim of nihilism, as discussed in Chapter 3. Following Agamben, however, we see that the time that remains is thus the time in which the part without part can make the diffuse noise of its murmuring be heard as a voice that demands its own place – this is exactly what it means that the capacity to use one's own voice is given (back).[48] Therefore, the centre of gravity of the pneumatic moment is the *creation* of a remnant and not the eschatological perspective of God being all in all.[49]

Such a conception of Paul is a true heir to a dialectic of exception that never culminates in a Hegelian sublation. This remnant is a surplus that exceeds that which Paul imagines as the completion of the dialectic mechanism: 'The messianic remnant exceeds the eschatological all, and irremediably so; it is the unredeemable that makes salvation possible.'[50] Unlike Hegel's dialectic, in which every moment is taken up and is assigned its own place in the totality of the dialectic movement, this time and remnant cannot themselves be saved but should be understood as the moment and the material, respectively, making salvation *possible*; yet, it is and remains the remnant that cannot be saved, since it cannot be assimilated into the soteriological machine.[51] This remnant already 'irreversibly' exceeds 'the eschatological all'. The principle of the spirit, then, is not the principle of completion, but the principle that makes a difference, creating remnants that can make their demand be heard.

In line with this form of Paul's political theology, it is Agamben who insists that the Pauline event is present – in the sense of *parousia* – when a community assumes the formlessness of a remnant and in this way sets itself up as nonconformist, not determined by any one identification, position, habit or attachment – not even by a new attachment to an identifiable, good cause: '*At a decisive instant, the elected people, every people, will necessarily situate itself as a remnant, as not-all.*'[52] The Pauline community is therefore not Badiou's community of subjects that attach themselves to the good cause and equally not the community of 'all Israel', as Taubes argues. The Pauline community is the community that remains in the presence of and as exception to every political community founded on the basis of any dichotomy. For this reason, Agamben describes the Pauline community as the community that 'can never coincide with itself, as all or as part, that which infinitely remains or resists in each division'.[53] The current form of the world, based on divisions and distinctions, is passing at the very moment this nonconformist, formless remnant announces itself by separating itself from the divisions that regulate the order of the world as pneumatic exception. It is the community that remains and that revivifies when the socio-political order has run out of steam.

NOTES

1. Wright, *Pauline Perspectives*, 405.
2. For an overview of several themes related to the question of Paul and community, departing mainly from Esposito's concept of *communitas*, see Weaver, *The Scandal of Community*, esp. chap. 5.
3. See Heller-Roazen, *The Enemy of All*, who, inspired by Agamben, points to the pirate as the enemy of all and shows the continuous reference to this paradoxical notion in political theory. The title of Popper's famous *The Open Society and Its Enemies* contains a similar paradox: open to all, but excluding its enemies. It is interesting to see that the example Popper, *The Open Society and Its Enemies*, 238, provides in reference to Christianity is the same as the one offered by Badiou, *Saint Paul*, 23–5/21–3, to account for his 'antidialectic', namely the struggle of Paul as described in Acts 10 and 15 (and in Gal. 2 in relation to Peter) against those who aim to maintain something from the Jewish laws and customs. In this way, however, the Pauline pneumatic and dialectic reinterpretation of these laws and customs is completely lost in a dualism.
4. Agamben, *Homo Sacer*, 22/19.
5. Note that the rendering of *ekklēsia* as church gives a completely different emphasis to the word since, etymologically, church is probably derived from *kurios*, lord, and means 'house of the lord'.
6. See Siedentop, *Inventing the Individual*, 51–78.
7. Taubes, *Die politische Theologie des Paulus*, 38/25.
8. Ibid., 38/25.
9. Ibid., 69/48. The discussion about '*pas* Israel' can be found esp. in ibid., 67–72/47–51.
10. This motif of no longer coinciding with oneself and detaching oneself from the first calling is extensively discussed by Agamben in his assessment of the second calling; see chap. 4.
11. Badiou, *Saint Paul*, 116/108.
12. Ibid., 115/107.
13. Ibid., 67/63.
14. Ibid., 60/56.
15. Ibid., 67/63.
16. Ibid., 67–8/64.
17. Also see Boyarin, 'Paul among the Anti-philosophers', 111.
18. Engberg-Pedersen, 'Paul and Universalism', 97.
19. Ibid., 92–3, 102–3.
20. See Badiou, *Saint Paul*, 43–57/40–54.
21. Žižek, 'The Necessity of a Dead Bird', 184.
22. Just as the account of Pentecost in Acts does not say that the apostles all of

a sudden speak a universal language, but rather that everyone hears them speaking in their own language. People are addressed in their particularity and the proclamation can be heard in particular languages.
23 In what follows, I refer specifically to Rancière, *La Mésentente*, 48–53/25–30.
24 Žižek, *The Fragile Absolute*, 115.
25 Rancière, *La Mésentente*, 52/29.
26 In Chapter 3, I noted that Rom. 8 offers an ontological version of this noise: the sigh of creation is but a noise that is at first not heard as a voice demanding salvation.
27 Rancière, *La Mésentente*, 53/30.
28 See. e.g., Depoortere, 'Badiou's Paul', 146–9.
29 Žižek, *The Puppet and the Dwarf*, 64.
30 Ibid., 65.
31 Ibid., 69: '[T]he Real is not external to the Symbolic: the Real is the Symbolic itself in the modality of non-All.'
32 See Van der Heiden, *The Voice of Misery*.
33 The latter passage is referred to in Agamben, *Il tempo che resta*, 47/44. The Greek verb *aphorizō* can also mean 'to ban'; see Liddell-Scott-Jones, *s.v. aphorizō* II.1. Even though Agamben does not point this out, it does show the link with banishment and exile, which for him are related to the state of exception, as extensively discussed in *Homo Sacer*.
34 It will come as no surprise that exactly this episode strongly inspires Badiou's account of Paul; see *Saint Paul*, chap. 2, as well as his – much earlier – play *The Incident at Antioch*, which was first conceived in 1982.
35 Agamben, *Il tempo che resta*, 47–8/44–5. This is also noted by Engberg-Pedersen in 'Paul and Universalism', as discussed above.
36 Agamben refers and objects to Badiou here, see Agamben, *Il tempo che resta*, 53–5/51–2.
37 Ibid., 48–50/45–7.
38 Ibid., 52/49.
39 Ibid., 52/50.
40 Ibid., 53/51.
41 'He who dwells in the law of the Messiah is the non-non-Jew.' Ibid.
42 Ibid., 54/52.
43 Ibid., 55/53.
44 Ibid., 55/52–3.
45 Ibid., 55/53.
46 Ibid., 58/56.
47 Ibid., emphasis added.
48 In a reading of Gaétan Soucy's *La Petite Fille qui aimait trop les allumettes*, I have argued how these two aspects of the human voice, the noise that murmurs and the voice that addresses and speaks, can be articulated; see Van der Heiden, *The Voice of Misery*, 33–51.
49 Agamben, *Il tempo che resta*, 58/56.

50 Ibid., 58/57.
51 'The truly unsaveable life is the one in which there is nothing to save, and against this the powerful theological machine of Christian *oiconomia* runs aground.' Agamben, *La comunità che viene*, 12/6.
52 Agamben, *Il tempo che resta*, 57/55. Elsewhere, he suggests that this people of God is a *multitude* – like the crowd that followed Jesus – rather than a *people*, if we understand people in the technical sense of an entity with a particular identity or unity and a *volonté générale*: 'In the New Testament, we thus find three terms for "people": *plēthos* (in Latin, *multitudo*) ... *ochlos* (in Latin, *turba*) ... and *laos* (in Latin, *plebs*) .... What is missing is the term with political value – *dēmos* (*populus*) – almost as if the messianic event had always already transformed the people in a multitude or a formless mass.' Agamben, *Stasis*, 72/64.
53 Agamben, *Il tempo che resta*, 58/57.

Epilogue: A Pauline Dialectic of Exception

Let us return to the two epigraphs of the Introduction. What about 'the words, the serious words, [that] have been used up' and which 'don't seem to fit the thoughts nowadays'? Have we been able to use them without abusing them or using them up? Have they regained the poetic power to speak to us 'as if we were hearing [them] for the first time'? To capture the nature of the unique word of a poet or a thinker – or of Paul, the poet-thinker – Heidegger uses the expression *die Erstlinge des Wortes*, the firstfruits of the word. This expression is a Pauline heirloom. 'Firstfruits' renders the Greek *aparchē*, which names the first fruit of the revivifying power of the spirit: 'we have the firstfruits of the spirit [*tēn aparchēn tou pneumatos*]' (Rom. 8:23). With this heirloom, Heidegger articulates the power of the word to quicken thought, to open up new ways for thinking and hearing, and to speak to us as for the first time, as on the first day. Freshness, newness and fruitfulness are returned to the word as on the first day of its creation or inception. The words that are part of our culture, presupposed by this culture as words belonging to its inception, belonging to our culture's 'in the beginning', *in principio*, regain their power to speak, become *initium*, words that speak here and now as for the first time and as on the first day. Looking back to the previous chapters, we may now ask to which extent the used-up words of the apostle can be said to have regained their poetic power. Have the explorations of ontology, ethics and political philosophy revivified another Pauline legacy for thinking? In which sense are the very stakes of the Pauline discovery of the outcast and the spirit found in this revivification?

Throughout this study, I have discussed several portrayals of this legacy. Some were judged to be limited and petrified. Some interpretations have indeed used up the serious words and were unable to revivify them. The Nietzschean lens that pervades, for instance, Derrida's and

Deleuze's assessment of the Pauline legacy, affects the portrait of Paul they paint. A similar concern arose with respect to those present-day readers who are incapable of resisting the Gnostic temptation to which all readers of Paul are exposed, beginning with Marcion of Sinope. Another limitation was found in the field of application assigned to his letters. I argued that another portrayal of Paul does not need to limit itself to 'the ongoing cultural and political functions of the Pauline legacy'.[1] It can also be revived *'before and apart from any need to profile it in an explicitly political manner'*.[2] Indeed, as I have argued, this legacy concerns first and foremost ontological and ethical questions, which subsequently do have important politico-theological variations and ramifications.

A new portrayal of Paul and another legacy of his letters that is worthwhile pursuing philosophically – such has been the argument in this book – equally moves away from a Nietzschean and a Marcionite frame, from both nihilism and dualism. Yet, when moving away from the Charybdis of dualism one should also steer clear of the Scylla of monism, represented by ancient Stoicism and its modern Hegelian legacy. Instead, I have argued that in Paul's letters a dialectic of exception may be discerned. This portrayal does not begin by filling in the socio-political colorations in the apostle's present-day countenance, but rather first draws the ontological and ethical features of his face, bringing out the mode of being, thinking and living that define the Pauline character.

POSITIONING PAUL IN ANCIENT THOUGHT

To capture how Paul navigates between the Scylla of monism and the Charybdis of dualism, I have discussed how present-day philosophy and new testamentary scholarship position Paul among the ancient philosophers.[3] This positioning comprises two distinct elements, which are dialectically related: (a) the reappraisal of ancient philosophy as a mode of living and (b) a particular, subtle detachment of Paul from ancient philosophy, in both vocabulary and ideas, that singularises his thought among the ancient philosophers and brings out the Pauline significance of the two basic motifs that guide my own study: the outcast or the scum (of the world) and the spirit (of God).

(a) Mode of Living, Thinking and Being

Chapter 2 discussed Foucault's account of ancient philosophy as an art of living, emphasising that ancient philosophy is not only guided by the ontological motif of the quest for another, higher world, but also always pursues the ethical motif, namely that of another mode of living that, in all its aspects, bears witness to a truth of human existence hidden from view. Paul belongs to the ancient world and his vocabulary is strongly indebted to ancient thought. Therefore, it is only a small step to approach his letters in light of this ethical motif as well. This is in part what happened in the 1990s. The Nietzschean-Marcionite portrait brings out features in Paul emphasising his ontological dualism and nihilism. However, the one-sidedness of these portraits becomes apparent as soon as the ethical motif is underlined. Indeed, the new philosophical portraits of Paul show how he is committed to a life according to the spirit. This turn in the assessment of the Pauline legacy can be understood along the following lines of thought.

First, the reappraisal of ancient philosophy and Paul alike concerns a shift from a dualistic ontology to an ethics or a new ethos, from seeking another, higher world to exercising another way of life in this world. This has several implications. For instance, the Nietzschean account of Pauline *pistis* or faith as *holding-to-be-true* the fiction of another world, as well as accompanying convictions – or, rather: con-fictions – is problematised. Faith is rather understood as a particular ethos adopted by believers. The account of *pistis* in terms of fidelity is a striking example: fidelity is not an epistemological notion but rather an ethical one. The emphasis on *chrēsis* or use is also part of this ethical reappraisal of Paul.

Second, by emphasising the ethical motif, the socio-political impact comes into view. Foucault's account of the ancient Cynics, his true heroes, shows that the exercise of living one's life in accordance with a truth that is not yet manifest in the current order of the world can have a strong, political outcome because this new way of living can turn into a political effort to transform the social, cultural world in line with this truth. Badiou's account of subject and event offers a Pauline version of Foucault's political, militant portrayal of Cynic life.

Third, once the idea of such a transformation of the social world becomes part of our understanding of the ethical motif, it becomes necessary to differentiate between the world as it is now and the world as it might or will be. This has an important hermeneutical consequence. Whenever we encounter passages in Paul's letters speaking of two worlds, we now have to decide whether they express a dualistic cosmology or rather concern two different social orders of this world. In the preceding chapters, we have seen several examples of this hermeneutic task. For instance, the Pauline difference between spirit and flesh, *pneuma* and *sarx*, need not signal a Gnostic dualism; rather, it may very well express that life according to the flesh complies with the current order of the world. Spirit, by contrast, is the principle that this order can change and is changing; by consequence, the life of the spirit accords with this change.

Fourth, however, the emphasis on the ethical motif does not mean that the term 'spirit' has lost its ontological sense, but rather that it needs to be reinterpreted. It would be wrong to read Paul's *pneuma* merely as a political spirit of change – for instance, towards emancipation or a genuinely equal world. This is true for ancient thought in general: the recommended other way of life is not motivated by the arbitrariness of a modern human will and its values or norms, but is rather grounded in a particular truth of being and existence. Ancient thought does not yet suffer from the modern dichotomy of freedom and nature, each equipped with their own metaphysics, as Kant has suggested. For the ancients, rather, ethos and ontology are closely connected: a mode of living corresponds to a mode of being. For instance, for Aristotle, the most desired life is one according to the *nous*, which has a metaphysical foundation. Similarly, Paul encourages life according to the spirit, *pneuma*. Hence, once the detour along the ethical motif has loosened the grip of a dualistic interpretation, a space opens up for more subtle ontological interpretations. My own proposal to think the Pauline legacy as a dialectic of exception belongs to this space.

An important example was encountered in the discussion of 1 Cor. 15, where Paul borrows *pneuma* from Stoic vocabulary and discusses *kosmos* in Stoic terms. Hence, *pneuma* is also an ontological and cosmological term. Yet, Paul deviates from Stoic monism as soon as he distinguishes between the spirit of God and the spirit of the *kosmos*. One could now take the hermeneutical decision that, in this way, Paul returns to dualism. Yet, by considering Paul's rhetorical strategy, another option reveals itself: he uses this Stoic term in a non-Stoic way – he is Stoic *as non*-Stoic, we might also say playing on his *hōs mē*-formula – thus disengaging it from its Stoic usage and releasing it for another use. Consequently, he is revising Stoic monism from the inside. Taking into account the ethical motif, we have to confront the question of what the ontological role of *pneuma* exactly is, if it endorses neither Platonic-Marcionite dualism nor Stoic monism. This question brought us to the ontological discussions explored in Chapters 3 and 4.

(b) Detachments

The reference to 1 Cor. 15 is important in yet another aspect. Paul's letters can be approached in a new way due to the reappraisal of ancient thought, but they also propose a genuinely different philosophical point of view because Paul deviates from ancient philosophical positions. In the course of this study, we have encountered several examples of such Pauline detachments. 1 Cor. 15 does this by using Stoic terminology in a non-Stoic way. Yet, there is another crucial example discussed in Chapter 2.

For Foucault, the ethical motif finds its completion in ancient Cynicism. In some aspects, Paul's phrasing of the ethical motif may remind us of a Cynic point of view and vocabulary, but is ultimately rephrased in a non-Cynic way. This rephrasing provides one more characteristic feature of Paul's present-day philosophical portrait, which we can track down when considering the figure of scandal, *skandalon*, in the ancient world. Not only Paul, but also ancient Cynicism, represents a way of life that the surrounding world experienced as radically nonconformist. As masters of suspicion *avant la lettre*, the Cynics are committed to ridding our existence of every embellishment and to revealing the bare truth of existence behind all of it. For them, this is no theoretical exercise, but is rather consummated in the Cynic life itself: it is shown in how they use their body, how they dress, how they behave themselves, and so on. Foucault therefore calls the Cynic a 'witness to the truth', *marturōn tēs alētheias*.[4] Their form of life is an expression of this truth: 'the [Cynic] body itself [is] the visible theater of the truth.'[5] This strongly resonates with Paul's remark that the body is a temple of the Holy Spirit (Cor. 6:19). In this body, the truth of the spirit manifests itself; and, in this body, it lives. According to the Cynics, this truth is a scandal for the members of society because it confronts them with their inability to live their lives in accordance with their thoughts and convictions, a motive also encountered in Paul's account of sin in Rom. 7. Courageously, the Cynic dares to denounce the gaping hole between thought and action, thus bearing witness to the truth.[6]

Hence, a clear affinity between Foucault's Cynic and the present-day philosophical Paul exists. The question, however, is: up to what point? Where exactly do the Cynic and Paul part ways? At which point can the scandal and the corresponding way of life Paul proclaims no longer be understood as a variation of (Foucault's portrayal of) Cynicism? To answer this question, we must first know *what* truth is experienced as scandal by the Cynics. Foucault understands the Cynic life in terms of the ancient desire for a sovereign life: '[S]overeign life is a life in possession of itself, a life of which no fragment, no element escapes the exercise of its power and sovereignty over itself. Being sovereign is first and foremost being one's own, belonging to oneself.'[7] The Cynics offer a radicalised version of this life, as the infamous meeting between Alexander the Great and Diogenes the Cynic illustrates. Diogenes faces

Alexander with his bare life: the former possesses 'nothing, no army, court, allies, or anything else'.[8] Diogenes may seem less sovereign; yet, he actually is in a less precarious position than Alexander, who stands to lose army, court, allies and so much more. The sovereignty of the latter is not truly and naturally his own and can thereby be overturned. Therefore, as Foucault summarises: 'The Cynic is a true king; only he is an unrecognized, unknown king who, by the way he lives, [...] deliberately hides himself as king. [...] He is a king of poverty [...] who hides his sovereignty in destitution.'[9]

This highlights an important difference between Paul and Cynicism. In Paul, the ideal of sovereignty is thwarted by the idea of the *doulos*, the slave or servant of Christ. Thus, after having noted that the body is the temple of the spirit, he remarks in that the Corinthians do not belong to themselves but to God (Cor. 6). Hence, there is no mention of sovereignty in the sense of self-ownership. The Pauline emphasis on use, *chrēsis*, in 1 Cor. 7, which is an *alternative* to possession, ownership and (self-)mastery, is therefore nothing less than a Pauline correction of the Cynic ideal of self-ownership and self-determination.[10]

More importantly, even if one sees a hidden, Cynic king in the figure of Christ – and why would this not be possible? – one should add that, for Paul, the true scandal of Christ is his crucifixion. The cross is not only scandalous because it is confrontational and offensive, as Diogenes' behaviour was, but also because it refers to a deeper layer of the bare life at stake in Paul's Christianity that is more unbearable than the Cynic one of austerity and poverty. Because the natural or bare life of the Cynics remains indebted to the ancient idea of sovereign self-ownership, it is incapable of reaching the depth of a Pauline form of bare life that I addressed under the heading of 'the outcast' and 'the scum of the world'. Paul's version of 'unbearable life', to borrow Bradley's striking term, manifested in the figures of slave, cross, scum and outcast radicalises the idea of the nakedness and bareness of existence, up to the point where natural self-sovereignty no longer makes any sense. This highlights a fundamental difference between the Cynic and the Pauline scandal. The Pauline version of the scandal therefore demands another sovereignty, another truly sovereign spirit that quickens – *zōopoieō* – the life that is unbearable and finds itself reduced to a deathlike state. In this particular sense, the Cynic unity of scandal and sovereignty is unhinged and transformed into the Pauline dyad of the scum of the world and the spirit of God, the death on the cross and the divine power to call to life what is dead.

To summarise: Paul's account of the spirit confronts us with a non-Stoic use of a Stoic term. Paul's account of the scandal confronts us with a non-Cynic use of a Cynic motif. In its non-Cynic use, the genuine scandal concerns the outcast and the scum of the world, a life 'simply deemed to be ontologically or politically nonexistent'.[11] Thus, by suspending the Nietzschean and Marcionite image of a dualistic, nihilist Paul, two ways in which Paul disengages from ancient thought become visible, disclosing a non-Stoic spirit and a non-Cynic outcast, respectively. These two concepts offer us the two poles of a thought that concerns ontology, ethics and politics alike and which, in the course of this study, I have termed a Pauline dialectic of exception.

By describing Paul's use of the terms of the spirit and the outcast as a distortion of and disengagement from their proper Stoic and Cynic use, we have already encountered a concrete dialectic in the formation of Pauline concepts – we might even call it an example of his pneumatic hermeneutics, not applied to Jewish texts, but to ancient Greek philosophical concepts. The distinguishing feature in the portrayal of Paul arising from 1 Cor. 15 is a distortion of Stoicism. Paul's spirit is an *exception* to the general rule that regulates the use of *pneuma* in Stoicism. By detaching *pneuma* from this regulated, Stoic usage, he opens up the linguistic space for a new use and for a new interpretation of this concept. Similarly, by detaching *skandalon* from its Cynic significance, he opens up the possibility of a new interpretation of the notions of scandal, scum, exile and outcast. We thus have come across a particular dialectic of exception in Paul's rhetorico-poetico-hermeneutical strategy by which *pneuma*, *skandalon* and *hōs perikatharmata tou kosmou*, scum of the world, can be heard as if for the first time. This strategy is mirrored in a conceptual dialectic of spirit and outcast in his ontology and ethics.

NAVIGATING DIALECTICALLY

Foucault's reappraisal of ancient thought distinguishes the Platonic ontological commitment to dualism from the Socratic ethical concern. My assessment of the implications of this reappraisal for reinterpreting the Pauline legacy suggests that this distinction between ontology and ethics cannot be maintained. Rather, the ethical concern presupposes *another* ontological commitment, which remains concealed as long as we take dualism for granted. Therefore, any attempt to disclose this other ontological commitment needs to keep track of the ethical counterpart as well – and, indeed, these go hand in hand in ancient thought and are interwoven in Paul's letters. For this reason, one cannot but treat the particular ontological and ethical commitments of Paul together.

Looking back on Chapters 3 and 4, which discuss Paul's ontological commitment and our philosophical assessment thereof, what is the dialectic of exception that is taking shape in them? As the Marcionite and Nietzschean readings form the background of the philosophical turn to Paul, two issues take precedence: How can Paul be detached from a Gnostic, Platonic dualism? How or to what extent does Paul offer an ontology that is not nihilistic, that is, does not discard the weight and gravity of the world in which we live?

(a) Meontology and Ethos

Let me begin with the second issue and recall the argument developed in Chapter 3 that the meontology presented in 1 Corinthians is not nihilistic. This letter is important because it offers the blueprint of Paul's understanding of the difference – and even the opposition – between the spirit of the world and the spirit of God. This distinction makes all the difference. The discussion of the *tou kosmou*-formulas in 1 Corinthians as well as the passing away of the present form or order of this world, *to schēma tou kosmou toutou* (Cor. 7) has shown that the goal of this opposition is not the affirmation of another, higher ontological dimension in reality. By contrast, the stakes of this distinction are found in a third term, namely *ta mē onta*, the things that are not or, simply, the non-beings. The nothingness of these things is the nothingness of the scum and the outcast. It is not mere nothingness, not *ouk on*, but rather a qualified one, *mē on*. It concerns that which is considered to be nothing or which is not allowed to flourish or even to exist in what Paul calls the world, *kosmos*. Yet, when considered from the perspective of the spirit of God, they somehow are.

Rather than signalling a dualism or nihilism, this conception of nothingness actually manifests a dialectic tension in the notion of *kosmos*. In the first place, *kosmos* concerns the totality of all that is; *kosmos* is the All, *ta panta*, in which every being has its ordered place and position. Yet, Paul's meontology shows that this identification is threatened by that which from the perspective of the *kosmos* as All is nothing, but which in another sense somehow *is*: the scum, the things that are not, the outcast, the cross, the slave and so on, are the remnants left out of the order represented by the *kosmos*; they form the *exception* to the identification of *kosmos* and All. In exactly this sense, these meontological notions manifest the *crisis* of the *kosmos* as All in Paul's cosmology: they are a part of the All without being a part of the order of the *kosmos*. In his letters, as the figures of slave and cross show, this cosmological crisis is mirrored in a crisis of the social order of the world and its outcasts.[12]

In light of this twofold crisis, a Pauline conception of God is introduced. Paul's God serves to *detach* from the ontological commitment that the *kosmos* is the All. Yet, this disengagement is not nihilistic. God is not the term for the destruction or bringing to nothing of the world, as some Bible translations read it. In this context, the discovery of *katargēsis*, deactivation or suspension, is of the utmost importance. When using this or related terms, Paul does not proclaim the forthcoming destruction of the world, but rather the suspension of the identification of world and All, *so that the scum and the outcast may be brought into view*.

Paul's God thus strongly deviates from the metaphysical one. The latter, as can be seen in Aristotle's *Metaphysics*, is the culmination point of the ontological order represented by the term *kosmos*. The spirit of God, by contrast, acknowledges the crisis of this world and displays a preference for the exception to the encompassing order of the *kosmos*. In 1 Cor. 1, this ontological concern is indeed mirrored in a social one. The majority of the members of the community in Corinth are not strong, intelligent, powerful or rich. This means that they are awarded no place or role of significance – or even no place at all – within the present order of the social world. Paul's God is not the peak of this order. Paul's God does not favour what is strong, intelligent, powerful or rich, but rather that which is reduced to nothing in and by this order. In this sense, it is not the Pauline God that is nihilistic; it is rather the identification of world and All as well as its mirror image in the socio-political world that has nihilistic effects: by not acknowledging the crisis of this identification, it produces outcasts and unbearable life and reduces to nothingness that which nevertheless is.

Let me add one more remark concerning the difference between the Pauline God and the ontotheological, Aristotelian one. The Pauline God cannot be understood as the object of the contemplative gaze of a subject enjoying and knowing the eternal being as well as the eternal order of beings that is grounded in this being. In relation to the self, the mode of being of the Pauline God is fundamentally different. To express this, the early Heidegger often uses the verb 'to have': the self *has* the beings it associates with or uses; the self *has* God; or the self *has* itself. For the early Heidegger, 'to have' does not express possession or a related sense, but rather expresses the enactment of the relation to other beings, to others, to itself or to God.[13] In this context, the Pauline self *has* God to the extent that, in using or associating with – *chraomai* – other beings, others or itself, the self enacts these relations in such a way that they gain a specific significance, namely a pneumatic one. The detachment from the way of the world and from the forms of dealings with – *chraomai, chrēsis* – the world, others and self that are prescribed by this way of the world thus displays its positive dimension. To have God means to enact one's relations to what is – one's worldly callings, one's relations to beings or people in the world and one's situation – *pneumatically*. Hence, *pneuma* does not refer to another entity, but is rather the name for the specific enactment and significance that characterises the self's having of God. This also implies that the Pauline God *is simply not accessible* to the objective gaze of the subject contemplating an eternal order. The Pauline God is only accessible in and as this particular pneumatic having of everything that is.

The awareness of the crisis of the world in both an ontological and social sense thus has a direct 'ethical' expression in the form of what Heidegger called enactment. The famous imperative in 1 Cor. 7 to live in the mode of 'as not' perfectly illustrates this. One lives and works in the present social order of the world, and one cannot simply step out of it. Yet, if this order were perfectly sound and without a crisis, one could fully identify with it as well as with the callings one has in it. Given the crisis, however, the task is to identify neither with this order nor with the role assigned to one. Hence, the Pauline ethos is not a simple rejection of the world; it is not *against* the world, and it does not call for a complete withdrawal from the *kosmos*. It rather calls for exercising the detachment from this order and its attachments and commitments because this disengagement opens up a space in which the crisis of this order is disclosed and releases the possibility for a deactivation of this order and its destructive effects. Due to the non-coincidence of order and All, the order is truly like a machine that is broken and therefore needs to be deactivated.

Hence, quite a specific ethos speaks from and mirrors Paul's meontology. In this sense, Badiou's description of the Pauline ethos in terms of *fidelity* to an event foreign to the world and coming from the outside runs the risk of reducing Paul to yet another subtle form of dualism. Yet, what we need to retain from Badiou's analysis is his anti-Nietzschean attempt to understand *pistis* not as a holding-to-be-true or as not-wanting-to-know but rather as a particular ethos. *Pistis* means trust and fidelity; yet, it concerns the trust that the suspension of the rule and the law of the world releases and discloses the possibilities of different ways of living and being than those that this order of the world has to offer. In this respect, Paul's account of *chrēsis* or use in the specific sense of using as not abusing is of crucial importance. This notion mirrors that of *katargēsis*. Because the latter notion does not concern the destruction of the world, the Pauline idea of a new creation is not another creation, but the same creation in which, nevertheless, to paraphrase Heidegger and Agamben, everything is different. This difference can ethically be understood in terms of *use*. In fact, this notion articulates the significance of the mode of living *hōs mē*. Life in the mode of 'as not' is a life that is in the process of *disengaging* from rather than *identifying* with the present order of the world. The enigmatic *hōs mē*-chorus from 1 Cor. 7:29–31 suggests this: neither in marriage, nor in sorrow, nor in joy, nor in economic exchange, nor in any dealings with the world, should we be wholly absorbed. However, it expressly does *not* say that we should not marry, mourn, rejoice, barter or associate. The 'as not' chorus, therefore, expresses something else. It says that all our forms and practices of life can always be accomplished in two ways. In the first mode of enactment, we blindly conform to the prevailing paradigms of the world and see no alternative – we do not even come up with the thought of an alternative. Without the 'as not' there is only marriage, mourning, rejoicing, bartering and dealing with the world as we know it from the prevailing worldly paradigm, so that they can only have the prevailing importance and significance. The expression 'as not', on the other hand, introduces a certain leeway and space to play between the particular practice – of mourning, rejoicing, bartering and so on – and its prevailing significance or form. The 'as not' thus opens up a space for finding or creating other meanings, other forms, other practices, other considerations and other thoughts. Such a life thus opens up a latitude with respect to this order. The space that thus appears is not that of a new order, but rather the space of a free, creative use of the world for the mutual dealings – *chrēsis* – of humans with each other and other beings as well as the space of a pneumatic interpretation of all there is in the world, granting everything a new sense in this mode of living. The last of the *hōs mē*-formulas, to use the world as not abusing it, emphasises that this new mode of living is one marked by its own tension, test and ordeal, that is, by a dialectic battle to ward off the intrinsic risk of degeneration – expressed by the Greek prefix *kata*- – in every use by which the exception proves to be true.

This ethos is mirrored in Paul's cosmology. The new creation is not a new, perfect(ed) order of the world. The notion of the new creation should not be explained in Gnostic terms as if the old *kosmos* and its order are the product of the evil creator-god, while the new creation is a new product, another *kosmos* and another order, created by the good father-god. The Pauline new creation rather implies that the *kosmos* itself must give way to a similar latitude, to a non-coinciding with the All, offering the remnant, the outcast and *ta mē onta* a space to be.

The kabbalistic tradition uses the term *tzimtzum* to describe the act of creation as a kenotic movement: the creator contracts itself and by contracting opens up the space for creation to be.[14] Pauline *katargēsis* can perhaps be understood in terms of such a contraction of the *kosmos* so that, within the All, a space of difference opens up between the *kosmos* and the All. This space is the space of play and latitude of the spirit. Although this description is rather speculative and might perhaps even be considered to be abstract or overtly theological, it is important to see how this proposal to rethink the Pauline notion of new creation and its implications for a mode of living and being, is actually concerned with heightening the creative capacity of creation. Creation is not identical to the *kosmos*. Creation rather concerns a basic difference between *kosmos*, as *created* creation or created order, and *creating* creation. In the course of this study, I have shown how my conception of this difference has several sources of inspiration. Let me only recall how it is a reinterpretation of Arendt's account of Augustine's twofold notion of beginning: while the order of creation, or *kosmos*, is in the beginning, *in principio*, the creative resources to begin something novel and original in this order are referred to by *initium*: *pneuma* is the very principle of grace, granting the creature the potential of *initium*.[15] At this point, one might raise the following suspicion. Does this cosmological approach through the lens of the notion of creation not lead us back to an ontotheological paradigm? And was not this paradigm the one we aimed to overcome by turning to Paul, as I suggested above?[16] I address this suspicion in the next subsection.

To end this subsection, though, let me offer an example to illustrate what is at stake in this differentiation in creation, and let me do this in terms of what the ethos of *chrēsis* means that guides this interpretation of Paul's cosmology.[17] As children we are taught our mother tongue. In the course of time, we are introduced to the full order of this language; we learn its grammar, its structural features, its semantics; we learn (part of) what has been said and written in this language; we learn its expressive power; and so on. Yet, our linguistic capacity is only truly manifest when we can freely use this language, discover our own style in our mode of writing, and discover our voice in our mode of speaking. This discovery is not the sign of our *possession* of this language – what would it mean to possess a language when one is not even able to grasp the totality of what is expressed therein? – but rather of our use of, of our continuous *Umgang* – our dealing or association, *chrēsis* – with the language that we inherited from our parents and our social world. Hence, this use is not free because it lacks linguistic constraints; rather, in our dealings with our mother tongue, possibilities of speaking and writing are released that belong to and happen *in our singular use alone*. When this happens, the possibility to speak with one's own voice is granted. Thus, the free use of language demonstrates performatively that language does not coincide with itself; the All of language does not coincide with the order of language or with the totality of everything that has been produced in or by language. Our linguistic capacity flourishes in the linguistic space of play in which our own voice and style are born. By contrast, our linguistic capacity suffers – much like Paul's creation does – when vocabularies are forced on it, suppressing our style and voice. Our capacity to think suffers – much like Paul's creation does – when it is forced to repeat, be it slogans and propaganda or mathematised theories and petrified concepts; and our capacity to understand is rendered helpless and passive in such circumstances.[18] Language and thought flourish by exceptional, singular voices that speak the words of language and thought as if for the first time, thus enriching and transforming language and thought, but they die when the voices that are heard are only particular instances and repetitions of what has been heard and said before, when their speech only abuses and uses up the words they inherit from language and thought.

(b) Gnostic and Stoic Temptations

The speculative description of the *kosmos* and its accompanying *ethos* is the first ingredient of a Pauline dialectic of exception. Yet, Paul's ontological legacy is not exhausted by his meontology. *Katargēsis* is the dialectic suspension of the order of the *kosmos*. By this *epochē*, a place and a voice are given to that which is excluded by this order: the non-coinciding of the All with itself discloses a remnant that demands a place in the world.

This dialectic movement, as noted several times in the course of this study, should avoid the Charybdis of dualism and the Scylla of monism. In modern thought, the latter confronts us with a particular problem. There are passages in which Paul indeed seems to suggest a monism; for instance, in the famous: 'For from him and through him and to him are all things [*ta panta*]' (Rom. 11:36), in which God seems to be described in more or less Stoic, monistic terms. The Stoic temptation reappears at the heart of one of the major dialectic systems that affirms this Pauline legacy, namely that of Hegel. To avoid a Hegelian, totalising monism, one has to rediscover Paul's non-Stoic use of this term and emphasise his distinction between the spirit of the world – Hegel's *Weltgeist* – and the spirit of God. Paul's account of the spirit of God has to be rescued from both its Nietzschean rejection and its Hegelian identification with the spirit of the world.

The spirit of the world is the principle of the rational order represented by the *kosmos*. In its modern, Hegelian instance, it is the principle of the rational self-realisation of the *kosmos* in a dynamic, dialectic form. Equating the spirit of the world with that of God would thus be a powerful reinstatement of a rational, dynamical order permeating the All in a dialectic form. Yet, for Paul, the spirit of God is nothing less than the principle of *initium*, of initiating and beginning; it is in this sense truly the *archē* that harbours a power of transformation by which the order of the world becomes transitory. It is described as quickening what is dead, as giving life to the dead, *zōopoiountos tous nekrous*. God is the one who calls to existence the things that are not: *kalountas ta mē onta hōs onta* (Rom. 4:17). In this sense, it is the spirit of God that names a basic motif in a philosophical reappraisal of the apostle's letters.[19]

The Pauline conviction that the spirit of the *kosmos* is not all there is, is closely related to the aforementioned difference of *kosmos* and *ta panta*. The space of latitude opened up by this difference is the space of play of the spirit of God in distinction to that of the world. In its present-day philosophical interpretation, brought out by Breton, the spirit of God represents with respect to the *kosmos* a specific type of *contingency* that Paul identifies as grace, *charis*. For bare life to be made alive and for bare existence to be endowed a flourishing existence, it is not enough to follow the spirit of the world; they require a contingent rupture with the rational order of the world; they require grace.

Conceptually, Pauline grace and its contingency appear under the heading of the event, which concerns that which cannot be deduced from or anticipated in the order of the world. Even though different authors tend to embrace different exemplary Pauline events – such as resurrection, Parousia and the time that remains – in each case, the event suspends the order of the world and demonstrates its transience, its passing away. The event is the contingent presence of the spirit of God in world history, granting new possibilities of existing and living. Without contingency, there would be no real history, but only changes that follow (from) the inherent principles of movement prescribed by the spirit of the world. To be fully human – thus seems to be the shared conviction of these three authors – means to witness this grace in its contingency.

Yet, one can be a witness in different ways. In the context of his transvaluation of Paul, Badiou's theory of the event implies that to witness grace is nothing less than to become loyal to it. For him, the subject of fidelity is a witness to the truth in the all-pervading and militant sense that Foucault already put forward in his account of ancient Cynicism. As opposed to Badiou's antidialectic approach to Paul, leading to a subtle form of dualism, Heidegger's and Agamben's conception of the grace of the event is genuinely dialectic. For them, the ethos of *hōs mē* enacts the disengaging from the order of the world. In this case, the event is not structured as an idea or a good cause, as Badiou's theory suggests, but the event rather concerns the human experience of the transience of the *kosmos* and the social world, as well as of the particular forms of existence that the *kosmos* and social world enable. This order and all that it entails are no longer experienced as stable and secure. This experience, as Heidegger notes, has its ethical mirror-image in the self-understanding of the Thessalonians: they know of their 'having-become', that is, of the rupture of contingency that happened in and to their existence and are encouraged to live their lives in accordance with the experience of contingency at stake in the phenomenon of the *parousia*.

The Pauline sense of an ending is therefore not nihilistic, but rather contains a particular promise. To experience the contingency of all that is means to affirm the promise and the possibility of a full existence for that which is barely allowed existence in the order; it means to see the potentiality-of-being-otherwise.[20] In this perspective, other features of *pistis* are brought out: it does not appear as a Badiouan fidelity to a good cause but rather as a particular trust. *Pistis* now is the trust that the experienced contingency is indeed grace, that is, trust in the promise of the event that the disengagement from the order of the world will indeed be quickening, life-endowing and existence-granting. That this contingency is grace cannot be known; it is rather an article of faith, trust and hope.

These notions of trust, promise and grace also determine, it seems to me, the politico-theological variation of this Pauline approach. Yet, before turning to this variation, we need to assess where the distinction between the spirit of the world and the spirit of God leaves us with respect to the alternative of dualism and monism. One could comment as follows: 'By introducing two spirits to avoid monism, we basically return to a Marcionite model; hiding this under the rubric of a dialectic, makes one a "crypto-Marcionite".' Do these attempts to overcome the Scylla of monism indeed drive us into the Charybdis of dualism? Breton perceptively describes how Paul's rhetoric navigates between these two alternatives in the form of a 'hesitation between a necessity that imposes itself and a gratuity that challenges it'.[21]

If we take the Pauline idea of creation seriously and truly aim to avoid a Marcionite conception of it, there seems to be only one solution, namely that the spirit of the *kosmos* is, in some way, another manifestation of God or, rather, another relation of God to what is. At this point, Kierkegaard's dialectic of exception is of crucial importance. His description of the relationship between the universal – which in his case is another term for God – and the exception shows that it has two modalities. As discussed in Chapter 4, these are reflected in two attitudes or tendencies in the relationship of the universal to the exception. On the one hand, the universal attempts to subsume the exception, include it, and grant it its proper position in the rational order of the universal. On the other hand, the universal demonstrates a peculiar preference for the exception; the universal silently and secretly hopes and prays that the exception proves to be worthy of its own position as exception, introducing a relationship between the universal and the exception that does not culminate in a reduction of the exception to a moment or element in the rational order of the universal.

In Kierkegaard's case, these two modalities serve his account of the ethical and the religious modes of existence. In the former, the human relationship to God is mediated by the rational, universal norms of ethics. In the latter, this relationship is immediate and understood in terms of a faith that cannot take recourse to these universal, rational norms. His account of the second ethos displays formal similarities with the Pauline ethos of *hōs mē* and *chrēsis*: in both cases, the pregiven normative structures cannot be relied upon and, instead, a particular sense of *pistis* is required. In line with the considerations in the previous sections, in which each ontological conception is mirrored in an ethical one, and vice versa, I have also brought into play the ontological mirror-image of this Kierkegaardian – and basically ethical – dialectic of exception. We can now draw the conclusion from this 'ontologisation' of Kierkegaard.

In the Pauline understanding, the relationship of God to what is has two modalities: in mediation, God is creator, while in immediacy, God is revivifying power.[22] These two modalities are described in terms of the spirit of the world and the spirit of God, respectively. The former concerns the first creation and its intrinsic, dynamic, rational order. The latter, by contrast, concerns another, immediate relation of beings to the life-granting, creative power of God, indicating that a being's reality or existence does not coincide with its mediated place in the *kosmos*. This difference marks in each being a particular surplus of reality and existence that surpasses the order of the *kosmos*; each creature is somehow more than it was created to be, or rather becomes more thanks to the possibilities that arise in this immediate relation. To describe the spirit of God as life-granting, as life from death, or as calling to life and being, means that this surplus of being is brought into play, quickening being, endowing it with another intensity of existence and reality: it exists as for the first time and as on the first day. In the Pauline vocabulary of creation, all beings share in the creative powers of God, but they first share in it mediately, in the *kosmos*, in the order of what has been created. This order distributes reality and existence to each being according to its place. Yet, due to the crisis of the *kosmos*, another sharing in and sharing out of the creative power of God has become necessary; the spirit of God concerns a supplementary, immediate sharing in this creative power, no longer depending on a mediating order, but directly quickening a being to a more intense mode of being, reality and existence.

This, then, allows us to offer a particular interpretation of Rom. 8:20–3, of its sense of creation and of the firstfruits of the spirit. When one touches on the weakness and futility of creation, one is no longer capable of recognising creation as the expression of a creating power. In its futility, in its bondage to decay, *kosmos* as creation is experienced as banned from these creative powers. Rom. 8:20–1 bears witness to this abandonment. In this futility, the non-beings that seem to be the exception to the order of the world in fact appear as the *pars pro toto* of the *kosmos*. However, the suspension of this order opens up the space of the quickening of the exception to its full being, now having – that is: enacting – the firstfruits of the spirit, as Rom. 8:23 says.

These two modalities of being are also crucial in our understanding of Paul's notion of the new creation; it is the very same creation that we know under the heading of *kosmos* – the same world that surrounds us populated by the same beings – but now one in which the order of the world is suspended so that its surplus of being is given the space and latitude to play. Along these lines of thought, inspired by Agamben and Kierkegaard, we may avoid being swallowed by the Charybdis of dualism. There is no destruction of the world in Paul; there is only a quickening of all that is, only seeing and creating possibilities beyond that which the order of the world has to offer, returning creative potentiality to what was once created as completed work and order.[23] There are not two ontological orders, but only two modalities of reality and existence[24] – two modalities of creation, if one prefers to use the theological notion – a twofold *partage de l'être*, to borrow Nancy's expression: two ways in which beings share in being and two ways in which being is shared out to all beings – mediately according to order and immediately according to the power that quickens, makes alive and calls to existence. In this sense, Nietzsche's opposition between the human power of creation and Pauline faith, as discussed in Chapter 2, becomes obsolete because the latter *is* commitment to the power of creation, with the additional note that this power is not naturally – *psuchikon* – given but is granted and called to life and existence by *pneuma*.

In such a conception, to come back to the suspicion raised above, creation is no longer an ontotheological notion. When Heidegger raises the problem of the ontotheological constitution of scholastic metaphysics in its understanding of the *ens creatum*, he does so because, in this framework, creation is understood in terms of causality and of the principle of sufficient reason as well as in terms of the divine, contemplative gaze in which each and every being is reduced to an object.[25] Hence, the *ens creatum* is only the created being, taken up in the created order of the *kosmos*. However, thought as a notion to describe the pneumatic and the revivifying power, creation is another characterisation of the pneumatic significance of all that we encounter in the situation in which we live and exist: it speaks of the quickening, the renewal, and the intensification of our relation to all that is.

(c) Politico-Theological Variations

The interplay of ethical and ontological considerations offers us a portrait of Paul in which the features of a dialectic of exception stand out. In Chapters 5 and 6, I have argued how the much-debated sociopolitical implications of the Pauline legacy can, in fact, be understood as a politico-theological variation of the portrayal that captures these features.

In this politico-theological variation, the scum of the world, the outcast and the non-beings appear as bare, unbearable and precarious life or, in Schmitt's terminology, as enemies of the people.[26] In Chapters 5 and 6, I used Taubes as point of departure because he argues how much of the 'theology' informing Schmitt's political theology actually stems from a particular, distorted Pauline legacy. Just like Nietzsche, to paraphrase Blanton, Schmitt 'failed radically to transform [...] the ongoing cultural and political functions of the Pauline legacy'.[27] How do the concerns explored in Paul's ontology and ethics affect the politico-theological understanding of law and community?

In Paul's political theology, law plays a role analogous to that of order in his cosmology. In Schmitt, the suspension of the law is understood in terms of a purification. The confusion and contamination in a community leading to a crisis calls for purification: the impure community needs to be divided in a community of friends, forming the new people, and their enemies. The state of exception is the space of this purification and the casting out of enemies. The latter are, from a socio-political point of view, genuinely nothing: they have no place and are not allowed to exist in the state or social order constituted in the state of exception. This, one might summarise all too briefly, is the Marcionite version of political theology, still inspiring forms of anti-Semitism in the twentieth century.

Following Schmitt's version, the suspension of the law opens up the space of the original constituting powers – or violence – of formation of the people and the constitution. The law as well as the actual political community are thus the order that is brought about by these constituting powers. Consequently, a given people can only relate mediately – through the unity of their political community and its constitution – to these constituting powers. As both Taubes and Agamben remind us, Schmitt sensed the profound political significance of Kierkegaard's notion of exception. The state of exception is exactly the realm in which these constituting powers act immediately.

Yet, concerning the nature of these constituting powers, a Marcionite and a Pauline account part ways. For Schmitt, the state of exception is the space of purification by means of a political distinction – that is, the dualism of friend and enemy. In Schmitt's raw conception of the political, this friend–enemy distinction, and the basic dispute undergirding it, offers the structural means to constitute a community. Its common enemy binds a people together as one. This constituting violence in turn grants the constitution its power. The Pauline version is not dualistic but dialectic. The outcast or 'the part without part' does not define the political; it is not the solution to but rather the very principle of the *crisis* of a political community and its constitution, since the production of unbearable or bare life intrinsically belongs to the constitution of this socio-political community. In the Pauline state of exception, however, we do not encounter a friend–enemy distinction, but rather a realm marked by the politico-theological variation of promise, trust and faith. Consequently, it points to fundamentally different constituting powers of both community and law.

In principle, the law mediates justice or righteousness, *dikaiosunē*. This is the Pauline logic: the law is supposed to be life-enhancing; this is how it is supposed to share in justice. A crisis of the law means that this mediation of justice in a society is obstructed. When the law no longer functions, it needs to be suspended in order to share in an immediate way in that which inspires the law. In this sense – and much closer to Kierkegaard than Schmitt's version – the state of exception is the politico-theological variation of the space of grace, where, despite the crisis of the law, justice is nevertheless accessible for a community in its free use of the world without abusing it.

Similarly, the constitution of a community is not the consequence of a primordial political dispute between friend and enemy, but rather concerns a contingent and singular promise that this particular set of humans can be a people, as long as they trust this promise and attest to their loyalty to it in and by their actions. As Heidegger emphasises, this promise is engraved in the existence of the members of the community: their existence is 'having-become [*Gewordensein*]'; they have experienced a rupture in their existence which marks their belonging to this community of the promise, this community of those who have experienced the potentiality-of-being-otherwise in their existence. A constituted political community is thus based neither on the casting out of enemies nor on a shared Badiouan conception of the good cause. Rather, it is based on the promise of being a community as well as on the people's attestation in speech and action that they are and can be true to this promise. The emphasis on promise, trust and attestation demonstrates that it is never a matter of certainty that a set of people can be a community, but rather of contingency; therefore, promise, trust and attestation are supplemented by the notion of grace. Here, another sense of exception is at stake: in the Schmittian state of exception, bare existence and unbearable life are created; in the Pauline state of exception, the quickening of living together and being a community in a new way is experienced.

As the discussion of *aphōrismenos* has shown, this Pauline version does include a separation, but it is not the separation of an enemy that, by this separation, defines the community. Separation from the constituted community is rather the way in which human beings are called to this promise of community. This is the dialectic meaning of 'Neither Jew, nor Greek': even though one culturally and socially belongs to particular groups in a society, one is not identical to or identifiable by these forms of belonging. If the political is understood in terms of such an identification, we simply embrace the Marcionite-Schmittian version of the Pauline legacy because then we consider this identification and the dispute among identities arising from it, as defining the political. The political, however, can also be understood according to another variation of the Pauline legacy. To be called means to be called not to coincide or identify with one's particular identities and forms of belonging, but rather to share, together with all others, in the promise of a community that is enabled by *aphōrismenos*. Pauline separation concerns neither the production of opposing groups or of unbearable life, but rather the creation of a remnant in us, 'chosen by grace', by which we are granted the use of our own voice and body to speak and to act. This, basically, is the politico-theological variation of Paul's new creation, which is not another creation, but rather the revivification of the old one in which each being that exists is granted the potential of creating and of *initium*.[28] The new people is not another people, constituted by a violently installed separation of equals and outcasts; rather, it is the same people, suspended and dissolved as people, but called as remnant, by and to the promise of the potentiality-of-being-otherwise.

FIRSTFRUITS OF THE SPIRIT

In his reassessment of the Cynic mode of life, Foucault underlines the importance of being a witness to the truth. Life according to the spirit may, perhaps, be described in similar terms. It witnesses to the bare existence of the outcasts who *demand* to be heard. This witnessing takes place when, varying on Rom. 8:22, a voice sighing for redemption is heard in the murmur of creation and the diffuse noise uttered by ontological and social outcasts. It is tempting to view the spiritual interpretation at stake in Paul's distinction between letter and spirit as being concerned with finding another, higher meaning – such that, for example, the vanity or purposelessness to which the creation is subject according to Rom. 8:20 is abolished in another, higher sense and another, higher order. However, the Pauline dialectic of exception developed in the course of this study suggests a more basic account of pneumatic hermeneutics.

Every interpretation, every attempt to understand and unfold the meaning of an event or phenomenon, assumes arranging and sifting. We create order by our attempts to understand a text, to form a community and to develop a legal system, but in this process we also sift the understandable from the incomprehensible. Our interpretations thus tend to leave behind the scum sifted out in this way; we subsequently regard what has been cast out as marginal, unreal or unimportant, and after a while do not even notice or pay attention to it anymore as we do when we block out background noise. In this way, the possibility of having significance is taken away from this outcast in the order that has thus arisen. Against the background of such a conception of hermeneutics, the urgency of a pneumatic hermeneutics becomes clear. The firstfruits of the spirit of this pneumatic hermeneutics creates the ability to hear (that there is) a remainder; to perceive the insignificant noise of a text, the murmur of an event, phenomenon or person as a demand to speak. The spirit quickens the insignificant noise of mere murmur to a voice that addresses.[29] It is thus that one partakes of the community of those 'who have the firstfruits of the spirit' (Rom. 8:23).

No voice is heard, only murmur and inward groaning. Yet, perhaps, who knows, the spirit lends a voice to the suppressed murmur of that which counts for nothing and is cast out. Perhaps, the spirit calls the noise to be a voice. And perhaps the witness living according to the spirit may be attentive and listen to the voice that thus begins to summon and to speak, establishing communication and community. How this happens and what this involves is a theme for another book.[30]

NOTES

1. Blanton, *A Materialism for the Masses*, 3–4.
2. Bloechl, 'Love and Law according to Paul and Some Philosophers', 151; the implication in this article that Agamben reduces Paul's letters to their political stakes seems incorrect to me. Abbott's suggestion in *The Figure of the World* to speak of a political ontology is more accurate: his politico-philosophical concepts are derived from particular ontological convictions; yet, I would emphasise that this ontology cannot be separated from its Pauline, theological bearings.
3. See also Van der Heiden and Van Kooten, 'Epilogue'.
4. Foucault, *Le Courage de la vérité*, 160/173.
5. Ibid., 168–9/183.
6. Ibid., 215–16/234; 168/182.
7. Ibid., 248/271.
8. Ibid., 254/276.
9. Ibid., 255/278.
10. For the relation between Agamben, Foucault and Cynicism, see also Van der Heiden, 'Exile, Use, and Form-of-Life'.
11. Bradley, *Unbearable Life*, 5.
12. The mirroring of the cosmological order in musical order and in the order of the soul, thus shaping a particular mode of living, is itself an important theme in ancient thought regulating the basic sense of *mimēsis*; see Gadamer, 'Kunst und Nachahmung', 34–5.
13. See Heidegger, *Phänomenologie des religiösen Lebens*, 91–2/63–4, 189–92/139–41 (in relation to Augustine); and Heidegger, *Einführung in die phänomenologische Forschung*, 249/193.
14. According to Sawczyński, 'The Significant Nothing', 76, 82–5, *tzimtzum* is present in Agamben's *Il tempo che resta*.
15. Beyond the scope of what I set out in the previous chapters, one may also suggest that it offers a contemporary reinterpretation of Spinoza's distinction between *natura naturans* and *natura naturata* in which the former is not only positioned in the beginning, as presupposition of the latter, but is returned to the latter as its original creativity.
16. In fact, for the early Heidegger the primary model for ontotheology is not Aristotle's metaphysical God, but rather the scholastic understanding

of God as creator and of every other being as *ens creatum*; see Van der Heiden, 'The Christian Experience of Life and the Task of Phenomenology', 211–12.

17 In *L'uso dei corpi*, Agamben offers other examples as well, namely, the body and the landscape.
18 'Now, precisely a language that is no longer related to truth can turn into a prison – a sort of machine that seems to work autonomously and from which it seems we cannot get out. Perhaps human beings have never been so helpless and passive in the face of a language that increasingly determines them.' Agamben, 'Where is Science Going?', 109.
19 Cf. Rom. 4:17, 1 Cor. 15:22 and 1 Cor. 15:45, but also 2 Cor. 3:6.
20 Heidegger's comments regarding the everyday incapacity to see these genuine possibilities are striking in this context, see *Sein und Zeit*, 194–5/181–2.
21 Breton, *Saint Paul*, 37/66.
22 Cf. Agamben's 'decreation' in 'Bartleby o della contingenza', 72–89/259–71.
23 Spinoza's distinction between *natura naturata* and *natura naturans* can also be understood in Agamben's terms as the distinction between creation as a completed work or *ergon* and creation as a potentiality; the latter form of creation concerns 'a constitutive excess of potential over any realization in the act'. Agamben, 'What is the Act of Creation?', 24.
24 See also Agamben's modal ontology and its link to Spinoza in *L'uso dei corpi*, 192–227/146–75.
25 See Van der Heiden, *Ontology after Ontotheology* and 'The Christian Experience of Life and the Task of Phenomenology'.
26 See also Bradley, *Unbearable Life* and Heller-Roazen, *The Enemy of All*.
27 See Blanton, *A Materialism for the Masses*, 3–4.
28 Agamben, *Il tempo che resta*, 43/40; *L'uso dei corpi*, 218–20/168–9.
29 'We can only, in an unjust and false society, attest to the presence of the right and the true. We can only, in the middle of hell, testify of heaven.' Agamben, 'Where is Science Going?', 109.
30 See Van der Heiden, *The Voice of Misery*.

Bibliography

Abbott, Mathew. *The Figure of this World: Agamben and the Question of Political Ontology*. Edinburgh: Edinburgh University Press, 2018.

Agamben, Giorgio. *Altissima povertà: Regole monastiche e forma di vita*. Vicenza: Neri Pozza, 2011. Translated by Adam Kotsko as *The Highest Poverty: Monastic Rules and Form-of-Life* (Stanford: Stanford University Press, 2013).

Agamben, Giorgio. 'Bartleby o della contingenza.' In Giorgio Agamben and Gilles Deleuze, *Bartleby: La formula della creazione*, 45–89. Macerata: Quodlibet, 2011. Translated by Daniel Heller-Roazen as 'Bartleby, or On Contingency', in *Potentialities: Collected Essays in Philosophy* (Stanford: Stanford University Press, 1999), 243–71.

Agamben, Giorgio. *La comunità che viene*. Turin: Giulio Einaudi, 1990. Translated by Michael Hardt as *The Coming Community* (Minneapolis: University of Minnesota Press, 1993).

Agamben, Giorgio. *Homo Sacer: il potere sovrano e la nuda vita*. Turin: Giulio Einaudi, 2005. Translated by Daniel Heller-Roazen as *Homo Sacer: Sovereign Power and Bare Life* (Stanford: Stanford University Press, 1998).

Agamben, Giorgio. *Potentialities: Collected Essays in Philosophy*, translated by Daniel Heller-Roazen. Stanford: Stanford University Press, 1999.

Agamben, Giorgio. *Il sacramento del linguaggio: Archeologia del giuramento*. Rome: Laterza and Figli, 2008. Translated by Adam Kotsko as *The Sacrament of Language: An Archeology of the Oath* (Stanford: Stanford University Press, 2011).

Agamben, Giorgio. *Stasis: La guerra civile come paradigma politico*. Turin: Bollati Boringhieri, 2015. Translated by Nicholas Heron as *Stasis: Civil War as a Political Paradigm* (Stanford: Stanford University Press, 2015).

Agamben, Giorgio. *Il tempo che resta: Un comment alla* Lettera ai Romani. Turin: Bollato Boringhieri, 2000. Translated by Patricia Dailey as *The Time That Remains: A Commentary on the Letter to the Romans* (Stanford: Stanford University Press, 2005).

Agamben, Giorgio. *L'uso dei corpi*. Vicenza: Neri Pozza, 2014. Translated by Adam Kotsko as *The Use of Bodies* (Stanford: Stanford University Press, 2015).

Agamben, Giorgio. 'What is the Act of Creation?' In *Creation and Anarchy: The Work of Art and the Religion of Capitalism*, translated by Adam Kotsko, 14–28. Stanford: Stanford University Press, 2019.

Agamben, Giorgio. 'Where is Science Going?' Interview by Andrea Pensotti. *Organisms* 4, no. 2 (2020): 105–9.

Anderson, Valerie Nicolet, and Sophie Fuggle, eds. 'Michel Foucault and St. Paul.' Special issue *Journal for Cultural and Religious Theory* 11, no. 1 (2010).

Arendt, Hannah. *Between Past and Future: Eight Exercises in Political Thought*. New York: The Viking Press, 1969.

Arendt, Hannah. *The Human Condition*. Chicago: The University of Chicago Press, 1998.

Arendt, Hannah. *Love and Saint Augustine*. Chicago: The University of Chicago Press, 1996.

Aristotle. *Metaphysics, Volume I: Books 1–9*, translated by Hugh Tredennick. Loeb Classical Library 271. Cambridge, MA: Harvard University Press, 1933.

Aristotle. *Metaphysics, Volume II: Books 10–14. Oeconomica. Magna Moralia*, translated by Hugh Tredennick and G. Cyril Armstrong. Loeb Classical Library 287. Cambridge, MA: Harvard University Press, 1935.

Aristotle. *Nicomachean Ethics*, translated by H. Rackham. Loeb Classical Library 73. Cambridge, MA: Harvard University Press, 1926.

Augustine. *City of God, Volume III: Books 8–11*, translated by David S. Wiesen. Loeb Classical Library 413. Cambridge, MA: Harvard University Press, 1968.

Augustine. *City of God, Volume IV: Books 12–15*, translated by Philip Levine. Loeb Classical Library 414. Cambridge, MA: Harvard University Press, 1966.

Azzam, Abed. *Nietzsche versus Paul*. New York: Columbia University Press, 2015.

Badiou, Alain. *L'Éthique: Essai sur la conscience du mal*. Caen: Nous, 2003. Translated by Peter Hallward as *Ethics: An Essay on the Understanding of Evil* (London: Verso, 2001).

Badiou, Alain. *L'Être et l'événement*. Paris: Seuil, 1988. Translated by Oliver Feltham as *Being and Event* (London: Continuum, 2005).

Badiou, Alain. 'From Logic to Anthropology: Affirmative Dialectics.' In *Badiou and the Political Condition*, edited by Marios Constantinou, 45–55. Edinburgh: Edinburgh University Press, 2014.

Badiou, Alain. *The Incident at Antioch. A Tragedy in Three Acts*. Introduction by Kenneth Reinheid, translated by Susan Spitzer. New York: Columbia University Press, 2013. Bilingual edition.

Badiou, Alain. *Logiques des mondes: L'être et l'événement II*. Paris: Seuil, 2006. Translated by Alberto Toscano as *Logics of Worlds: Being and Event II* (London: Continuum, 2009).

Badiou, Alain. *Saint Paul: La fondation de l'universalisme*. Paris: Presses universitaires de France, 1997. Translated by Ray Brassier as *Saint Paul: The Foundation of Universalism* (Stanford: Stanford University Press, 2003).

Barclay, John M. G. 'Paul and the Philosophers: Alain Badiou and the Event.' *New Blackfriars* 91, no. 1032 (2010): 171–84.

Barclay, John M. G. 'Stoic Physics and the Christ-event: A Review of Troels Engberg-Pedersen, *Cosmology and Self in the Apostle Paul: The Material Spirit* (Oxford: Oxford University Press, 2010).' *Journal for the Study of the New Testament* 33, no. 4 (2011): 406–14.

Barnes, Julian. *England, England*. New York: Vintage International, 2000.

Benjamin, Andrew. 'Reading, Seeing and the Logic of Abandonment: Rembrandt's Self-Portrait as the Apostle Paul.' In *Saint Paul and Philosophy: The Consonance of Ancient and Modern Thought*, edited by Gert-Jan van der Heiden, George van Kooten and Antonio Cimino, 21–46. Berlin: DeGruyter, 2017.

Blanton, Ward. 'Mad with the Love of Undead Life: Understanding Paul and Žižek.' In *Paul in the Grip of the Philosophers: The Apostle and Contemporary Philosophy*, edited by Peter Frick, 193–216. Minneapolis: Fortress Press, 2013.

Blanton, Ward. *A Materialism for the Masses: Saint Paul and the Philosophy of Undying Life*. New York: Columbia University Press, 2014.

Blanton, Ward. 'Reappearance of Paul, "Sick": Foucault's Biopolitics and the Political Significance of Pasolini's Apostle.' *Journal for Cultural and Religious Theory* 11, no. 1 (2010): 52–77.

Blanton, Ward, and Hent de Vries, eds. *Paul and the Philosophers*. New York: Fordham University Press, 2013.

Bloechl, Jeffrey. 'Love and Law according to Paul and Some Philosophers.' In *Phenomenologies of Scripture*, edited by Adam Y. Wells, 144–58. New York: Fordham University Press, 2017.

Boulnois, Olivier. *Saint Paul et la philosophie: Une introduction à l'essence du christianisme*. Paris: Presses universitaires de France, 2022.

Boyarin, Daniel. 'Paul among the Antiphilosophers: or, Saul among the Sophists.' In *St. Paul among the Philosophers*, edited by John D. Caputo and Linda Martín Alcoff, 109–41. Bloomington: Indiana University Press, 2009.

Boyarin, Daniel. *A Radical Jew: Paul and the Politics of Identity*. Berkeley: University of California Press, 1997.

Bradley, Arthur. *Unbearable Life: A Genealogy of Political Erasure*. New York: Columbia University Press, 2019.

Breton, Stanislas. *Saint Paul*. Paris: Presses universitaires de France, 1988. Translated by Joseph N. Ballan as *A Radical Philosophy of Saint Paul* (New York: Columbia University Press, 2011).

Breton, Stanislas, et al. 'L'événement saint Paul: juif, grec, romain, chrétien.' Special issue *Esprit* 292 (2003).

Caputo, John, and Linda Martín Alcoff, eds. *St. Paul among the Philosophers*. Bloomington: Indiana University Press, 2009.

Chase, Michael, Stephen R. L. Clark and Michael McGhee, eds. *Philosophy as a Way of Life: Ancients and Moderns. Essays in Honor of Pierre Hadot.* London: Wiley-Blackwell, 2013.

Cicero. *Orations. Pro Lege Manilia. Pro Caecina. Pro Cluentio. Pro Rabirio Perduellionis Reo*, translated by H. Grose Hodge. Loeb Classical Library 198. Cambridge, MA: Harvard University Press, 1927.

Cimino, Antonio. 'Agamben's Political Messianism in *The Time That Remains.*' *International Journal of Philosophy and Theology* 77, no. 3 (2016): 102–18.

Cimino, Antonio. *Enactment, Politics, and Truth: Pauline Themes in Agamben, Badiou, and Heidegger.* London: Bloomsbury, 2018.

Cooper, John M., ed. *Plato: Complete Works.* Indianapolis: Hackett Publishing Company, 1997.

Coyne, Ryan. *Heidegger's Confessions: The Remains of Saint Augustine in Being and Time and Beyond.* Chicago: The University of Chicago Press, 2015.

Critchley, Simon. *The Faith of the Faithless: Experiments in Political Theology.* London: Verso, 2012.

Crockett, Clayton. *Radical Political Theology: Religion and Politics after Liberalism.* New York: Columbia University Press, 2011.

Crowe, Benjamin. 'Heidegger on the Apostle Paul.' In *Paul in the Grip of the Philosophers: The Apostle and Contemporary Philosophy*, edited by Peter Frick, 39–56. Minneapolis: Fortress Press, 2013.

Davis, Creston, John Milbank and Slavoj Žižek, eds. *The Monstrosity of Christ: Paradox or Dialectic?* Cambridge, MA: The MIT Press, 2009.

De Kesel, Marc. *Eros and Ethics: Reading Jacques Lacan's Seminar VII*, translated by Sigi Jöttkandt. Albany: SUNY Press, 2009.

Delahaye, Ezra. '"It Is No Longer I Who Lives": Heidegger, Badiou and Agamben on Subjectivity in the Letters of Saint Paul.' PhD diss., Radboud University, 2017.

Deleuze, Gilles. *Différence et répétition.* Paris: Presses universitaires de France, 1993. Translated by Paul Patton as *Difference and Repetition* (New York: Columbia University Press, 1994).

Depoortere, Frederiek. 'Badiou's Paul: Founder of Universalism and Theoretician of the Militant.' In *Paul in the Grip of the Philosophers: The Apostle and Contemporary Philosophy*, edited by Peter Frick, 143–64. Minneapolis: Fortress Press, 2013.

Derrida, Jacques. *Donner la mort.* Paris: Galilée, 1999. Translated by David Wills as *The Gift of Death* (Chicago: The University of Chicago Press, 1995).

Derrida, Jacques. *L'Écriture et la différence.* Paris: Seuil, 1967. Translated by Alan Bass as *Writing and Difference* (London: Routledge, 2001).

Derrida, Jacques. *Force de loi.* Paris: Galilée, 1994. Translated by Mary Quaintance as 'Force of Law: The "Mystical Foundation of Authority"', in *Deconstruction and the Possibility of Justice*, edited by Drucilla Cornell, Michel Rosenfeld and David Gray Carlson (London: Routledge, 1992), 3–67.

Derrida, Jacques. *Marges de la philosophie*. Paris: Minuit, 1972. Translated by Alan Bass as *Margins of Philosophy* (Chicago: The University of Chicago Press, 1982).
De Veen, Thomas. '"Het is veel spannender om met imaginaire personages te leven." Interview met Paul Auster.' *NRC*, 8 August 2017. https://www.nrc.nl/nieuws/2017/08/08/het-gaat-om-het-onverwachte-12253314-a1569522
De Vries, Hent. *Kleine filosofie van het wonder*. Amsterdam: Boom, 2015.
De Wilde, Marc. 'Politics between Times: Theologico-Political Interpretations of the Restraining Force (*katechon*) in Paul's Second Letter to the Thessalonians.' In *Paul and the Philosophers*, edited by Ward Blanton and Hent de Vries, 105–26. New York: Fordham University Press, 2013.
Dunn, James D. G. *The New Perspective on Paul*. Grand Rapids: Eerdmans, 2007.
Engberg-Pedersen, Troels. *Cosmology and Self in the Apostle Paul: The Material Spirit*. Oxford: Oxford University Press, 2010.
Engberg-Pedersen, Troels. 'Paul and Universalism.' In *Paul and the Philosophers*, edited by Ward Blanton and Hent de Vries, 87–104. New York: Fordham University Press, 2013.
Euripides. *Cyclops, Alcestis, Medea*, translated by David Kovacs. Loeb Classical Library 12. Cambridge, MA: Harvard University Press, 1994.
Euripides. *Medea*, translated by George Gilbert Aimé Murray. New York: Oxford University Press, 1912. See: https://gutenberg.ca/ebooks/murrayeuripides-medea/murrayeuripides-medea-00-h.html
Filiz, Kadir. 'Event and Subjectivity: The Question of Phenomenology in Jean-Luc Marion and Claude Romano.' PhD diss., Radboud University, 2023.
Foucault, Michel. *Le Courage de la vérité (Le Gouvernement de soi et des autres II): Cours au Collège de France, 1983–1984*, edited by Frédéric Gros. Paris: Seuil, 2009. Translated by Graham Burchell as *The Courage of Truth (The Government of Self and Others II): Lectures at the Collège de France 1983–1984* (New York: Palgrave Macmillan, 2011).
Foucault, Michel. *Le Gouvernement de soi et des autres: Cours au Collège de France, 1982–1983*, edited by Frédéric Gros. Paris: Seuil, 2008. Translated by Graham Burchell as *The Government of Self and Others: Lectures at the Collège de France 1982–1983* (New York: Palgrave Macmillan, 2010).
Frederiksen, Paula. 'Historical Integrity, Interpretive Freedom: The Philosopher's Paul and the Problem of Anachronism.' In *St. Paul among the Philosophers*, edited by John D. Caputo and Linda Martín Alcoff, 61–73. Bloomington: Indiana University Press, 2009.
Frick, Peter, ed. *Paul in the Grip of the Philosophers: The Apostle and Contemporary Continental Philosophy*. Minneapolis: Fortress Press, 2013.
Gadamer, Hans-Georg. 'Kunst und Nachahmung.' In *Ästhetik und Poetik I*, 25–36. *Gesammelte Werke*, vol. 8. Tübingen: Mohr Siebeck, 1990.

Gadamer, Hans-Georg. *Wahrheit und Methode. Gesammelte Werke*, vol. 1. Tübingen: Mohr Siebeck, 1990. Translated by Joel Weinsheimer and Donald G. Marshall as *Truth and Method* (London: Bloomsbury, 2013).
Gignac, Alain. 'Agamben's Paul: Thinker of the Messianic.' In *Paul in the Grip of the Philosophers: The Apostle and Contemporary Philosophy*, edited by Peter Frick, 165–92. Minneapolis: Fortress Press, 2013.
Hadot, Pierre. *Qu'est-ce que la philosophie antique?* Paris: Gallimard, 1995. Folio Essais. Translated by Michael Chase as *What is Ancient Philosophy?* (Cambridge, MA: Harvard University Press, 2004).
Harnack, Adolph von. *Lehrbuch der Dogmengeschichte. Erster Band. Entstehung des kirchlichen Dogmas*. Freiburg: Mohr, 1888.
Hegel, Georg Wilhelm Friedrich. 'Glauben und Wissen.' In *Jenaer Schriften, 1801–1807. Werke 2*, 287–433. Frankfurt: Suhrkamp, 1986. Translated by Walter Cerf and H. S. Harris as *Faith and Knowledge* (Albany: SUNY Press, 1977).
Hegel, Georg Wilhelm Friedrich. *Phänomenologie des Geistes*. Hamburg: Meiner, 1952. Translated by A. V. Miller as *Phenomenology of Spirit* (Oxford: Oxford University Press, 1977).
Heidegger, Martin. *Einführung in die phänomenologische Forschung*. Frankfurt: Klostermann, 1994. Translated by Daniel O. Dahlstrom as *Introduction to Phenomenological Research* (Bloomington: Indiana University Press, 2005).
Heidegger, Martin. *Grundbegriffe der aristotelischen Philosophie*. Frankfurt: Klostermann, 2002. Translated by Robert D. Metcalf and Mark B. Tanzer as *Basic Concepts of Aristotelian Philosophy* (Bloomington: Indiana University Press, 2009).
Heidegger, Martin. *Hölderlins Hymne 'Der Ister.'* Frankfurt: Klostermann, 1993. Translated by William McNeill and Julia Davis as *Hölderlin's Hymn 'The Ister'* (Bloomington: Indiana University Press, 1996).
Heidegger, Martin. *Metaphysische Anfangsgründe der Logik im Ausgang von Leibniz*. Frankfurt: Klostermann, 1978. Translated by Michael Heim as *The Metaphysical Foundations of Logic* (Bloomington, IN: Indiana University Press, 1984).
Heidegger, Martin. *Nietzsche I*. Stuttgart: Neske, 1961.
Heidegger, Martin. *Nietzsche*. 4 vols. Translated by David Farrell Krell. San Francisco: Harper & Row, 1979–87.
Heidegger, Martin. *Nietzsches metaphysische Grundstellung im abendländischen Denken. Die ewige Wiederkehr des Gleichen*. Frankfurt: Klostermann, 1986.
Heidegger, Martin. *Parmenides*. Frankfurt: Klostermann, 1982. Translated by Richard Rojcewicz and André Schuwer as *Parmenides* (Bloomington: Indiana University Press, 1992).
Heidegger, Martin. *Phänomenologie des religiösen Lebens*. Frankfurt: Klostermann, 1995. Translated by Matthias Fritsch and Jennifer Anna Gosetti-Ferencei as *The Phenomenology of Religious Life* (Bloomington: Indiana University Press, 2010).

Heidegger, Martin. *Sein und Zeit*. Tübingen: Niemeyer, 2001. Translated by Joan Stambaugh as *Being and Time: A Translation of* Sein und Zeit (Albany: SUNY Press, 1996).

Heidegger, Martin. *Wegmarken*. Frankfurt: Klostermann, 1976. Translated by William McNeill as *Pathmarks* (Cambridge: Cambridge University Press, 1998).

Heller-Roazen, Daniel. *The Enemy of All: Piracy and the Law of Nations*. New York: Zone Books, 2009.

Jennings, Theodore W. *Outlaw Justice: The Messianic Politics of Paul*. Stanford: Stanford University Press, 2013.

Kearney, Richard. 'Paul's Notion of *Dunamis*: Between the Possible and the Impossible.' In *St. Paul among the Philosophers*, edited by John D. Caputo and Linda Martín Alcoff, 142–59. Bloomington: Indiana University Press, 2009.

Kierkegaard, Søren. *Fear and Trembling. Repetition*. Vol. VI of *Kierkegaard's Writings*, edited and translated by Howard V. Hong and Edna H. Hong. Princeton: Princeton University Press, 1983.

Knox, Ronald A. *Enthusiasm: A Chapter in the History of Religion*. Oxford: Oxford University Press, 1950

Lacan, Jacques. *Le Séminaire. Livre VII. L'éthique du psychanalyse. 1959–1960*. Paris: Seuil, 1986.

Laity, Paul. 'Paul Auster: "I'm going to speak out as often as I can, otherwise I can't live with myself".' *The Guardian*, 20 January 2017. https://www.the guardian.com/books/2017/jan/20/paul-auster-4321-interview.

Lilla, Mark. *The Shipwrecked Mind: On Political Reaction*. New York: New York Review of Books, 2016. iBooks.

Løland, Ole Jakob. *Pauline Ugliness: Jacob Taubes and the Turn to Paul*. New York: Fordham University Press, 2020.

Løland, Ole Jakob. *The Reception of Paul the Apostle in the Works of Slavoj Žižek*. Cham: Palgrave MacMillan, 2018.

Loose, Donald, ed. 'The Apostle Paul in Modern Philosophy.' Special issue *Bijdragen. International Journal for Philosophy and Theology* 70, no. 2 (2009).

Marion, Jean-Luc. *Dieu sans l'être: Hors-texte*. Paris: Fayard, 1982. Translated by Thomas A. Carlson as *God without Being* (Chicago: The University of Chicago Press, 2012).

Martin, Dale M. 'The Promise of Teleology, the Constraints of Epistemology, and Universal Vision in Paul.' In *St. Paul among the Philosophers*, edited by John D. Caputo and Linda Martín Alcoff, 91–108. Bloomington: Indiana University Press, 2009.

Meillassoux, Quentin. *Après la finitude: Essai sur la nécessité de la contingence*. Paris: Seuil, 2006. Translated by Ray Bassier as *After Finitude: An Essay on the Necessity of Contingency* (London: Continuum, 2008).

Morgan, Teresa. 'Narratives of *Pistis* in Paul and Deutero-Paul.' In *Saint Paul and Philosophy: The Consonance of Ancient and Modern Thought*, edited

by Gert-Jan van der Heiden, George van Kooten and Antonio Cimino, 165–87. Berlin: De Gruyter, 2017.
Morgan, Teresa. *Roman Faith and Christian Faith*. Oxford: Oxford University Press, 2015.
Muller, Jerry Z. *Professor of Apocalypse: The Many Lives of Jacob Taubes*. Princeton: Princeton University Press, 2022.
Nietzsche, Friedrich. *Werke. Kritische Gesamtausgabe*. Edited by Giorgio Colli and Mazzino Montinari, continued by Volker Gerhardt, Norbert Miller, Wolfgang Müller-Lauter and Karl Pestalozzi. Berlin: De Gruyter, 1967ff.
Nietzsche, Friedrich. *Also sprach Zarathustra. Ein Buch für Alle und für Keinen (1883–1885)*. In *Werke. Kritische Gesamtausgabe*, vol. VI/1.
Nietzsche, Friedrich. *Der Antichrist*. In *Werke. Kritische Gesamtausgabe*, vol. VI/3:162–252. Translated by Judith Norman as 'The Anti-Christ', in *The Anti-Christ, Ecce Homo, Twilight of the Idols, and Other Writings* (Cambridge: Cambridge University Press, 2005), 1–68.
Nietzsche, Friedrich. *Ecce Homo. Wie man wird was man ist*. In *Werke. Kritische Gesamtausgabe*, vol. VI/3:253–372. Translated by Judith Norman as 'Ecce Homo: How to Become What You Are', in *The Anti-Christ, Ecce Homo, Twilight of the Idols, and Other Writings* (Cambridge: Cambridge University Press, 2005), 69–152.
Nietzsche, Friedrich. *Die fröhliche Wissenschaft*. In *Werke. Kritische Gesamtausgabe*, vol. V/2:11–320. Translated by Josefine Nauckhoff as *The Gay Science* (Cambridge: Cambridge University Press, 2001).
Nietzsche, Friedrich. *Die Geburt der Tragödie*. In *Werke. Kritische Gesamtausgabe*, vol. III/1:1–152. Translated by Ronald Speirs as *The Birth of Tragedy* (Cambridge: Cambridge University Press, 1999).
Nietzsche, Friedrich. *Götzen-Dämmerung oder Wie man mit dem Hammer philosophiert*. In *Werke. Kritische Gesamtausgabe*, vol. VI/3:49–154. Translated by Judith Norman as 'Twilight of the Idols or How to Philosophize with a Hammer', in *The Anti-Christ, Ecce Homo, Twilight of the Idols, and Other Writings* (Cambridge: Cambridge University Press, 2005), 153–230.
Nietzsche, Friedrich. *Jenseits von Gut und Böse*. In *Werke. Kritische Gesamtausgabe*, vol. VI/2:1–255. Translated by Judith Norman as *Beyond Good and Evil* (Cambridge: Cambridge University Press, 2001).
Nietzsche, Friedrich. *Morgenröthe. Gedanken über die moralischen Vorurtheile*. In *Werke. Kritische Gesamtausgabe*, vol. V/1:1–335. Translated by R. J. Hollingdale as *Daybreak: Thoughts on the Prejudice of Morality* (Cambridge: Cambridge University Press, 2003).
Nietzsche, Friedrich. *Nachgelassene Fragmente Herbst 1887*. In *Werke. Kritische Gesamtausgabe*, vol. VIII/2:1–248.
Nietzsche, Friedrich. *Nachgelassene Fragmente Sommer-Herbst 1882*. In *Werke. Kritische Gesamtausgabe*, vol. VII/1:39–108.
Nietzsche, Friedrich. *Über Wahrheit und Lüge in aussermoralischen Sinne*. In *Werke. Kritische Gesamtausgabe*, vol. III/2:367–84. Translated by Daniel Breazeale as 'On Truth and Lies in a Nonmoral Sense', in *The Nietzsche*

Reader, edited by Keith Ansell Pearson and Duncan Large (London: Blackwell, 2006), 114–23.

Nietzsche, Friedrich. *Zur Genealogie der Moral. Eine Streitschrift*. In *Werke. Kritische Gesamtausgabe*, vol. VI/2:257–430. Translated by Carol Diethe as *On the Geneology of Morality* (Cambridge: Cambridge University Press, 2007).

Petersen, Anders Klostergaard. 'Paul's Use of *Pistis/Pisteuein* as Epitome of Axial Age Religion.' In *Saint Paul and Philosophy: The Consonance of Ancient and Modern Thought*, edited by Gert-Jan van der Heiden, George van Kooten and Antonio Cimino, 231–48. Berlin: De Gruyter, 2017.

Plato. *Euthyphro. Apology. Crito. Phaedo. Phaedrus*, edited and translated by Christopher Emlyn-Jones and William Preddy. Loeb Classical Library 36. Cambridge, MA: Harvard University Press, 2017.

Plato. *Republic, Volume I: Books 1–5*, edited and translated by Christopher Emlyn-Jones and William Preddy. Loeb Classical Library 237. Cambridge, MA: Harvard University Press, 2013.

Plato. *Republic, Volume II: Books 6–10*, edited and translated by Christopher Emlyn-Jones and William Preddy. Loeb Classical Library 276. Cambridge, MA: Harvard University Press, 2013.

Popper, Karl. *The Open Society and Its Enemies*. New One-Volume Edition. Princeton: Princeton University Press, 2013.

Raffoul, François. *Thinking the Event*. Bloomington: Indiana University Press, 2020.

Rancière, Jacques. *La Mésentente: Politique et philosophie*. Paris: Galilée, 1995. Translated by Julie Rose as *Disagreement: Politics and Philosophy*. Minneapolis: University of Minnesota Press, 1999.

Ricœur, Paul. *De l'interprétation. Essai sur Freud*. Paris: Seuil, 1965. Translated by Denis Savage as *Freud and Philosophy: An Essay on Interpretation* (New Haven: Yale University Press, 1970).

Ricœur, Paul. *La Métaphore vive*. Point Essais. Paris: Seuil, 1975. Translated by Robert Czerny with Kathleen McLaughlin and John Costello, SJ, as *The Rule of Metaphor: The Creation of Meaning in Language* (London: Routledge, 2004).

Ruin, Hans. 'Faith, Grace, and the Destruction of Tradition: A Hermeneutic-Genealogical Reading of the Pauline Letters.' *The Journal for Cultural and Religious Theory* 11, no. 1 (2010): 16–34.

Salaquarda, Jörg. 'Dionysus versus the Crucified One: Nietzsche's Understanding of the Apostle Paul.' In *Studies in Nietzsche and the Judaeo-Christian Tradition*, edited by James C. O'Flaherty, Timothy F. Sellner and Robert M. Helm, 100–29. Chapel Hill: University of North Carolina Press, 1985.

Sawczyński, Piotr. 'The Significant Nothing: Agamben, Theology, and Political Subjectivity.' In *Subjectivity and the Political: Contemporary Perspectives*, edited by Gavin Rae and Emma Ingala, 75–90. New York: Routledge, 2018.

Schatz, Oskar, and Hans Spatzenegger, eds. *Wovon werden wir morgen geistig leben? Mythos, Religion und Wissenschaft in der 'Postmoderne.'* Salzburg: Anton Pustet, 1986.
Schelling, Friedrich Wilhelm Joseph. *Philosophische Untersuchungen über das Wesen der menschlichen Freiheit und die damit zusammenhängenden Gegenstände.* Edited by Thomas Buchheim. Hamburg: Meiner, 2011.
Schelling, Friedrich Wilhelm Joseph. *System der Weltalter: Münchener Vorlesung 1827/28 in einer Nachschrift von Ernst von Lasaulx.* Frankfurt: Klostermann, 1998.
Schmidt, Dennis J. 'Hermeneutics as Original Ethics.' In *Difficulties of Ethical Life*, edited by Shannon Sullivan and Dennis J. Schmidt, 35–47. New York: Fordham University Press, 2008.
Schmitt, Carl. *Der Begriff des Politischen. Text von 1932 mit einem Vorwort und drei Corollarien.* Berlin: Duncker & Humblot, 2002. Translated by George Schwab as *The Concept of the Political* (Chicago: The University of Chicago Press, 2007).
Schmitt, Carl. *Die politische Theologie. Vier Kapitel zur Lehre von der Souveränität.* Berlin: Duncker & Humblot, 2004. Translated by George Schwab as *Political Theology: Four Chapters on the Concept of Sovereignty* (Chicago: The University of Chicago Press, 2005).
Sellars, John. *Stoicism.* Durham: Acumen, 2006.
Sextus Empiricus. *Outlines of Pyrrhonism*, translated by R. G. Bury. Loeb Classical Library 273. Cambridge, MA: Harvard University Press, 1933.
Siedentop, Larry. *Inventing the Individual: The Origins of Western Liberalism.* Cambridge, MA: Harvard University Press, 2014.
Sierksma-Agteres, Suzan. 'Paul and the Philosophers' Faith: Discourses of Pistis in the Graeco-Roman World.' PhD diss., University of Groningen, 2023.
Stowers, Stanley. 'Paul as a Hero of Subjectivity.' In *Paul and the Philosophers*, edited by Ward Blanton and Hent de Vries, 159–74. New York: Fordham University Press, 2013.
Taubes, Jacob. '"Frist" als Form apokalyptischer Zeiterfahrung.' In *Wovon werden wir morgen geistig leben? Mythos, Religion und Wissenschaft in der 'Postmoderne'*, edited by Oskar Schatz and Hans Spatzenegger, 89–98. Salzburg: Anton Pustet, 1986.
Taubes, Jacob. *Die politische Theologie des Paulus*, edited by Aleida Assmann and Jan Assmann. Munich: Fink, 1993. Translated by Dana Hollander as *The Political Theology of Paul* (Stanford: Stanford University Press, 2004).
Taubes, Jacob. *Vom Kult zur Kultur. Bausteine zur einer Kritik der Historischen Vernunft.* Edited by Aleida Assmann and Jan Assmann. Munich: Fink, 1996. Translated as *From Cult to Culture: Fragments towards a Critique of Historical Reason* (Stanford: Stanford University Press, 2009).
Terpstra, Marin. 'The Management of Distinctions: Jacob Taubes on Paul's Political Theology.' In *Saint Paul and Philosophy: The Consonance of Ancient and Modern Thought*, edited by Gert-Jan van der Heiden, George van Kooten and Antonio Cimino, 251–68. Berlin: De Gruyter, 2017.

Topolski, Anya. 'The Islamophobic Inheritance of the Resurrected Saint Paul: From F. C. Baur's Judeo-Christianity to the Event.' *ReOrient* 2, no. 2 (2017): 126–45.

Van der Heiden, Gert-Jan. 'The Christian Experience of Life and the Task of Phenomenology: Heidegger on Saint Paul, Saint Augustine, and Descartes.' *Forum Philosophicum* 26, no. 2 (2021): 207–26.

Van der Heiden, Gert-Jan. 'Contingency and Skepticism in Agamben's Thought.' In *Contemporary Encounters with Ancient Metaphysics*, edited by Jacob Greenstine and Ryan Johnson, 289–304. Edinburgh: Edinburgh University Press, 2017.

Van der Heiden, Gert-Jan. 'The Dialectics of Paul: On Exception, Grace, and Use in Badiou and Agamben.' *International Journal of Philosophy and Theology* 77, no. 3 (2016): 171–90.

Van der Heiden, Gert-Jan. 'Exile, Use, and Form-of-Life: On the Conclusion of Agamben's *Homo Sacer*-series.' *Theory, Culture & Society* 37, no. 2 (2020): 61–78.

Van der Heiden, Gert-Jan, ed. 'Geloof als levenshouding: *Pistis* en *ēthos* bij Paulus en de filosofen.' Special issue *Tijdschrift voor Theologie* 54, no. 3 (2014).

Van der Heiden, Gert-Jan. 'Interpreters of the Divine: Nancy's Poet, Jeremiah the Prophet, and Saint Paul's Glossolalist.' *Angelaki* 26, no. 3–4 (2021): 90–100. With a short response ('Echo') by Jean-Luc Nancy.

Van der Heiden, Gert-Jan. *Metafysica: Van orde naar ontvankelijkheid*. Amsterdam: Boom, 2021.

Van der Heiden, Gert-Jan. 'On What Remains: Paul's Proclamation of Contingency.' In *Saint Paul and Philosophy: The Consonance of Ancient and Modern Thought*, edited by Gert-Jan van der Heiden, George van Kooten and Antonio Cimino, 115–30. Berlin: De Gruyter, 2017.

Van der Heiden, Gert-Jan. *Ontology after Ontotheology: Plurality, Event, and Contingency in Contemporary Philosophy*. Pittsburgh: Duquesne University Press, 2014.

Van der Heiden, Gert-Jan, ed. 'Paul in Philosophy Today.' Special issue *International Journal of Philosophy and Theology* 77, no. 3 (2016).

Van der Heiden, Gert-Jan. *Het uitschot en de geest: Paulus onder filosofen*. Nijmegen: Vantilt, 2018.

Van der Heiden, Gert-Jan. *The Voice of Misery: A Continental Philosophy of Testimony*. Albany: SUNY Press, 2020.

Van der Heiden, Gert-Jan. 'Witnessing the Uninhabitable Place: On the Experience and Testimony of Refugees.' *Research in Phenomenology* 52, no. 2 (2022): 223–41.

Van der Heiden, Gert-Jan, and George van Kooten. 'Epilogue: Saint Paul and Philosophy – The Consonance of Ancient and Modern Thought.' In *Saint Paul and Philosophy: The Consonance of Ancient and Modern Thought*, edited by Gert-Jan van der Heiden, George van Kooten and Antonio Cimino, 325–45. Berlin: De Gruyter, 2017.

Van der Heiden, Gert-Jan, George van Kooten and Antonio Cimino, eds. *Saint Paul and Philosophy: The Consonance of Ancient and Modern Thought*. Berlin: De Gruyter, 2017.

Van Kooten, George. *Paul's Anthropology in Context: The Image of God, Assimilation to God, and Tripartite Man in Ancient Judaism, Ancient Philosophy and Early Christianity*. Tübingen: Mohr Siebeck, 2008.

Van Kooten, George. 'Paul's Stoic Onto-Theology and Ethics of Good, Evil and "Indifferents": A Response to Anti-Metaphysical and Nihilistic Readings of Paul in Modern Philosophy.' In *Saint Paul and Philosophy: The Consonance of Ancient and Modern Thought*, edited by Gert-Jan van der Heiden, George van Kooten and Antonio Cimino, 133–64. Berlin: De Gruyter, 2017.

Van Kooten, George. 'Paulus als anti-filosoof en messiaans nihilist? Kanttekeningen vanuit antiekwijsgerig perspectief bij Badious, Taubes' en Agambens interpretatie van Paulus.' *Tijdschrift voor Theologie* 54, no. 3 (2014): 277–94.

Van Tongeren, Paul. *Friedrich Nietzsche and European Nihilism*. Newcastle: Cambridge Scholars Publishing, 2018.

Vedder, Ben. *Heidegger's Philosophy of Religion: From God to the Gods*. Pittsburgh: Duquesne University Press, 2007.

Wasserman, Emma. *The Death of the Soul in Romans 7: Sin, Death, and the Law in Light of Hellenistic Moral Psychology*. Tübingen: Mohr Siebeck, 2008.

Wasserman, Emma. 'Paul among the Ancient Philosophers: The Case of Romans 7.' In *Paul and the Philosophers*, edited by Ward Blanton and Hent de Vries, 69–83. New York: Fordham University Press, 2013.

Watkin, Christopher. *Difficult Atheism: Post-Theological Thinking in Alain Badiou, Jean-Luc Nancy and Quentin Meillassoux*. Edinburgh: Edinburgh University Press, 2013.

Weaver, Taylor M. *The Scandal of Community: Pauline Factions and the Circulation of Grace*. Lanham: Lexington Books/Fortress Academic, 2021.

Weber, Max. *Die protestantische Ethik und der 'Geist' des Kapitalismus*, edited by Klaus Lichtblau und Johannes Weiß. Wiesbaden: Springer, 2016. Translated by Talcott Parsons as *The Protestant Ethic and the Spirit of Capitalism* (London: Routledge, 2001).

Welborn, Larry L. 'The Culture of Crucifixion and the Resurrection of the Disposed: The Interpellation of the Subject in the Roman Empire and Paul's Gospel as "truth event."' In *Paul and the Philosophers*, edited by Ward Blanton and Hent de Vries, 127–40. New York: Fordham University Press, 2013.

Welborn, Larry L. 'Jacob Taubes – Paulinist, Messianist.' In *Paul in the Grip of the Philosophers: The Apostle and Contemporary Philosophy*, edited by Peter Frick, 69–90. Minneapolis: Fortress Press, 2013.

Welborn, Larry L. *Paul's Summons to Messianic Life: Political Theology and the Coming Awakening*. New York: Columbia University Press, 2015.

Wright, N. T. *Pauline Perspectives: Essays on Paul 1978–2013*. Minneapolis: Fortress Press, 2013.
Yazıcıoğlu, Sanem. 'The Anonymous: The Invisibles of Society.' *International Yearbook of Hermeneutics* 19 (2020): 36–54.
Yazıcıoğlu, Sanem. 'Arendtian Beginning under the Threat of Violence.' In *Continental Perspectives on Community: Human Existence from Unity to Plurality*, edited by Chantal Bax and Gert-Jan van der Heiden, 79–91. London: Routledge, 2020.
Žižek, Slavoj. *The Fragile Absolute: Or, Why is the Christian Legacy Worth Fighting For?* London: Verso, 2008.
Žižek, Slavoj. 'The Necessity of a Dead Bird.' In *Paul and the Philosophers*, edited by Ward Blanton and Hent de Vries, 175–85. New York: Fordham University Press, 2013.
Žižek, Slavoj. *On Belief*. London: Routledge, 2001.
Žižek, Slavoj. *The Puppet and the Dwarf: The Perverse Core of Christianity*. Cambridge, MA: MIT Press, 2003.
Žižek, Slavoj. *The Ticklish Subject: The Absent Centre of Political Ontology*. London: Verso, 1999.

Index

absolute, 4–5, 40, 41, 42
actuality (*energeia*), 71–2, 73, 75, 77
adiaphora, 83, 88, 164
affect *see pathos*
afterlife, 17, 46, 56, 62, 107
Agamben, Giorgio, 7–8, 27
   eschaton, 174
   event, 175, 193
   flesh-spirit distinction, 170–1
   grace, 149
   justice and law, 138
   katargeō, 71
   katargēsis, 73
   mode of living 'as not' (*hōs mē*), 82, 84, 85–7, 193
   ontological squandering, 110
   potentiality, 145–6
   promise, 147
   relation of exception, 155
   vocation, 173
agōn, 49
Alexander the Great, 183–4
allegorical meaning, 31–2
Allegory of the Cave, 15
ancient philosophy, 14–16, 61–2, 63, 64, 88–9, 180–5; *see also* Aristotle; Plato; Socrates; Stoicism
anomia, 129
Anti-Christ, The (Nietzsche), 47, 50, 51, 52, 55, 56–7, 60
anti-Semitism, 30
antidialectic (Badiou), 101–11, 193
antinomianism, 128–9, 135, 138, 147, 149
aphōrismenos (separation), 169–76, 198

aporia, 88, 89, 114, 146, 148
archē (beginning), 36, 37, 41, 58, 81, 97, 105, 192; *see also* beginning
Arendt, Hannah, 37, 81, 123, 190
Aristotle, 15, 16, 51, 71–3, 182, 187
art of living, 14, 61–2, 63, 64, 180; *see also* mode of living
asceticism, 62, 110
astheneia (weakness), 41, 145, 146
Aufhebung (sublation), 33–4, 40, 74, 100, 104, 112, 114
Augustine, 37, 81, 190
Auster, Paul, 118, 122

Badiou, Alain, 4, 8–9, 13, 27
   antidialectic, 101–11, 193
   event, 97, 102–4, 105–6, 107–8, 110, 161–3, 192–3
   flesh-spirit distinction, 19
   grace, 140
   on Nietzsche, 49, 50–2
   Pauline ethos, 188
   on Paul's universalism, 7, 161–6, 172
   sin, 143
Barth, Karl, 35–6, 78
beginning, 190
   and transformation, 12–14
   see also archē (beginning)
being, mode of, 12, 16, 63–4, 70, 78, 119–20, 182, 187, 195; *see also* event; potentiality-of-being-otherwise
Benjamin, Walter, 35–6
Beyond Good and Evil (Nietzsche), 46
Blanton, Ward, 3, 6, 9, 18, 45, 196

215

Index

Bloechl, Jeffrey, 5–6
Breton, Stanislas, 32, 42, 90, 122, 141, 192, 193
brokenness of creation, 90–1

calling *see* vocation
capitalism, 4, 13
charis see grace (*charis*)
chrēsis (use), 85–8, 150, 181, 184, 188–9, 190, 194
Christ *see* Jesus Christ
'Christ-event', 104, 107, 140, 161, 162, 163
Christianity
  asceticism, 62
  dispute between Judaism and, 30
  Nietzsche's view of, 46, 47–8, 51, 52–3, 55, 97–8, 107
  'perverse core of', 40
Cicero, 109
circumcision, 107, 137–8, 158
City of God (Augustine), 37
community, 154–6
  Rancière's notion of, 166–9, 173–4
  and separation, 169–76, 198
  and universalism: Badiou, 161–6; Israel, 156–60
concepts, 57
constitutive power, 135
contemporary European philosophy
  other(ness), 100–1
  time and event, 96
  turn to Saint Paul, 3–8: criticism of selectivity, 8–12; leitmotifs, 12–20
  see also individual philosophers
contingency, 78, 89–90, 102, 111, 115, 117–19, 122, 140–1
conversion, 119, 121, 122
cosmology, 25–6, 35, 54; *see also kosmos*
Courage of Truth, The (Foucault), 61–4
creating, 59–60
creation, 26, 32, 40, 189–90, 195–6
  beginning of, 37
  interruption of, 41
  and Nietzsche, 47
  and nihilism, 50
  in Paul's meontology, 75, 81, 90–1

Critchley, Simon, 6–7, 12, 27, 42, 69
crucifixion, 108–11, 132, 184
Cynicism, 61, 62, 63, 181, 183–4

Daybreak (Nietzsche), 49, 52–3, 60
De Vries, Hent, 102
death
  Badiou's antidialectic of, 104
  of God, 99
  in Hegel, 103, 104
  of Jesus Christ, 16, 97–8, 99–100, 108–10, 132 (*see also* crucifixion; resurrection)
  v. life, 141–2
Deleuze, Gilles, 3, 76
Derrida, Jacques, 3, 23n8, 100–1, 139
detachment / disengagement, 7, 38–9, 182–5, 188, 189
dialectic
  of exception, 42, 111–15, 119–20, 121, 171, 194
  between monism and dualism, 33–8 (*see also* pneumatic hermeneutics)
dialectic method, 30–1
dialectic movement, 33–4
dialectic process, 88
dialectic struggle, 112–15, 123
dialectic thought, 74
Diogenes the Cynic, 61, 183–4
doulos (slave), 86, 105, 109, 184
dualism
  Badiou, 108
  of law and grace, 139–44, 164, 172: *katargēsis*, 145–50
  monism-dualism tension, 26–7: dialectic between monism and dualism, 33–8 (*see also* pneumatic hermeneutics); Gnostic dualism, 28–9; Gnostic temptation, 30–2
  as nihilism, 46–7
  Platonic, 28, 57
dunamis (power), 41, 72–4, 124, 145–6

emergency, state of, 130
empirical knowledge, 77
enactment of life, 55, 188
ending, sense of, 77–81, 84, 89–90, 193

enemies *see* friend-enemy distinction
energeia (actuality), 71–2, 73, 75, 77
Engberg-Pedersen, Troels, 164–5
England, England (Barnes), 1
epochē (suspension), 88, 114, 191
equality, 154–5, 168
eschaton, 150n2, 160, 174–5
esteem, 35
eternal return of the same, 37–8, 54
ethical motif, 181–2, 183
ethics, 181, 185
ethos, 53–4, 90, 181, 188–99
Euripides, 143
event, 20, 26, 119
   in Badiou's antidialectic, 102–4, 105–6, 107–8, 110
   and community, 175
   and exception, 99–100
   as gift, 111
   and grace, 140, 192–3
   and outcasts, 169
   and time, 96–7, 123–4
   and universalism, 161–2, 163–4
exception, 99–100
   dialectic of, 42, 111–15, 119–20, 121, 171, 194
   relation of, 155
   state of, 129–32, 135–7, 143–4, 156, 196–8
   and universal, 111–15, 157–8, 194
existence *see* human existence; *sur-existence*

'Faith and Knowledge' (Hegel), 98, 99
Faith of the Faithless (Critchley), 12, 27
faith (*pistis*), 16–18, 193
   Badiou's understanding of, 104–5, 106, 188
   being called to, 82
   and community, 162–3
   and law, 146–7, 148
   Nietzsche's understanding of, 55–61, 181
Fall, the, 40, 135
fidelity, 7, 163, 181, 188, 193
firstfruits, 135, 179, 195, 199–200
flesh-spirit distinction, 19, 29, 32, 159–60, 163–4, 170–2, 181–2

Foucault, Michel, 61–4, 180, 181, 183, 184, 199
Frederiksen, Paula, 8–9, 10
Frick, Peter, 9, 10
friend-enemy distinction, 131–2, 133–4, 136, 154–5, 156, 166, 197–8

Gadamer, Hans-Georg, 10, 11
genesthai, 119, 120, 123
ghost, spirit as, 39
Gnostic dualism, 28–9
Gnostic temptation, 30–2, 41
Gnosticism, 6–7, 39, 62
God
   death of, 99
   as father of Jesus Christ, 28
   in ontotheology, 70–1
   Paul's conception of, 7, 14, 187–8, 194
   as sovereign, 132
   spirit of, 18–20, 27, 33, 34–5, 36, 49, 99, 186, 187, 192 (*see also pneuma*)
   of the world / of creation, 75
   Žižek's description of, 39
Gorgias (Plato), 114
grace (*charis*), 174
   dualism of law and grace, 139–44, 164, 172: *katargēsis*, 145–50
   and event, 140, 192

Hegel, G.W.F.
   death and resurrection, 103, 104
   dialectic movement, 33–4
   Weltgeist (spirit of the world), 19–20, 34
Hegelian dialectic, 40, 74, 98–100, 101, 104, 110, 112, 114, 115
Heidegger, Martin, 27
   archē, 97
   on Aristotle, 51
   beginning, 13
   brokenness of Christian life, 90
   community, 198
   enactment of life, 188
   Erstlinge des Wortes (firstfruits of the word), 179
   faith (*pistis*), 59, 61

Heidegger, Martin (*cont.*)
  genesthai, 119
  metaphysics, 70, 71, 196
  mode of living 'as not' (*hōs mē*), 82–3, 193
  Nietzsche's interpretation of Paul, 54–5
  non-being, 76
  Parousia, 120
  Pauline God, 187
  phenomenology of religion, 5
  reading of Paul, 78, 79
  temporality, 116–17
  thrownness, 39
hermeneutic experience, 11
hermeneutics *see* pneumatic hermeneutics
hermeneutics of suspicion, 11, 48
hermeneutics of trust, 11
historical meaning of text, 31
history, 116–17
hōs mē (as not)-formula, 81–90, 147–8, 173, 188, 189, 193
human existence, 117–20
humanism, 39
hyperbole, 102–3

immanentism, 35–6
immortality, 15
indifference, 46, 83–5, 86, 88, 107, 160, 162, 172
infinity, 98–9
initium, 37, 81, 124, 179, 190, 192
interpretation, Paul's method of, 31–2
Israel, 30–1, 39, 40, 133–5, 136–7, 156–60, 170–6

Jennings, Theodore W., 3, 138, 139
Jesus Christ
  crucifixion, 108–11, 132, 184
  death, 14, 16, 97–8, 99–100, 108–10, 132
  faith in, 148
  law of Christ, 144
  mode of living, 51, 55
  resurrection, 14, 16, 20, 51–2, 53, 97–8, 99–100, 101–2, 132: Badiou's antidialectic of, 102–11

Judaism, 28, 30, 32, 107; *see also* Israel
justice, 138–9, 145, 147–8, 197–8
justification, 144

katargeō, 71, 129, 138, 145
katargēsis, 71–2, 73–5, 81, 88, 89, 114, 187
  and *charis*, 145–50
  and *kosmos*, 190, 191
katechon, 129, 150–1n2
Kearney, Richard, 14
Kierkegaard, Søren, 111–15, 124, 157–8, 194
knowledge, 56–7, 58–9, 77
Knox, Ronald A., 13
kosmos, 70, 74, 182, 186–7, 191–2, 193, 194–5

la police (Rancière), 167, 174
la politique (Rancière), 167–8
language, 57, 147, 153n49, 190–1
law, 128–9, 170, 172–3
  of Christ, 144
  dualism of law and grace, 139–44, 164, 172: *katargēsis*, 145–50
  of faith, 146
  and faith, 146–7, 148
  and justice, 138
  resistance to *see* antinomianism
  of works, 146, 147
  see also la police (Rancière); political theology
Leibniz, Gottfried, 102, 140
life v. death, 141–2
living, art of, 14, 61–2, 63, 64, 180
living, mode of, 14–18, 63, 64, 70, 79–80, 142, 144
  ancient philosophy as, 180–2
  and event, 161, 163
  Jesus Christ, 51, 55
  'as not' (*hōs mē*), 81–90, 188, 189, 193
  see also enactment of life; other life

Marcion of Sinope, 27, 28–9, 30, 32, 84
Margins of Philosophy (Derrida), 100–1

Marion, Jean-Luc, 80, 81
Medea, 143
meontology, 68, 69–77, 186–7, 189–90
  brokenness of creation, 90–1
  mode of living 'as not' (hōs mē), 81–90
  sense of an ending, 77–81, 84, 89–90, 193
metaphors, 57
metaphysics, 70–1, 196; *see also* meontology; ontotheology
Metaphysics (Aristotle), 71, 72, 187
miracle, 102, 136
mode of being, 12, 16, 63–4, 70, 78, 119–20, 182, 187, 195; *see also* event; potentiality-of-being-otherwise
mode of living, 14–18, 63, 64, 70, 79–80, 142, 144
  ancient philosophy as, 180–2
  and event, 161, 163
  Jesus Christ, 51, 55
  'as not' (hōs mē), 81–90, 188, 189, 193
  see also art of living; enactment of life; other life
mode of thinking, 16, 63, 64, 70, 142; *see also* pneumatic hermeneutics
monism, 25, 191
  monism-dualism tension, 26–7: dialectic between monism and dualism, 33–8 (*see also* pneumatic hermeneutics); Gnostic dualism, 28–9; Gnostic temptation, 30–2
mortality, 15

natural-spiritual distinction, 25–6; *see also* flesh-spirit distinction
Nazism, 30
negation, 98, 108, 110
negativity, 38–9
neoliberalism, 4, 13
Nicomachean Ethics (Aristotle), 15
Nietzsche, Friedrich, 3, 31
  death of God, 99
  on Paul's ontological dualism, 45, 46–9

polemic / struggle with Paul, 49–54, 97–8
understanding of faith, 55–61, 181
nihilism, 45, 46–7, 50, 53, 54, 55, 59, 62, 99; *see also* meontology
nomos see law
nomos empsuchos, 144
non-beings, 69–70, 72–3, 74–7, 79, 80, 186, 195
  and crucifixion, 110
  and politics, 167
nonconformism, 78–9, 81
'not..., but...'-formula, 164
nous, 15, 16, 182

Old Testament, 28, 29, 31, 53
On Truth and Lies (Nietzsche), 57
ontotheology, 70–1, 116, 187, 196
other life, 61, 62–3
other(ness), 36, 100–1, 113
outcasts, 7, 21, 90–1, 154–6, 184–5, 186–7, 197
  and crucifixion, 109, 110–11
  and event, 169
  Paul's identification with, 2, 3
  see also 'scum of the world'

paideia, 15
paragō, 80
Parmenides (Heidegger), 1
Parousia, 106, 116–17, 119, 120–3
part without part (*part des sans-part*, Rancière), 155, 166–9, 173–4
particularism, 4, 23n8, 156, 165
particularity, 156, 158, 161
pathos, 48, 60, 101, 113–15, 160
pathos-logos nexus, 143
permanent-transitory distinction, 26
Phaedrus (Plato), 28
Pharisee, 170
Phenomenology of Religious Life (Heidegger), 5
philosophy, 55, 56; *see also* ancient philosophy; contemporary European philosophy; Stoicism
pistis see faith (*pistis*)
Plato, 15, 16, 73, 76, 114
Platonic dualism, 28, 57

Platonism, 46, 47, 61, 117
pneuma, 15, 25–6, 27, 28, 36–7, 39, 185, 188; *see also* flesh-spirit distinction; spirit
pneumatic hermeneutics, 30–2, 34–5, 36–7, 40–2, 136, 199
  Žižek's interpretation, 38–40
pneumatic principle, 34–5, 37
polemos, 49
political community *see* community
political theology, 196–9
  Carl Schmitt, 129–32, 133, 135, 136, 196–7
  Saint Paul, 132–9, 196: dualism of law and grace, 139–44; *katargēsis and charis*, 145–50
  see also community
Political Theology of Paul, The (Taubes), 6
politics *see la politique* (Rancière)
possession, 87, 89
Posthumous Fragments (Nietzsche), 58
postmodernism, 3, 4
potentiality, 40, 72, 145–6; *see also dunamis* (power)
potentiality-of-being-otherwise, 81–90, 106, 118, 122, 123, 193
power *see dunamis* (power)
principium, 37
principle of sufficient reason, 36–7, 102, 140
principles, 36–7
promises, 147
Protestant German theology, 30
psuchē, 25–6, 38–9

Rancière, Jacques, 155, 166–8, 173–4
relation of exception, 155
relativism, 4
repetition, 26, 38–9, 40, 83, 85–6
Repetition (Kierkegaard), 111, 112
resentment, 50
resurrection, 14, 16, 20, 51–2, 53, 97–8, 99–100, 101–2, 132
  in Badiou's antidialectic, 102–11
Ricœur, Paul, 57
righteousness, 138–9, 146, 149, 150, 197
Roman Empire, 154

Sacrament of Language, The (Agamben), 147
Saint Paul
  effect of letters on church history, 12–13
  philosophical turn to, 3–8, 179–80: criticism of selectivity, 8–12; leitmotifs, 12–20 (*see also individual philosophers*)
  positioning in ancient thought, 180–5
Saint Paul: The Foundation of Universalism (Badiou), 7
salvation, 30, 36, 40, 41, 157, 159, 173–4
scandal *see skandalon*
Sceptics, 88–9, 114, 148
Schelling, F.W.J., 75
schēma, 77–9
Schmitt, Carl, 6, 30
  exception, 111–12
  genealogy of the legal order, 154–5
  political theology, 129–32, 133, 135, 136, 196–7
  'scum of the world', 10, 21, 79, 90, 91, 109, 184–5, 196; *see also* outcasts
Second Coming *see* Parousia
sense of an ending, 77–81, 84, 89–90, 193
sensus allegoricus, 31–2
sensus historicus, 31
sensus nudus, 31
separation (*aphōrismenos*), 169–76, 198
Sextus Empiricus, 88–9
sin, 141–3, 144, 147
skandalon (scandal), 61–2, 183, 184–5
slave *see doulos* (slave)
slave uprising of Spartacus, 103, 105, 111
Socrates, 61, 142, 144
Sophist (Plato), 73, 76
sovereign / sovereignty, 130–1, 132, 133, 135–7, 144, 149–50, 183–4
spirit, 52, 158–9, 185
  firstfruits, 199–200
  flesh-spirit distinction, 19, 29, 32, 159–60, 163–4, 170–2, 181–2

as ghost, 39
of God, 18–20, 27, 33, 34–5, 36, 49, 99, 186, 187, 192
of the world, 27, 28, 33, 36, 186, 192: *Weltgeist* (Hegel), 19–20, 34
see also pneuma
spiritual life, 14–16, 99
spiritual meaning, 38
spiritual-natural distinction, 25–6; see also flesh-spirit distinction
state of emergency, 130
state of exception, 129–32, 135–7, 143–4, 156, 196–8
Stoic *adiaphora*, 83, 88
Stoic cosmology, 25–6, 35, 54
Stoicism, 15, 19–20, 34, 38–9, 77, 182
Stowers, Stanley, 18–19, 20
subjects, 105, 107–8
sublation (*Aufhebung*), 33–4, 40, 74, 100, 104, 112, 114
suffering, 48, 90, 104, 114
sur-existence, 52
suspension see *epochē* (suspension)
suspicion, hermeneutics of, 11, 48

Tanakh see Old Testament
Taubes, Jacob, 20
  on Benjamin and Barth, 35
  cosmos, 36
  eschaton, 160, 174–5
  on Hegel, 33
  law, 128
  Marcionism's relation to Paul, 28, 29, 30
  mode of living 'as not' (*hōs mē*), 84
  on Nietzsche's interpretation of Paul, 50, 52
  on Paul's political theology, 132
  Paul's universalism, 157–8
  time, 6
temporality see time
text, meaning of, 31
theōria, 15, 16
thinking, mode of, 16, 63, 64, 70, 142; see also pneumatic hermeneutics
thrownness, 39
time, 5, 6, 96–7, 116–17, 120–2, 123–4, 174–5

Time That Remains, The (Agamben), 7–8, 82
tolerance, 162–3, 173
tou kosmou-formulas, 69, 78–9, 86, 186
transcendence, 21, 36, 37
transitory-permanent distinction, 26
transvaluation, 49, 52, 129, 192
trust, 11, 16, 17, 188, 193
truth, 15, 55, 56, 57, 58, 59, 60, 105–6
Truth and Method (Gadamer), 10
truth procedure, 105–6

Universal Declaration of Human Rights, 154
universal, relation between exception and, 111–15, 157–8, 194
universalism, 156, 157–8
  in Badiou's interpretation, 7, 161–6, 172
  and separation, 169–76
use see *chrēsis* (use)

values, 49, 50, 52; see also transvaluation
Van Kooten, George, 88
vocation, 74, 82–9, 91, 171, 173
Von Harnack, Adolph, 30

Wasserman, Emma, 143
weakness see *astheneia* (weakness)
Weltgeist (spirit of the world, Hegel), 19–20, 34
'Whole of Society' (Žižek), 168
word
  firstfruits of, 179
  passing of, 77–81, 84 (see also sense of an ending)
  spirit of, 27, 28, 33, 36, 186, 192: *Weltgeist* (Hegel), 19–20, 34
Wright, N.T., 154

Žižek, 4
  Badiou's spirit of the event, 106
  capitalism, 13
  Christianity, 62, 165–6
  detachment / disengagement, 38–40
  exception, 135–6

Žižek (cont.)
    God, 110
    non-beings, 80
    particularism, 23n8

resurrection and faith, 17–18
true speculative meaning, 41
universal singularity, 168–9
universality and fidelity, 7

EU representative:
Easy Access System Europe
Mustamäe tee 50, 10621 Tallinn, Estonia
Gpsr.requests@easproject.com

www.ingramcontent.com/pod-product-compliance
Lightning Source LLC
Chambersburg PA
CBHW051122160426
43195CB00014B/2310